The Complete Idiot's Reference Card

Day Trading Is...

➤ High-performance
➤ Information-intensive
➤ Real-time
➤ Disintermediated
➤ Do-it-yourself securities trading
➤ Done like a pro, with the pros

The Day Trader's Equipment List

Information Tools

➤ Daily financial news
➤ High-performance professional news and quote feeds
➤ Specialized day-trader information, recommendations, and chat

Trading Tools and Venues

➤ Use different types of orders to your advantage.
➤ Use margin where it makes sense, but be careful!
➤ Internet brokers provide inexpensive trading from almost anywhere.
➤ NASDAQ Level II screen provides market "transparency,"—the ability to see the whole market and what lies ahead.
➤ Specialized trading rooms give power, training, and community at a reasonable price—if available in your area.
➤ High-performance in-home trading platforms bring it to your home office, if you're ready to make the investment.

For Do-It-Yourselfers

➤ Modern PC (or PCs) with the most memory
➤ The biggest monitor you can afford
➤ High-speed, high-bandwidth Internet and direct connections

alpha
books

W9-BAM-688

Major Day-Trading Strategies

- ➤ **Scalping teenies:** Capture the spread between the bid and the ask price.
- ➤ **Playing momentum:** Finding the big movers (up or down) and playing them for what they're worth.
- ➤ **Gap openings:** Profit from market behavior when a stock's opening price is very different—gapped—from its close the previous day.
- ➤ **Shadowing the Ax:** Follow "heavy" or active market makers and profit from their moves.
- ➤ **Event play:** Trade on earnings news, acquisition rumors, splits and IPOs.

What Makes a Successful Day Trader

- ➤ **Knowledge:** Understand inner market workings and key trading techniques.
- ➤ **Confidence:** Act on what you know and what you perceive.
- ➤ **Ability to act:** Pull the trigger.
- ➤ **Willingness to learn:** When it doesn't work, figure out why instead of getting mad.
- ➤ **Willingness to try new things:** Learn by doing—and by the way, stock behaviors change over time.
- ➤ **Ability to accept failure and responsibility:** Don't blame others—learn and move on.
- ➤ **Ability to manage money:** For better or for worse.
- ➤ **Passion:** Live it, breathe it. If money, numbers, and fast action don't thrill you, choose another way to spend your time.
- ➤ **Patience:** At times, practice not only patience, but restraint.
- ➤ **Facility with Numbers:** Quick, which is bigger: $^{13}/_{32}$ or $^{1}/_{4}$? No fast answer? Hate fractions? Could be a problem.
- ➤ **Concentration:** Stay focused. Day trading requires intensity.
- ➤ **Discipline:** Above all else, make a set of rules—and stick to them.
- ➤ **Stamina:** Stay in good mental—and physical—shape. Intense brain and eye work required.
- ➤ **Know how your brain works:** Self explanatory.

Five Ways to Predict Short-Term Market Movement

- ➤ Closely follow market indicators like the S&P 500, TICK, and ARMS.
- ➤ Watch NASDAQ Level II to keep tabs on market-maker activity and determine underlying strategies.
- ➤ Get the news when the pros do—and before everyone else.
- ➤ Use charts to track past stock behavior and visualize future moves.
- ➤ Use technical indicators to determine strength, weakness, and buy or sell signals.

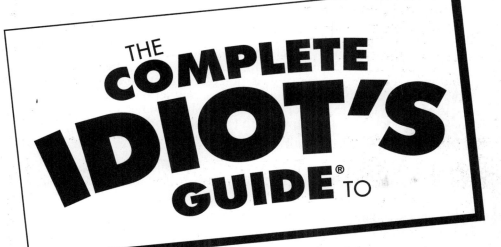

THE COMPLETE IDIOT'S GUIDE® TO

Day Trading Like a Pro

by
Jennifer Basye Sander
Peter J. Sander

alpha books

A Division of Macmillan General Reference
A Pearson Education Macmillan Company
1633 Broadway, New York, NY 10019-6785

Alpha Development Team

Publisher
Kathy Nebenhaus

Editorial Director
Gary M. Krebs

Associate Publisher
Cindy Kitchel

Associate Managing Editor
Cari Shaw Fischer

Acquisitions Editors
Jessica Faust
Michelle Reed

Development Editors
Phil Kitchel
Amy Zavatto

Assistant Editor
Georgette Blau

Production Team

Development Editor
Phil Kitchel

Production Editor
Faunette Johnston

Cover Designer
Mike Freeland

Illustrator
Jody Schaefer

Book Designers
Scott Cook and Amy Adams of DesignLab

Indexer
Joy Dean Lee

Layout/Proofreading
Angela Calvert
Julie Trippetti

Contents at a Glance

Appendices

Contents

Appendices

Introduction

You hear about it everywhere—it's splashed all over the financial pages and blaring at you from your car radio—ads for seminars that promise to teach you all the secrets. And you've heard the mythical stories of the folks who are doing it—that guy who used to sit in the cube down the hall from you, your aunt's former boss, even the room-service waiter who just delivered your breakfast. The rumors, the buzz, the hype—what is this all about? Why did all these seemingly normal people quit their jobs to sit at home in front of their computer hour after hour? Listen closely: The reason—the *phenomenon*—is day trading.

Day trading has arisen from the convergence of sustained stock-market growth, new personal-investment savvy, improved market rules, reduced transaction costs, and most of all, the profound revolution in personal technology. Day trading has been made possible by technology, becoming available to "the rest of us" with the same dizzying speed as most other Internet-enabled commerce. Who woulda thunk of buying a book with three mouse clicks a few years ago? The same revolution that is transforming the landscape of consumer commerce has also transformed the landscape of personal investing.

But the personal technology revolution isn't the whole story. The day-trading phenomenon owes a lot to changes in the way the investment world works, and to new tools and techniques that have become easy for average folks to get—and use.

The Place to Start

The Complete Idiot's Guide to Day Trading Like a Pro will provide a complete journey through this rapidly expanding world. We'll talk about markets. We'll talk about tools, strategies, and techniques. We'll talk about resources. We'll talk about lifestyles and what it takes to be a good day trader.

And who are *we*? Are we professional day traders who'll give you a little info and then hope you'll pay us big bucks to buy the whole class? Just like during a gold rush, the folks who make most of the money aren't the ordinary Joes who break their backs mining for the shiny stuff—it's the guys who sell the picks and shovels!

Well, "we" aren't selling picks and shovels. We are Peter and Jennifer Sander—a husband-and-wife writing team. Between us, we have many years of investing experience (most of it successful) and we fit the classic profile of ordinary, middle-class Americans who are deciding to day trade nowadays. We've set out to learn as much about this new phenomenon as we can, so we can explain it all clearly to you, in plain and simple language, with examples that will make sense even if you haven't yet taken the day-trading plunge.

And if, by the end of this book, you decide this nerve-wracking business of day trading isn't for you, we believe that the new high-tech tools you'll learn about here will help make you a better investor, regardless of your style and objectives.

How to Use This Book

This book is divided into five parts. **Part 1, "A Day at a Time,"** teaches you more about the day-trading phenomenon: what it is, how it started, and who's out there doing it now.

Part 2, "A Trip to the Markets," leads you further into what day traders actually do: how they make their money, and where they make it. You'll learn what day traders are trading, and what they aren't; how the markets work; and best of all, *why* they are trading.

Part 3, "Tools to Keep You Informed," teaches you more about the resources and tools available to help you become a successful day trader. Where should you go for technical stock analysis? Quotes and news feeds? How do you place a stop order? And what the heck is a NASDAQ Level II screen?

Starting with **Part 4, "Tools of the Trade,"** we will begin to delve into the real but mysterious trading world. How to decide which stock to trade and when to buy and sell. How to turn all those charts and numbers (hopefully) into trading profits.

In **Part 5, "Reading the Tea Leaves,"** you will learn some of the many, many techniques used by pros and common investors alike to read the direction of markets and individual stocks. These tools are important not only to predict price movement but also to pick which stocks to trade.

And in **Part 6, "Developing Your Own Day-Trading Style,"** we'll help you build your own day-trading game plan. From basic trading strategies to basic decisions about whether day trading is even the right thing for you to try. It's not for everyone, you know. A day-trading plan—and even the decision to get into it—must be well thought out.

Extras

No one learns by dry, dull information alone, and we've tried to spice up your day-trading lessons with a few sidebars to keep you reading.

Behind the Screen

These are longer anecdotes and odd bits of info meant to broaden your insider knowledge of the investment world.

Alarm Bells

Those pitfalls that you would be well served to avoid.

Trading Terms

Here you'll find words that you will need to know: the vocabulary of the day trader.

Daily Specials

Look here for trading hints and tips from the pros.

Acknowledgements

All writers sit before the keyboard with a hidden host of helpers behind them. Friends, family, and colleagues—no one really writes a book alone. We'd like to acknowledge a few members of the chorus here:

Our agent and friend, Sheree Bykofsky. Our friends at Macmillan—Jessica Faust and Gary Krebs. Our sympathetic family—the Basyes, always willing to babysit a grandchild or two while we write into the night. And our own two little guys—Julian and Jonathan Sander—as fine a reason to keep writing books (and saving up for college tuition) as an author could have.

Special Thanks to the Technical Reviewer

The Complete Idiot's Guide to Day Trading Like a Pro was reviewed by an expert and experienced trader who checked the accuracy of what you'll be reading and provided valuable insights and suggestions along the way to help us give you as complete a picture of day trading as possible. Our special thanks to Thomas Burton of Davis, CA.

Tom epitomizes the do-it-yourself trader. Just over two years ago, he left his position as an engineer at the local electric company to venture forth into day trading, first as a futures trader. He then helped start the only day trading firm in Sacramento, CA—which eventually merged into Cornerstone Securities, one of the country's premier day-trading firms. Tom runs the local branch today, doing all training, account management, and computer network engineering himself. Tom has an MBA and NASD Series 7, 24, and 63 licenses, and is particularly fond of technical analysis systems with several hundred hours of study and application under his belt. We'd like to not only acknowledge Tom's knowledge and hard work in helping us with this project, but also mention his exceptional teaching abilities as well.

Part 1
A Day at a Time

Exactly what is day trading, and what are traders trading all day long? In Part 1, you will gain an understanding of what this new phenomenon is all about (you'll also learn that it isn't really so new after all), and the technological and sociological forces that gave rise to it.

What do day traders trade, and how exactly do they trade? What do you need to get started? And what does it take to succeed as a day trader? It's all here.

And lastly, we'll take a look at why there is such a big fuss about the idea of day trading. Who thinks it is a good idea and why? Who thinks it is a bad idea (a very bad idea) and why? The more you know, the better you'll be able to decide what kind of an idea you think it is!

Just What Is Day Trading?

"Day trading." Everybody's talking about it, but what the heck is it? It sounds like a couple of waiters swapping shifts—"You work Wednesday for me and I'll cover for you on Friday..." Trading days, right?

Nope. This *day trading* is stock trading during the day. Seems simple. All trading must be day trading—aren't the financial markets only open for a few hours every day? Who ever heard of "night trading"?

Well, if it were this simple, we wouldn't need a book, would we? Nope again. There's something very new, different and special going on here. In this chapter, we'll describe what day trading is (and isn't), and talk about what makes it possible, and—most important—what makes it *profitable*.

In and Out

Strictly speaking, "day trading" is an investment position entered into and closed out during the same trading day.

Let's repeat that critical information: in and out, same day.

That's right. No positions held overnight. One hundred percent cash while the stars shine. You buy or sell, then reverse or "close" the position before quitting time. For the pure day trader, no exceptions. In fact, day traders quip that "long-term investments" are simply day trades that didn't work!

Trading Terms

Day trading is buying and selling stocks throughout the course of a day, and closing out the last trade, not holding any positions past the close of the market. A **swing trader** is a stock trader who holds onto a position for more than one day, but closes out all trades at the end of the week.

Discipline: The Big "D"

Sharp readers will quickly see that true day trading requires a lot of *discipline*. Yes, trades or positions that didn't work (earn a profit) must be disagreeably dispatched regardless of how financially painful it is. Likewise, the really sweet upswing must be cashed out regardless of how certain you are of an even stronger push the next day. Technique, information, luck—they all play a role—and in this book we'll talk in depth about each. But it's trading discipline that makes the system work, and work consistently, for the successful trader. We'll get back to talking more about the "big D" in a later chapter.

NOTHING Held Overnight?

So, you're wondering, if the techniques, information, and resources available to the day trader are wonderful enough to produce profitable trades in a single day, why can't they also prove profitable over longer periods? Good question.

Trading Terms

Teenies are stock-market slang for a sixteenth of a point. The cash value of a teenie is 6.25 cents per share, which translates to $62.50 on a 1,000-share trade.

While the focus is the day trade, and while many a true day trader loses sleep at night counting eighths and "teenies" (sixteenths) jumping over a fence, it's true that day-trading techniques can also be employed by the short-term, or "swing," trader. A *swing trader* may keep a position for a few days or even a week, but will almost always close it out before the weekend, to reduce vulnerability to uncontrollable world events.

For the most part this book will address the tools and techniques of short-term trading, which generally apply to "pure" day trading, too.

A High-Performance Jet

Some day trading can be more accurately described as "minute trading." Through sophisticated information and ordering systems, a trader can stay with market movements and place trades in intervals measured in *seconds*. Many of these traders hold positions for two minutes or less. They act more like dealers or "market makers" than retail traders. Like flying a jet fighter, this form of day trading requires the highest degree of skill, stamina, discipline, and concentration—not to mention the most high-powered computer equipment and the fastest access lines. (You don't attempt this sort of thing on your old 486 with a 14.4K modem.) It's not for everyone, but we will share some of the tools and methods of high-performance day trading in Parts 4 through 6 of this book.

A New Revolution, an Old Idea

Ever heard of a "bucket shop"? No, we're not talking about the corner hardware store, nor the five-star dealership where you bought that bucket of bolts sitting in your driveway. *Bucket shops* were short-term trading houses that appeared around the turn of the century and flourished during the great 1920s bull market.

Put It in the Bucket

Bucket shops were the first real day-trading venues. Kind of like off-track betting parlors, bucket shops provided a smoky venue for customers to buy and sell stocks with each other, or with the "house" (kinda like in Vegas), and only sometimes through the stock exchanges! Bucket-shop speculators were essentially gaming for every up or down move that came across the old ticker tape. Many were illegal, and dealt illegal or even non-existent securities. For many, they provided a source of income, and for most a source of good fun. Even more fun was to be had with *margin money:* You could have your fun, with up to 90 percent of the money furnished by the house.

Trading Terms

Margin money is borrowed from a broker to purchase securities. It is a form of credit. Most brokers allow you to borrow up to 50 percent of the value of securities at relatively modest interest rates: usually between 7 and 10 percent depending on the broker and the amount borrowed.

The Dark Ages

The disastrous events and new public disfavor regarding stock speculation brought on by October 1929 brought a host of industry regulations and increased margin-equity requirements. You could no longer borrow 90 percent of the value of your stock; now you had to put up initial "equity" of 50 percent. Licensing rules eliminated the bucket shops and forced a return to a tradition already 136 years old—high, regulated (that is, fixed) commission rates. The concept of day trading had been born, but it would lie dormant for decades. It faded into sort of a "dark ages," suppressed by the regulating commissions and a securities trading and broker-age system that simply didn't support fast, cheap executions.

But in the early 1970s, several factors came together to change the climate—rule changes, market changes, and the advent of the computer and Internet age. We'll take a closer look at how those '70s changes created this '90s phenomenon in Chapter 2. Disco is back, and so is day trading!

But I Thought This Was an Investing Book

In and out in a day, huh? Positions held only for two or three minutes? The speed of business has become faster, all right, but can a company's fortunes really change in a few minutes? As day traders, are we betting on funda-mental changes in a company's value? Or are we simply gambling on small price movements that have no real supporting basis or underlying cause? If so, how can this be called investing? Isn't it gambling?

> **Daily Specials**
>
> In England, you really can gamble on the stock market. British bookies are famous for their willingness to handle just about any bet. When London banks suffered massive layoffs last year, some of those bankers became—you guessed it—bookies who lay odds on the financial spreads. You can bet that the stock-market index will finish higher than predicted, or wager that it will finish lower. You can even buy and sell call and put options on sporting matches.

In any financial paper on almost any given day you can find articles and professional commentary aimed at this very issue. And, we must confess, some day traders really are compulsive gamblers. But most are just ordinary Joes and Janes trying to earn a living.

While we concede that day trading is speculative and based on market factors *additional* to fundamental company value, we stop short of calling it gambling. Day trading is only gambling—and this is only a gambling book—if you're a gambler.

> **Behind the Screen**
>
> It's a safe bet Federal Reserve Chairman Alan Greenspan thinks day trading is gambling, since he thinks that simply investing in Internet stocks for the long-term is like playing the lottery: "What lottery managers have known for centuries is that you could get somebody to pay for a one-in-a-million shot more than the [pure economic] value of that chance."
>
> And Arthur Levitt, head of the Securities and Exchange Commission, casts a gimlet eye toward day traders, too: Traders should do so, he warns, only "with funds they can afford to lose."

Help for All Mankind

Our hope is that the information in this book will help *all* investors—short- *and* long-term traders, gamblers, and investors alike. Even if you are a poster child for long-term, "value-oriented" investors, this book should help you better understand the way the markets move and do a better job when you *do* buy and sell. And who knows? Maybe you'll decide to plunge headfirst into day trading!

Pure Capitalism

Never mind personal beliefs and habits—just what does day trading do for the world economy? For society? People make a living at this, yet just what have they contributed? Aren't they just collecting crumbs that fall off the huge cake of capitalistic finance? How can one feel good about that?

Just in case you're concerned about this sort of thing, we (and many others) think day trading plays an important role. It keeps market makers and other industry insiders honest by providing visibility and introducing viable competition to make prices more truly reflect supply and demand. Or, another way of putting it: It provides *liquidity* to the markets.

Maximum Liquidity

Suppose you want to buy a roast for dinner tonight. Imagine that only one butcher had all the roasts available. What if all your neighbors wanted a roast the same day? What if the butcher's supply chain were interrupted? Do you think you would get the best price? Do you think buying the roast would be easy and free of uncertainty? Probably not. You may or may not get the roast, and you probably won't get it at the price you had in mind.

The stock market, and especially the NASDAQ, bring multiple players from all over the world into the market. So the situation is a little better than the one-butcher-in-town model. Still, if you want to buy a roast, you have to find another player who wants to sell it, and they may have their own agenda. Competition reduces the risk, but how often do you see the same availability and price at all the groceries in town? More "liquidity," but still not a perfect market or entirely level playing field.

Trading Terms

Liquidity refers to the availability of enough buyers and sellers to quickly and easily execute transactions in a market. The effects of liquidity are fast, reliable executions and predictable prices.

The Public Market

Now let's say you go to a public market to buy the roast. At that market you'll find many small players, and each one can see and hear the quantity and the price the others are buying and selling for. The sellers know how many buyers there are and vice versa. Anyone who quotes a price that is "outside the market" will quickly be brought back in. What happens? You *will* end up with a roast, and it will be at the best price available at that moment. This kind of open situation creates the most liquid market.

What Does This Have to Do with Day Trading?

We know you didn't buy this book so you could spend your day in front of the computer trading rump roasts and oxtails. But the same principles apply in the stock market. Simply put, day trading brings more (a lot more) buyers and sellers into the market. The result is greater liquidity and a more "pure" market. What do we mean? A highly liquid market responds more to pure supply and demand, not the whimsy, the agenda, or predictions of a single or limited few buyers and sellers. Day traders and short-term traders bring liquidity and an increase in supply and demand. More supply and demand cause the markets to more truly reflect supply-and-demand conditions. A true supply-and-demand driven market is the purest form of capitalism.

Not Just a Job

Now that you feel good about the contribution you're making to society, let's talk for a minute about what day trading can do for you.

Can I Quit My Job?

In the introduction, we reminded you of the mythical folks you've heard about, such as your cousin's best friend, who…

➤ Quit work.

➤ Makes as much (or more) as you do in your full-time job.

➤ Spends only two hours a day doing it and plays golf the rest of the day.

Daily Specials

Paper trading is a great way to start. You just make trades on paper, without real money. This is the day-trading version of "hypothetical investing." Spot the trades, pretend you made them, and track the results. To learn the most from your paper trading, do it for a long time under a variety of market conditions.

No bosses, no deadlines save for closing out his investment positions at the end of the day.

Sound good? Well, it can be done, and many have done it. But it seems like just as many folks get rich showing others how to do it with books, tapes, Web sites, and seminars. Day trading isn't without risk, and it certainly isn't without some skill, diligence, discipline, startup capital, and investment in tools, training, and technique. Just like any job, it requires investment, learning, attitude, and time. To coin a new phrase—*something ventured, something gained!*

But day trading is certainly not for everyone, so don't quit your day job yet. Plan to get some solid training and then paper trade for awhile. Develop a trading system, a philosophy, and an attitude *that works*. Try it long enough to prove yourself—in all market conditions—before taking the plunge. In Chapter 3, "Is This Bud for You?," we'll talk more about what it takes to be a good day trader, a *professional* day trader.

Just How Much CAN I Make?

The $64,000 question—how much? Well, it depends on two things:

➤ How much you invest

➤ How aggressively you invest it

Most electronic brokers, especially the ones providing "high-performance" trading product, require a minimum of $25K in investment capital. But we've also seen it as low as $5K and as high as $75K. This can be leveraged by using margin funds to invest twice that amount.

Behind the Screen

"I went to a weekend-long course and learned just enough to become dangerous!" laughs Diane. A striking blonde who lives in the California beach town of La Jolla, Diane shared her most recent day-trading income statistics with us: "I was up 60 percent from November to January. But in February and March I made no money at all. And most of the other traders I know had crummy months then, too. We all got killed in a high-tech downturn."

Some day traders trade in minimum 1,000-share lots, others stick to 100-, 200-, 500-share lots, depending on the price of the stock traded and how much capital they want to risk. Obviously small price changes mean more realized profit (or loss) with larger share amounts—an uptick of an eighth of a point on a stock you own can earn you $125 with 1,000 shares.

Your exact profit depends on

➤ The net gain per trade, and

➤ The number of trades

➤ Commission (transaction) costs

Some day traders make 100 or more trades in a day, and may win on 5 or 10 more trades than they lose on. This is a very credible strategy if it can be maintained.

There's the bottom line: It really doesn't take a large number of profitable trades to realize a net of $300 or so a day. Three hundred bucks times about 240 trading days per year yields $72,000 in gross income per year. Not enough to make you rich, but not bad. This is the goal of many day traders. Many have earned considerably more.

Tax Time

Tax treatment of day-trading profits is evolving. For many years, trading gains were treated as investment or "capital" gains, subject to a maximum 28-percent tax rate. The recent capital-gains tax reduction to a 20 percent maximum for long-term gains helped long-term investors. But, alas, not the day trader, whose short-term gains are now taxed as ordinary income at the going rate. Check with your tax advisor to see the latest rules, as the IRS is starting to notice day traders and the rules could change before this book makes it into print!

Also note that good record keeping is *required*. And if you're a very active day trader, it'll take quite awhile to figure out what you did over the past year. You'll be up late for many an evening preparing your tax returns!

Who Wins and Why?

"Isn't this a zero-sum game?" you ask. If someone wins, then someone's gotta lose, right? You pick up an eighth of a point, someone else loses that eighth.

A true statement, in the strictest sense. If you buy low and sell high, the person who bought from you buys at the higher price and "loses" the difference between high and low. But that person wasn't in the market when you bought at the low. He/she may not really care about that eighth—for them it might be a long-term investment.

If you buy a stock as a day trader, you aren't necessarily buying it from another day trader who is about to lose or miss out on a gain if the stock goes up. Often you are buying and selling between other longer-term holders who just didn't reach the market at the same time. So, yes, your win comes at the expense of these traders in a sense. It doesn't necessarily come at the expense of another day trader who now has to beg to get his old day job back!

Likewise, if you lose, you can't really blame other day traders! In the day-trading game, winning and losing isn't about beating or getting beat by others. It's about seeing things, making correct judgements about what you're seeing, acting quickly, and sticking to your rules and your system. If you see more, judge better, act faster, and stick to your plan, you'll win. The other guy may not have the time or information, wasn't there, or just plain doesn't care about the short-term result. As a day trader, you're providing liquidity, so why shouldn't you get paid for it?

Does Anyone Important Do This?

Do any of the high-profile investment gurus do this? Strange we should ask. The investment landscape is littered with famous investment gurus—Peter Lynch and the rest—who have seemingly patented investing systems they convey to the mass believers in the form of personal-finance books and magazine articles. Day trading is kind of a new thing.

But moreover, as we quickly found while researching this book, day trading is a bit of a loner's game. It's done by individuals, not funds or institutions. Day traders make money for themselves, not their clients. They don't have to report their results to anyone (other than the IRS) and have no reason to. Think about it—when you are a really successful day trader, are *you* gonna share your secrets with anyone? Aside from chat rooms and the few day-trading rooms here and there, most day traders have very little contact with each other.

So, at the time of this writing, there is really no one who has become the Michael Jordan of day trading. There's plenty of fortune in this game, but not much actual fame. There are a few books written by emerging names in the day-trading business (thanks for selecting ours), but they are far from household names, and in some cases the purpose is as much to market their own day-trading products as to share experience, educate, or lead the public.

What We Assume You Already Know

Please bear in mind, this book isn't *The Complete Idiot's Guide to Making Money on Wall Street,* which is the best place for stock-market beginners to start. If that was what you meant to buy, take this book back to the bookstore right now and plead your case to the clerk.

This book will review the major securities markets and dig a little into how they work, but we assume you already know what a stock is and what it represents, how to read basic financial data, and a little about other types of securities. We assume you've traded stocks before, at least through a conventional broker. We also assume you've used a Windows-based computer and are at least a little familiar with the Internet. And we assume that you're interested in the dynamics, inner workings, techniques, and excitement of trading stocks!

Warning, Warning!

Day trading is not a game for beginners. And as authors, we would not be able to sleep at night if we thought we were encouraging readers to sell everything and risk it all on the off-chance that they might make a fortune day trading. Do not quit your job, mortgage your house, cash out your children's college fund, or dip into your retirement account in order to become a day trader. Day traders can make money, yes, but they can just as easily lose money in the blink of an eye.

Alarm Bells

Don't hock your grandmother's jewels to day trade. Trading is highly speculative and should not be undertaken with any money you can't comfortably afford to lose.

If you're a new investor, please go back to the bookstore and buy one of the many good books on beginning investing.

What NOT to Expect

Do we guarantee that by reading this book you will become a successful day trader? Hardly. Hey, if we could do that, we probably wouldn't need to write this book.

We're not going to make you a securities analyst or a great stock picker. We're not going to tell you what mutual fund to buy, nor how to invest your 401(k). And we're not going to tell you how to do your taxes, or reduce them. And we're not encouraging you to quit your job.

Now, if all of these strongly worded warnings about the risks and dangers of day trading haven't scared you off, then read on....

The Least You Need to Know

➤ Day trading is an investment position that is opened and closed on the same day.

➤ Day trading requires the discipline to let go of the losers rather than hang on in the hopes that the price will rise again soon.

➤ Short-term trading houses flourished in the 1920s but disappeared after the stock market crashed.

➤ Your exact profit depends on the net gain per trade and the number of trades you place.

➤ Do not day trade with money you can't afford to lose.

Chapter 2

The (Re-) Emergence of Day Trading

In This Chapter

➤ How the personal-technology revolution revived day trading

➤ What you need to day trade: information and trading access

➤ New tools and rules make it easier

➤ Low commissions make it affordable

In Chapter 1 we told you all about the bucket shops of the 1920s and the dark ages of day trading. And we promised to tell you more about how it re-emerged into the light. So here goes:

The Electronic Revolution

The "renaissance" that led to the re-emergence of day trading really started in the early 1970s with a one-two punch of market and rule changes and the advent of the personal computer. Like everything else in the information age, change and capability accelerated to blinding speed with the advent of the Internet. The Internet; low-cost, fast PCs; and some underlying social changes have not only brought day trading roaring back, but back into the hands of the masses! And this time it's here to stay.

Vacuum-Tube Logic

Most of us over 30 probably remember the stock-buying olden days, when the process worked like this:

1. You made an appointment to see a stockbroker.

2. Sat down with the broker, told him (yes, it was pretty much always a "him") what you were interested in buying.

3. The broker checked the stock's current price on the (then highly advanced) Quotron screen.

4. Once you decided what you wanted, the broker would scratch it down on a five-part carbon form about the same size and legibility of a drug prescription.

5. He would then walk it (or in bigger offices, vacuum-tube it) to a clerk (always a "she") in the back, who would teletype or phone it to the firm's agent in New York, who would communicate it to another agent or "floor broker" at the NYSE, then to the "specialist" for execution (every one a "he," if you're still interested.)

The process would be reversed to communicate the results of the transaction back to your broker through the firm's infamous "back office." Your broker might get a confirmation from the back office, and might call you. If your line wasn't busy and you were home to receive the call, you would learn that the trade had gone through. Remember, this was back before the days of voicemail.

Little would happen until five days later when the invoice came rolling into your mailbox. You wrote a check and mailed it off. A few weeks later you received a big brown envelope with your certificate. The commission on your trade would average 100 bucks or so, no matter which broker you went to. Then, when you sold your stock, you would be popped again—sometimes for several hundred bucks.

Imagine trying to trade frequently with such a system!

The Renaissance Trading Faire

The technology and rule changes that started in the early '70s combined to change the world so that day trading could flourish. Technology brought the prospect of true electronic trading: trading at the speed of light. Progress until then had given us electronic quotes and trade *reporting*, but hadn't automated trading itself beyond the speed of people, pens, and paper.

Federal regulators (the SEC), responding to emerging consumerism and ever-fading memories of the Depression, relaxed some of the stifling rules and regulations that had made investing inaccessible and expensive.

The Electronic (Market) Age

NASDAQ (which stands for National Association of Securities Dealers Automated Quotations) came into being on February 5, 1971. NASDAQ was essentially the first truly electronic market. *Market makers* would post their bids and offers and execute their orders with each other at the speed of light with the right keystrokes. No more unanswered phones, pokey clerks, and stressed-out agents.

While the New York Stock Exchange still maintains its human-powered "specialist" system to match buy and sell orders, the mechanisms for consumer-sized order placement have also been automated. Not as many phones, clerks, agents. Your order moves at nearly 186,000 miles per second to the trading floor.

Net Gains

Electronic markets and the real-time information exchange revolutionized the internal workings of the securities industry. Did this change bring on the day-trading phenomenon? Not really, unless you were a stockbroker yourself or were working very closely with a brokerage firm. As an individual you couldn't do the type of day trading we will describe.

But another revolution was around the corner— a revolution in *personal* technology. In the '80s, both the personal computer and the Internet were, for all practical purposes, born. But no one knew how to use them. If you did, it was no faster (and often slower) than picking up the phone and calling your broker (or "telebroker," for those of us in cyberspace, early-'80s style). And perhaps less dependable.

Trading Terms

A **market maker** makes a market in a security, buying and selling the security on behalf of his/her firm (usually an investment bank or brokerage) and the firm's clients. Think of it this way—a Ford dealer is a market maker for Ford cars, new and used.

NASDAQ is the National Association of Securities Dealers Automated Quotations system, or, as their new slogan recently bragged—"The Stock Market for the Next Hundred Years."

By the mid '90s, PCs and modem connections got pretty fast (and cheap!) Software could pull up graphics almost as fast as you could click your mouse. The Internet became "packaged," with usable browsers like Netscape Navigator or Microsoft Internet Explorer. Even more important, Internet-enabling languages such as Java and HTML made it possible for Web site hosts to create powerful, fast, easy-to-use sites very quickly. These sites became tied together and easily accessible through the World Wide Web structure and set of standards. Through the Web and more direct forms of network access, these high-performance sites are tied at the speed of light to quote databases and execution systems anywhere in the world.

Getting Connected

The final technological puzzle piece came into existence in 1996 with the advent of the 56K modem, which allows you, the user, *fast* access to the Web. Now you can access information and perform transactions with anyone at near real-time speed with an inexpensive PC and phone line. At the same time, other high-speed lines evolved (and are still evolving) such as ISDN and DSL, which give you still faster access and information download. And if you really want to fly the high-performance trading jet, you can connect directly through a dedicated direct line, "frame-relaying" with your trading firm as if you were an employee hooked into their network.

It Drives Fast, but What Good Is It?

But, you might ask yourself, doesn't this much horsepower just increase my chances of getting a speeding ticket? Well, sure, if you abuse it. But like any other high-performance "toy," when used right, it opens up incredible possibilities and can give stupendous results. Just fasten your seatbelt and hold on!

In a nutshell, the new technology provides fast, practical personal access to two critical things:

➤ Trading information

➤ Trading execution

The Three I's: Information, Information, Information

Check out Yahoo!Finance (quote.yahoo.com) someday, if you haven't already. At the click of a mouse, you can get delayed detailed quotes, stats, company research and profiles, analyst expectations, and graphs of a company's stock performance for one day, five years, or anything in between. For *any* stock, mind you, not just those tracked in the latest issue of Value Line.

Remember what you used to have to do to research a stock you were considering buying? Go to the library. Get the six-inch-thick Standard and Poor's that had your stock in it. Read something that—if you were lucky—was less than two months old. Want a quote? Wait until tomorrow's paper arrives, or call your broker and hope the weather kept him off the golf course. Want a graph? Get out the graph paper, ruler, and colored pens and make one. The hoops you had to jump through to get anything close to real-time information were small and always on fire.

Did we say "delayed" quotes? Yes, the free quotes you can find on Yahoo! and most other "portals" are delayed 20 minutes for New York Stock Exchange (NYSE) and 15 minutes for NASDAQ. Why? It has nothing to do with technology, just pure capitalism in action. It doesn't take that long for the info to crawl through those skinny wires and reach your part of the country, it has to do with money. These markets provide real-time quotes only for a fee. Yahoo! and other portals choose not to pay the fee. But ample access to *real-time quotes* is available through online brokers and certain other free or paid-for data sources.

Trading Terms

Real-time quotes reflect the price at which the stock is currently trading. Delayed quotes are quotes that reflect the price at which the stock sold 15 (for NASDAQ stocks) or 20 (for NYSE stocks) minutes ago.

If you have a modern PC and a phone line, you can instantly access the latest prices and price patterns on almost any stock, just like most traders, brokers, or anyone else, whether you live in Key West, Keystone, or Kona! Wanna know how to use this information? Keep reading.

Behind the Screen

Do all day traders live in big urban cities like New York, San Francisco, or Miami? Far from it (and we do mean *far*). All over the country, day traders are setting up their computers in front of windows that look out onto the beach, the farm, or the mountains. You don't need to live down the street from the stock market to trade this way. All you need is your computer and a high-speed modem.

High-Performance Information

You can step up your personal radar screen even further to get access to once-sacred Level II trading screens previously available only to market makers and certain large institutional players. Like anything else "high performance," there's a price and certain know-how required. If the idea of a Level II screen doesn't make sense to you at this point in the book, don't despair. We will explain Level II screens *ad nauseum* in a later chapter.

The Three A's: Access, Access, Access

You have the information to keep abreast of market changes and quickly decide what you want to do. If you still have to call your broker and get that vacuum-tube thing going, well, what good is it all?

Behind the Screen

Does online trading work perfectly every time? Alas, no. Hardly a week goes by without a glitch on one of the online broker's systems. E*Trade's computers faltered for parts of three days in the early part of 1999. Even behemoths like Schwab have had their systems go down, leaving anxious traders sweating it out in front of their screens. Is the Net the problem? Or the online broker's hardware? No, not always. Host servers and software upgrades seem to be the common culprits.

Internet trading, combined with electronic-trading platforms created by the major markets, gives you the ability to access—buy and sell—*almost* instantaneously. It isn't perfect, but it's darned close. Datek, one of the leading electronic brokerages, advertises confirmed 60-second trades or no commission paid. Most "market" orders placed for actively traded stocks through electronic brokers will execute within seconds and electronic acknowledgements are provided. We'll talk more about this in the next section.

High-Performance Access

In addition to high-performance information tools available to "high-end" traders, there are also high-performance trading tools. Often they are bundled together with the information tools, so that the advanced "pilot" can read the radar and, through a couple of keyboard strokes, immediately trade directly with a market maker or other electronic player. No brokers at the party, not even the slightest delay transmitting orders through an e-broker's network. And no "paid for order flow."

New Rules and Tools

In Chapter 1 we talked about the two big changes that fostered the re-emergence of day trading:

➤ **Tool change:** The 1971 advent of electronic trading with NASDAQ (1971)

➤ **Rule change:** The 1975 elimination of regulated commissions

In addition to those major shifts in the way business is done, other changes have gone a long way to facilitate all forms of electronic trading, including day trading. The result of most of these changes is to make trading faster, cheaper, and fairer, and to reduce the "spread," or profit margin, collected by market makers. A more level playing field has been created, one where you can compete side by side with the big guys.

Trading Terms

Paid for order flow occurs when a retail broker sells your orders to another firm for execution. The second firm will often bundle your orders together to get a better price (which you, of course, don't get). Obviously, this delays the process and causes loss of price control for market orders. Note that some, but not all, retail brokers do this.

Trading Terms

The **bid** price is the price at which the market maker (NASDAQ) or specialist (NYSE) is willing to buy the stock from you. The **ask**, or "offer" price is the price at which he/she will sell the stock to you. The difference is the **spread**. In a sense, bid is wholesale, ask is retail, and the spread is the profit margin.

Tool Change: DOT and SuperDot on the NYSE

DOT stands for *designated order turnaround system* (SuperDot is the "super" version of same). DOT and SuperDot are the NYSE's electronic-order routing system. Orders can be routed directly to a specialist's "book" (more in Chapter 6). DOT/SuperDot give the trader almost instant access to the floor and to trade confirmations usually inside 60 seconds.

Tool Change: SOES on NASDAQ

If you were around (and trading) on October 19, 1987, you probably remember a very ugly day in the markets. As the market began to crash, investors who tried to unload stock in the panic over this 22-percent drop simply couldn't. And brokers, if available, couldn't find a market maker who would even answer a phone, let alone post a bid and buy a NASDAQ stock.

NASDAQ had created SOES, or *small-order execution system*, a few years earlier. SOES automates trading for orders less than 1,000 shares, allowing a customer or broker to automatically transact a stock with a market maker at the posted bid or ask price. With the 1987 crash, the SEC decided to make SOES mandatory for NASDAQ market makers. That meant all market makers have to post quotes on "both sides of the market" (that is, to buy and to sell) that can be executed automatically by someone else in the market. The result: a faster and more liquid market.

Rule Change: Limit Order Protection Rule

In response to a great deal of criticism from both the public *and* the SEC, the NASDAQ implemented limit order protection in 1997. There are two parts to this rule. One part requires a market maker to post any limit order that improves on the existing price. If your order improves the price over the going market, it becomes next in line and will get posted in the market for everyone to see. The market maker can't hide it to preserve a spread and inflate his or her *own* profits. The other part of the 1997 rule prohibited market makers from displaying better prices in "private" or electronic-network markets than they do to the public through NASDAQ systems. With this change, the playing field was leveled even more.

Rule Change: Teenies

In 1997, both the NASDAQ and the NYSE implemented minimum quotable trading intervals of one-sixteenth (6.25 cents) per share. Previously these had been in eighths. The result was to drive down "spreads" and require a smaller price movement to allow an investor to "cover the spread and move ahead." Even more math changes are ahead—coming soon to a market near you is decimal trading, which will make spreads a little bigger, but free us all from dealing with those darned fractions!

Future Rules and Tools

At the time of this writing, the NYSE is looking to establish a form of pure electronic trading to supplement the specialist system. And a new trading system called "Optimark" will bring multiple fragmented markets and very large and very small players together into one screen-based trading system. The exact effect these coming changes will have on day trading isn't clear, but it's safe to assume that changes will happen continually.

Behind the Screen

The NYSE is in no danger of being left behind in the high-tech dust. A recent report in *The New York Times* suggests that, although traders have met in person on the exchange floor for the past 207 years, the NYSE has said it might build or buy its own electronic trading network. Not everyone is pleased at the prospect. Some experts fear that "as the NYSE competes for business with other trading networks, it will be less insistent on enforcing the tough standards on companies that want to be listed there."

Commission Remission

The seeds of the day-trading revolution were planted in the 1920s and began to germinate with climate changes brought on by electronic transaction technology. But the revolution was really triggered on "May Day," May 1, 1975, when costly, fixed brokerage commissions became a thing of the past. New "discount" brokers popped up, reducing the standard industry commission of several hundred dollars to something less than $100. The commission revolution, started by firms like Charles Schwab, has taken on new strength in recent years with the advent of electronic Internet trading, which has driven down the same commissions to less than $30 for most and as low as $5 for many trades.

Behind the Screen

How can online brokers possibly be making money on the commissions they charge? At $29.95 a trade, Charles Schwab certainly seems to be, announcing big profit increases in the late spring of 1999 (and sending their own stock price soaring). Online brokers are getting more efficient and are handling much higher volumes, making them more profitable—perhaps the first form of e-commerce to really profit from the Internet.

If you do the math, you'll see that the effect on day trading is obvious. A one-day turnaround on 1,000 shares of XYZ, instead of costing $400, now costs $14! You, the day trader, get to keep the profit now! Put another way, your trade only has to be about 3 percent as successful to break even as it would have had to be in 1969!

For the really serious day trader, some firms waive the commission altogether if you buy their information services and make enough trades!

A Bigger Roller Coaster

Enter the "V" word. Volatility. You hear about it almost nightly on the news: Global stock markets are getting more volatile. What does that mean? Simply that they go up more and they go down more. Faster. A swifter, more exciting roller coaster ride.

Why? There is more interest in the stock market than ever before, to be sure. There are more players, with more opinions behind the moves they make. But one key reason is electronic trading—with so many people able to trade at the speed of light, what would we expect the market to do? Any little change of direction can be magnified by a deluge of buy or sell orders, then when folks change their minds, it can reverse just as quickly. And the instantaneous availability of information helps stir the pot—faster and faster.

Is this a bad thing? For the faint of heart or those who sleep easier at night knowing they own "a piece of the rock," it isn't so desirable. Folks like that should limit themselves to conservative investments, professional advice, and diversification— a.k.a. good old mutual funds.

But for the day trader, volatility is most definitely a *good* thing. The day trader lives off price changes, the sooner and the more of them the better. You've probably figured out that day traders help to create volatility and at the same time benefit from it. Day traders could be described as investors who like roller coasters!

Alarm Bells

The market is up. The market is down. The market is fast. Fast? In an effort to protect themselves against complaints, more online brokers are warning their customers about "fast market conditions." Characterized by wide price fluctuations and heavy trading (the very conditions day traders need to flourish) during which, according to a brochure recently mailed to all Schwab account holders, "even real-time quotes may be far behind what is currently happening in the market."

The New Right-to-Work State

Any other revolutions at work here? Yes, there is one more recent revolution that has made the increasing popularity of day trading possible: the huge numbers of folks who have gone home to work. With just a computer and a phone line, folks all across the country have decided to turn their backs on corporate jobs and try something different. All the better if it turns out they can make more money at it, too!

Whereas in past generations, quitting your day job and trying something else would have been viewed with deep suspicion and considered downright un-American, now it is considered an inalienable right! Many of us are now seeking to work from home, to balance family and work life, avoid having a boss, and engage in a little entrepreneurial endeavor.

Add up all of these factors and voila! The day-trading tradition emerges.

The Least You Need to Know

➤ Buying and selling stock used to be a slow process, done in person, on paper, and through the mail.

➤ New computer technology gives fast access to trading information and trading execution, and levels the field for the small trader.

➤ Up-to-the-minute stock information is available all over the Net.

➤ Regulated commissions on stock trades were abolished in 1975, allowing the rise of discount brokers.

➤ The small-order execution system (SOES) creates a faster and more liquid NASDAQ market. SuperDot speeds up trading on the NYSE.

Chapter 3

Is This Bud for You?

In This Chapter

➤ The many types of traders

➤ What it takes to succeed

➤ A day in the life of a day trader

➤ What you need to get started

➤ About the cost of day trading

So, this day-trading stuff sounds pretty hot all right, but are you really cut out for that life? After all, this wasn't one of the career choices your high school advisor discussed with you; how can you tell if your parachute has "Day Trader" written all over it?

In this chapter, we'll examine day trading a little more personally. We'll take inventory of what makes a good day trader, and what it takes to get started. This might not make complete sense until you learn more about some actual day-trading tools and techniques, so we recommend you read this now to prepare for those specifics, then read it *again* after you read Parts 2 through 5. Heckuva way to read a book, but we think it's the best way.

Day Traders Come in Different Colors

No two day traders are alike. In fact, diversity is a *very good thing* in this business. For if all day traders were alike, day trading wouldn't work! Everybody would do the same thing at the same time! They would buy the same stocks, respond to the same charts and indicators, and stay in the trade for the same amount of time.

Markets depend on different opinions about what is being traded. For every buyer, there must be a seller. If everyone did the same thing at the same time, there would be no market. No market, no day trading. The sheep would all be trying to hit the same entry or exit gate at the same time. Orders wouldn't get filled, and day traders would have to beg for their old jobs back.

Behind the Screen

What makes a stock move? What makes the market move? Everyone has an opinion, a superstition, or a pet theory. Thankfully, all those opinions, superstitions, and theories are different. Some traders have developed rigid buy signals that they adhere to; some have equally rigid sell signals. In order for there to be constant movement in and out of the market, day-in and day-out, everyone has to be doing it for a different reason.

Alarm Bells

You may decide that "this Bud" (day trading) isn't for you. That's *fine*. We aren't trying to convince anyone to run out and do this. If it sounds good, you'll be able to approach day trading with greater confidence and skill. Those of you who are tentative in life are likely to be tentative day traders—not a formula for success. If your parachute says "day trader" but has a few holes in it, better to recognize them now. This is a good chance for self-assessment. To repeat our old tag line: *Even if you don't day trade, what you learn in this book will help you do better with any form of investing.*

As in the workplace, day trading is enriched by diversity. Diversity of opinion, diversity of objectives, diversity of style. Let's explore….

Day traders can be grouped according to

➤ What they trade
➤ Trading style
➤ Time horizon

We'll talk a little more about each.

Peas, Carrots, Beans, or Corn

What a day trader trades tells a lot about the trader and what he/she needs to know. The *what* question is answered at two levels: what *markets* and what *securities*.

You can find day traders trading in almost all of the financial markets. Most day traders trade common stocks on either the NYSE or NASDAQ. But there is a bushel-basket of alternatives: equity options (for individual stocks), commodity futures (pork bellies, etc.), financial futures (stock indices), futures options, bonds, foreign markets, and so on. We'll explore these different types of markets a bit in Chapter 4, "There Are So Many Good

Things to Buy." To keep it a little simpler, we'll mainly focus on the common-stock day trader.

Now that we know the market, a day trader has to pick which individual stock or stocks to trade. Traders can pick a single stock and thoroughly immerse themselves in it, or a few stocks that they watch and trade continuously or in rotation, maybe in a single industry group. Or some will simply trade whatever's hot that day, even if they'd never heard of it before the opening bell.

The point that is common to all these choices: Day traders must decide where and what to trade, and wholly immerse themselves in acquiring knowledge and experience with choice. Research, watch, watch some more, learn, do, watch, learn, do, watch, research some more. Become a devoted student.

A Question of Style

Now that we know *what* they trade, let's talk a little about *how* they trade. Different strokes for different folks:

Scalpers are the most active group. They may make 50, 100, or more trades in a single day, trying to reap small gains of an eighth or a quarter of a point each. They thrive on action. Concentration, quick thinking, and reliable, high-speed access to the markets are essential. Timing is everything.

Then come the *momentum* traders. Momentum traders like to spot a stock that is "in play," that is, seems to be moving consistently in one direction either in response to rumor or fact. Rumors are more fun—and usually more profitable—so the momentum trader has one eye on the market itself and the other two eyes on news feeds and the chat rooms. *Three* eyes? Most day traders, especially momentum players, would trade a loved one or two for an extra eye....

Next, the *technicians*. These aren't guys in white coats in a laboratory, but they do like their numbers. They like them best when they're expressed as charts and graphs. All the better if those charts and graphs come with statistical interpretations of "buy signals" and "sell signals." Theoretical buzzers that go off when a stock reaches a

Daily Specials

Day trading has gotten a ton of press lately, and so too have mutual funds. Much ink about the tons of money pouring into the mutual-fund market. So can you day trade it? No. Trade frequently, yes. Mutual funds are priced just once daily and can't be traded intraday, but a hardy band of mutual-fund investors dart in and out of funds several times a week. You can find more about their strategies at www.fundsinteractive.com.

Trading Terms

Scalpers engage in the most active, high-stress style of day trading, trying to make money by trading in large enough blocks of stock that an eight or a quarter of a point gain brings in a small profit. And then it's on to another stock.

certain price, signaling opportunity based on the stock's prior behavior. Technicians may not need three eyes at once, but may need to replace their own eyes after years of looking at detailed charts!

Now, the *fundamentalists*. These Bible-totin' day traders look at the fundamental financial value and change of value in that company. Since companies (other than a few Internet companies these days) don't change a great deal in the course of a day, as a general rule, there aren't a lot of intra-day profit opportunities looking at fundamentals alone. But fundamentalists *will* trade on events specific to a company, such as an upcoming earnings report, stock split, reorganization, or acquisition.

Finally, the *dabblers*. Some of us, for whatever reason, can't or don't choose to make day trading a full-time job. Our *other* full-time job may prevent us from three-eyed or even one-eyed day trading. But for fun—and for money every now and then—we still might buy 100 shares of Amazon.com at the opening bell and use a stop order or a beeper signal to sell out. For fun—and for money every now and then.

Behind the Screen

You've seen them in action. Those sneaky folks at work who toggle back and forth between a work-related spreadsheet and an online trading screen. Those fingers fly fast when the boss approaches! They're either smirking at lunch because they're having an up day on the market, or sitting depressed and alone in the corner of the company lunchroom because they just lost a bundle. Sound familiar? Maybe because it's *you?*

Timing—What Makes You Tick?

The final feather that identifies day traders' "species" is the timeframe in which they operate. This relates somewhat to their style.

➤ **Minutes or less:** The *scalper* operates in minutes or seconds, picking up the little upward and downward pulses in the market. Sometimes the scalper makes money in NASDAQ stocks only by reacting faster than the market makers themselves. Market makers have a lot of jobs to do and can't always respond fast enough to price changes—scalpers will snap up outdated ("out-seconded!") bids and offers for profit. Other times, scalpers are grabbing pieces of a momentum-based move in the stock's price.

➤ **A few times a day:** The *momentum* trader may act as a scalper, capitalizing on fine little bits of momentum that come his way. A stock that has been trading sleepily all day might have a short burst up in volume and price as a large order comes in. The mo scalper will trade with it until the move and volume "peter out." Or, a momentum trader might trade up and down cycles that occur usually a few times within each day. In, out, two, three, four times a day, but always out at the end of the day.

➤ **Swing high, swing low:** The technician stays in as long as his indicators tell him to, maybe a few days as a *swing* trader. Likewise the fundamentalist will time trades according to the events followed. Finally, the dabbler usually makes only one or two trades a day, varying the timing according to when price objectives are reached.

What It Takes

Now you know a little more about other day traders, what kinds are out there in the woods. But you're probably asking (and why not?), "What does it take for *me* to become a day trader?"

We're going to run you through a rather lengthy checklist of traits and items that we think are important for successful day trading. You'll notice most of these are *personal* traits. Only a few are possessions. You airplane pilots in the audience may notice a lot of similarities between these traits and those of a good pilot. We recommend a casual walk through this list before going to "ground school," then another review once your familiar with day-trading tools and techniques.

So, before we take off, let's hit the checklist:

❏ **Knowledge:** An understanding of the inner workings of the market and stock that you're trading, what makes it move and why.

❏ **Confidence:** This is absolutely critical. Can't act without it. Second-guessing will result in missed opportunities, missed gains, and extended losses.

❏ **Ability to act:** Ditto. You have to be able to pull the trigger, both to get in and get out. No room for the tentative.

❏ **Willingness to learn:** ...From your mistakes. When something doesn't work, don't get mad or back away. Figure out *why* it didn't work.

❏ **Willingness to try:** Nothing ventured, nothing gained. The willingness to try new things opens doors to new information, strategies, and tactics. Also important: What works today may not work tomorrow, as market makers and other traders get familiar with it. Too many people in the market doing the same thing can crowd a trader out. Take measured risks; seek new experiences.

❏ **Willingness to accept failure and responsibility:** This one's huge. The losing day trader who blames someone else or bad luck for his troubles is doomed. Don't dwell on it.

❏ **Passion:** You've gotta love it. If money, lots of numbers, and fast, independent action turn you off, then day trading is probably not for you.

❏ **Patience:** "Willingness to act" and similar adages don't suggest shooting from the hip in hopes of hitting a bullseye. Pick your targets and aim carefully. If you see a new opportunity, especially on a stock heretofore unheard of, watch it for a while. You probably won't starve in the meantime. It's OK not to have any positions open if the time just isn't right. Sometimes you will have to practice not just patience, but also restraint.

❏ **Reverse psychology:** Always a little room for the contrarian. There's a lot of dumb money (and novice day traders) out there. Think—don't always follow the crowd.

❏ **Facility with numbers:** This one's hard for some, and isn't easily acquired if you don't have it. Is $^{13}/_{32}$ bigger or smaller than $^1/_4$? If you guessed bigger, you're right, but if you have to do it on your fingers, you'll be left behind (and will run out of fingers!) Recognizing number and number patterns—in fast, real-time action—is important.

❏ **Concentration:** Ah, the "C" word. In day trading, so much information flys by at Mach I speed, especially for the scalper or "Level II" trader, which we'll describe later on. You've gotta stay on top of it, be able to avoid distractions, and stay focused.

There are some forms of day trading you should *not* try in a house filled with barking dogs and tiny children wandering in and out.

❏ **Discipline:** And now, the "D" word. In order to day trade successfully, you must stick to your plans, despite the turbulence in the market. Don't hold out for that extra sixteenth if you know that momentum is slowing on an up move. Get out when you hit your objective. Sell a small loss before it becomes a big loss (which they usually do). Avoid greed, hope, and fear! Keep track of what you do: Write things down. It's perfectly OK to take a day off whenever you want, but while you're "on the job," you must practice both concentration and discipline.

❏ **Skill:** Know your tools and how to use them. Enough said.

❏ **Stamina:** This can be hard work! Watching all the numbers go by, interpreting, keeping track of what's going on. A good day trader is conditioned for short, intense periods of brain and eye work. Nobody said this was easy—if it were easy, everybody would be doing it!

❏ **Money:** Hmm … it took us awhile to mention this requirement. You thought the list should have started here? Just how much does it take to get started? Opinions vary, as do broker requirements. You should probably figure $10K to $50K *uncommitted* investment capital, plus $5,000 or so to buy computer hardware and connectivity, data feeds, and trading tools. Check your piggybank. And please,

please, remember our stern warnings from Chapter 1: Don't mortgage your house, dip into your children's college fund, or cash out your retirement funds to day trade!

❏ **Connections:** In earlier decades this would have meant a *personal* network. Now, we mean one for your *computer*. Home-based day traders will want a fast and especially dependable hardware connection and ISP (Internet service provider). High-performance day traders might want high-speed Internet access (ISDN, DSL) or even direct network (WAN/frame relay) connections. Many traders have redundant connect capability, so if one blows up, the other is ready.

Alarm Bells

"This can be an exhausting way to live," one active day trader confided in us. "Sure, I'm done by the time the market is closed for the day, but then I find I need a nap!" Many traders keep a rigorous exercise routine just to stay in trading shape!

❏ **Information:** Information is the instrument panel of day trading. Sure, you can fly without it, but the more, the better, the faster, the easier to read—you get the picture. Includes raw data, news feeds, graphics, and interpretation.

❏ **Goals:** Sit down and think about what you're trying to achieve. $200 a day? $300? $1,000? Enough to pay bills or are you saving for a college education? Is this a long-term career choice or a transition? What do you want to achieve by day trading?

❏ **Strategies:** Once the goals are in place, you need strategies to achieve them: trading strategies, strategies for allocating your time, and so forth.

❏ **Rules:** Goes hand in hand with strategies—these are rules you set for yourself and maintain through your experience. For instance, selling a trade that "goes bad" by a quarter of a point in five minutes.

❏ **Agreements:** What's this? You thought day trading was an independent activity. No more endless team meetings, deals, demanding bosses, whining subordinates, and other office headaches. Just you and your computer in a tiny little room. Sure, this is true if you're single, but if not, well, it's a good idea to share what you're doing with your spouse. Like with any other major decisions in life and marriage, share your plans with your partner to avoid any unpleasant surprises.

OK, How'd You Do?

All of the above was really just sort of a personal inventory to help you figure out if "this Bud's for you." Do you have to have all of these traits? Well, you might get away with slightly less than 100%, but not too much less.

We'll say it again—day trading isn't for everyone. If it's for you, great. If it *isn't*, well, we hope you'll share our book with a friend. And if you're not sure, read on!

The Least You Need to Know

➤ The markets move up and down because hundreds of thousands of traders each have a different opinion and act accordingly.

➤ Most day traders trade common stocks, but some do trade commodities futures, options, or other types of markets.

➤ "Scalpers" are very short-term day traders who try to make a profit on fractional gains. Momentum traders try to spot stocks on the move and go along for the ride.

➤ Some day traders hold onto a stock for mere minutes before selling; others may hold for several hours.

➤ Day trading requires several personality traits: confidence, the ability to act, patience, stamina, and a facility for numbers among them.

Chapter 4

There Are So Many Good Things to Buy

In This Chapter

➤ What can you day trade?

➤ Which is better—stocks, options, or commodities?

➤ Or maybe a stock index?

➤ Why we like stocks best

We know that you were much more selective during your dating days, but remember that old expression: "Some guys will chase anything that moves." Well, here's your chance to act on it! As a day trader, you can trade anything you darn well please, as long as it *moves*. (The *price*, that is.) Why? If it didn't move, only the broker would get rich. And we wouldn't want that, would we?

Sure, you could day trade baseball cards, beanie babies, or even tulip bulbs (they actually did back in the 1600s). But as a practical matter, while popular and full of wild price movement, these might not work for day trading. Why not? We'll get to that, and tell you what you should look for in a day-trading market and instrument.

Making the Shopping List

What makes something a candidate for day trading?

They say a pilot's best friends are altitude and airspeed. You need both, or you're in real trouble! For a day trader it is *action* and *access*, which involve the following:

➤ Liquidity

➤ Volume

➤ Movement

➤ Access to information

➤ Access to trade

Let's look at them one at a time:

Liquidity

We defined liquidity in Chapter 1 as "the availability of enough buyers and sellers to quickly and easily execute transactions in a market." Liquidity results in fast, reliable executions at predictable prices. Easy entry, easy exit from the market.

There is no quantitative measure of liquidity. It is driven by a combination of

➤ Capitalization (number of shares outstanding).

➤ Volume.

➤ Breadth of ownership—number of share or contract owners.

➤ Number of market makers.

➤ Familiarity of market players with the company or commodity.

Daily Specials

Yahoo!Finance is our favorite charting tool for beginners—for stocks anyway. Type a symbol, bring up the quote, then click "Graph" and look at the "1-day" and "5-day" charts. If the charts resemble the Grand Tetons, it's a candidate. Flat as Kansas? Better look elsewhere. Make sure the automatically scaled "y-axis" on the left is scaled in large enough units. A stock trading in an eighth-point range through the day will look like *one* Grand Teton replicated across the page. Not exactly what you want.

For stocks, assume that any stock in an index (Dow Jones averages, S&P 500, S&P 100) is liquid. Futures and options are generally less liquid, although many of the leading financial and commodity futures can be as liquid as the most liquid stocks. Liquidity may change over time, as commodities change with the seasons.

Remember, the greater the liquidity, the smaller the spread (usually). A smaller hill to climb for profit.

Volume

Volume is both an indicator and an element of a liquidity, but it is measurable. A good day trading stock should trade minimum 100,000 shares each day. Futures and options—100 contracts or so passing through the market on any given day should be the minimum. The higher, the better.

Movement

As we said in the opener, you can go for anything that moves! Well, not *anything*. But to make it worthwhile it obviously has to move, and since it's a *day* trade, it should be reasonably fast. And we'd *like* it to be predictable, but that's a whole 'nuther can of worms, which we'll open in Part 4, "Tools of the Trade."

Most traders say your day-trading selection should move at least four or five times the trading unit (sixteenths, eighths, cents, dollars, whatever) in a day to make it worthwhile. More is better. We say the day's trading range should be at least $1, that is, the average difference between the highest price of the day and the lowest. Again, more is better for most day-trading strategies.

Sophisticated statistical measures called *volatility* measures, are available to measure movement. You remember sleeping through this in freshman statistics class—standard deviations and all that icky stuff. More practical for you as an everyday day trader is to simply look at a chart and use a little common sense.

Access to Information

This one's kind of obvious, we think. If it's hard to get quotes or news stories, you're flying blind. If nobody's heard of it, chances are nobody's trading it, and when you want to get out, nobody's buying it. Which leads to…

Easy Access to Trade

The stock, commodity, option, or tulip bulb must be easy to trade at a moment's notice. Online, real time. That rules out the bulbs unless you run the world's best roadside stand. Essential are immediate access to up-to-the-minute quotes and push-button or mouse click trading.

Stocking Up on Stocks

When most people talk about day trading, they talk about stocks. In fact, we've noticed nowadays when any two people talk about *anything* they talk about stocks! Our assumption is that you have a basic knowledge of what stocks *are*—shares of ownership in a corporation whose value is determined in a stock *market*. We're talking about *common* stocks here.

Stocks offer most of the advantages—liquidity, volume, movement, information access, ease of trading. At least, *some* stocks. You can't just decide stocks—it's *which* stocks, *which* markets.

> **Alarm Bells**
>
> Day traders keep one eye on the computer screen, and another on the clock. Better make sure that clock is right! In early April 1999, hoping to take advantage of momentum in the online brokers' stocks, Jennifer bought 100 shares of SIEB, intending to close it out before the end of the day. Alas, she hadn't changed her clock over the weekend to reflect daylight savings time…. She missed the close of the market—and so a swing trade was born! She held the stock for three days, selling for a $600 gain.

Stock Markets

We'll explore the inner workings of the major stock markets starting in Chapter 6, "Trading Places: The NYSE," and 7, "Trading Places: The NASDAQ." Both markets provide suitable liquidity, information, easy access to trading for the day trader. In fact both markets provide excellent real-time access to quote and activity data through computerized trading systems. The NASDAQ, being sort of an "open" electronic market, provides still greater visibility to underlying supply and demand useful to the serious or "high-performance" day trader. We'll explore that further too. You'll learn how both of these markets operate, and how to use their information to your advantage.

There are other markets. The American Stock Exchange (AMEX, or "annex" as some Wall Streeters refer to it) is much smaller than the NYSE or NASDAQ. Most stocks trade at much lower volume levels with less liquidity and less electronic visibility. For the most part, we'd stay away from AMEX, although the effects of the recent merger with NASDAQ are still unknown.

Regional markets also dot the landscape. The Philadelphia, Midwest, Cincinnati, and Pacific stock exchanges are the largest. For the most part, the stocks traded on these exchanges are also traded on the major exchanges, so these markets aren't part of the average day trader's strategy.

Stock Prices

For the most part, stock prices are simply a matter of supply and demand. At least, that's what every book about investing tells us. Let's go along with that basic explanation but please keep in mind the fact that an awful lot of things can influence supply and demand! (Some of them will be discussed in Chapter 8, "On the Move"—fundamentals, technicals, and all that stuff.) But it's exciting for the day trader that technology can now provide a short-term crystal ball.

In the next chapter we will give some more details about stock prices and quotes.

Now the homework begins. It's important to learn more about not only the market but individual stocks and the companies they represent. Then about the stock's behavior. And how the industry moves and how the company's stock moves in comparison. How it responds to news, how it trades, how the professionals view the company and the stock. How to chart and interpret behavior patterns.

And so ends our lecture on stocks. Now it's time you met some *other* popular items on the day trader's menu.

Trading Terms

An **option** is a contract to buy or sell a stock, commodity or a futures contract at a particular price by a particular date.

Other Options?

An option is a contract to buy (or sell) something at or before a specific time at a specific price. This fairly simple idea has evolved into a major trading platform for institutional and individual investors alike.

Options come in three types: equity options, futures options, and index options. For simplicity, we'll stick to equity options.

What Is an Equity Option?

An equity option contract is a contract to buy (or sell) 100 shares of a stock by a certain time (the expiration) at a certain price (strike price). A Dell JUNE 40 CALL is an option to buy 100 shares of Dell Computer between now and the third Friday in June at $40 per share. A Dell JUNE 30 PUT is an option, with the same expiration date, to *sell* 100 shares at $30 each. Options trade on several exchanges, the largest being the Chicago Board Options Exchange, or CBOE.

Daily Specials

To research the options symbol for any stock you might be thinking of trading, go to your online broker and look for the option chain search function. It is different from the stock symbol research function. You can also log onto the Chicago Board Options Exchange Web site at www.cboe.com.

Behind the Screen

You've no doubt noticed over the years that most stock symbols bear some kind of relationship to the company name: MSFT for Microsoft, HWP for Hewlett-Packard, SCH for Charles Schwab. But when trading options on NASDAQ stocks, there's a whole 'nuther alphabet at work. What do you suppose KQBAC might mean? It is a January 115 call for the Internet portal Excite, XCIT. ZQNDQ would be an April 185 call for Amazon.com stock, AMZN.

The Chicago Board Options Exchange Web site…for more about equity options.

Option Prices

Options are usually traded in strike-price increments of $5 for a price range that's relevant to the stock price. For higher volume options, often there will be a smaller strike-price increment of $2.50. For our Dell example, put and call options are likely to be found at strike prices of $30, $32.50, $35, $37.50, $40, $42.50, and $45 at the time of this writing. The greater the price swings of the stock, the broader the band of option prices. The time horizon is usually monthly for the "closest in" three months, then quarterly for the next six months. For some stocks you can buy LEAPS (long-term equity appreciation options) with strike dates going out to two years.

A Transfer of Risk

An equity option is really no more than a transfer of risk from the seller to the buyer at a market price. A call *writer* (seller) gives up the potential for future price gains but gets a *premium* (the option price) for doing so. Cash is collected, reducing risk by lowering the effective cost of the security. It also gives the stockholder more protection in a downturn.

The call *buyer*, on the other hand, is taking on additional risk. An option price is inflated to account for the uncertainty of events and movement between now and the expiration date. Unless the stock moves upward enough to cover this part of the premium, the call buyer will lose his investment (which usually happens!). On the other hand, a call buyer gets *leverage*—higher returns as a percent—if he does pick the right stock, strike price, and time period.

Equity-Option Pricing

Hours have been burned by hopeful business school Masters and Ph.D. candidates on developing theoretical option-pricing models, but it's still a big mystery. Equity option prices are a function of three things:

➤ **Intrinsic value:** If Dell is trading today at $37, it is easy to see that a June 30 call is worth a lot more than a June 40 call. The intrinsic value is pretty simple. Fifteen bucks for the former, zip for the latter.

➤ **Volatility** is more interesting. Suppose Dell traded between 30 and 60 during the last 6 months, and Static Communications Inc, also selling today at $37, moved only between $35 and $38 during the same 3-month period. Between a Dell June 40 Call and a Static June 40 Call, which is worth more? Which option appears to have the greatest profit potential given recent stock price history? The answer is… Dell, of course. (Please, raise your hand quietly, don't just blurt it out!) Normally, the Dell option will sell for more than the Static option because of volatility. How much more? Only the Ph.D.s know for sure. When stocks, or markets in general, get more volatile, volatility premiums go higher. So do option prices.

➤ **Time until expiration** is the third and final factor. The more time between today and the expiration date, the more that can "go right" with this option. A June 40 call will be worth more than a May 40 call. How much? You know the answer: Ask a Ph.D.

At, In, or Out of the Money

Don't panic, this isn't a preposition proposition, we aren't in a freshman English class, or even watching "Schoolhouse Rock"! What we're talking about is the choice of "strike" prices for options and what they mean.

Take Dell at $37. An (almost) at-the-money option would be a June 37.50 call. An out-of-the-money option would be the June 40 call, and an in-the-money would be a June 35 call. Why is this important? Because the behavior of intrinsic value, volatility, and time-premium components change. An out-of-the-money call has a greater chance to "win big," percentage-wise, and will get a greater time and volatility premium as a result. "Deep" in-the-money call prices will owe more to the intrinsic value, less on volatility and time.

What About Day-Trading Options?

It would seem that options would be a pretty good tool for the day trader. Big percentage price moves, right? Actually, there are two problems. First, the time premium tends to dampen price moves. Second, spreads are usually higher than for stocks, sometimes a quarter to a half a point.

If you day trade options expiring several months out, you might be disappointed. Small gains and losses in the stock will be virtually invisible in the option price, which is built on time and volatility premiums. As we get closer to expiration, the price is based more on intrinsic value, so underlying stock price changes will have greater effect.

So a possible day-trading strategy is to buy stock options close to expiration (less than one month) and in-the-money. Both will get you closer to intrinsic value, which get you closer to realizing point-for-point the moves of the stock. Advantages: 1) Less capital invested than if you actually bought the stock, 2) Some downside protection—you can only lose the amount invested.

And, options can be used to hedge other day trades. Buy a put to get downside disaster protection for the next few months on a particular stock, while trading that same stock daily for short upside moves.

Finally, combinations of options can reduce risk and increase profit possibilities. Buy or sell a put *and* call at the same or different strike prices. Buy an in-the-money call and sell an out-of-the-money call. Buy a call with a long expiration, sell another with a short one. You can read about straddles, strangles, spreads, and other sexy option techniques in any option-strategy book.

Huh? Still don't understand options? You're not alone. Understanding options takes patience and experience. We recommend trading options only after getting experience trading stocks and visiting your favorite bookstore to find a good option book.

Fire in the Bellies

Now let's switch to futures. Futures are a bit like equity options: a contract to buy an amount of something at a specified price at or by a specified time. The idea is similar to equity options—a transfer of risk and leverage from a seller to a buyer for a price. The pricing behavior of futures is similar to options.

Commodity Futures

Corn, wheat, soybeans, pork bellies, the whole hog. Oil, gas, gold, silver, platinum. All of these commodities can be traded as futures. Producers use these futures to collect some cash and hedge against market downturns, buyers use them to hedge against price upturns or to speculate. For instance, Starbucks buys a lot of coffee futures in order to make sure they can buy coffee beans at fairly stable prices, which allows them to offer a stable price when a customer buys a latte this week, next week, or next month.

Some day traders trade commodity futures and do it quite well. But you really have to know the business—market *internals* (trends, directions, momentum) and market *externals* (what the weather is like in Iowa). Most commodity traders are professionals. You gotta be good to make money at this, and this isn't where most day traders (or other investors, for that matter) are recommended to start.

Behind the Screen

Commodities traders are an odd breed, but who'd have guessed that some of them are... moonies? Yes, some Chicago traders put great faith in their belief that the changing lunar phases increase market volatility and change trends. A recent article in the *Wall Street Journal* brought these beliefs to light. When asked about it, one expert suggested that "people like having something they can put their finger on." So believing that the market will move with the phases of the moon is as good a reason as any.

Financial Asset Futures

In the case of financial futures, we're talking about T-bonds, bills, notes, Deutschmarks, yen, Swiss francs. Most of these futures are less volatile than commodity futures, for one thing, they aren't subject to random acts of weather! Further, governments and central banks try to keep things stable. For the day trader, lots of liquidity but not much price fluctuation, and difficult to keep up with and interpret all the news.

Fingering the Indexes

Unless you've been living in a cave (and even some of them are probably wired for the Internet now) you've probably heard of the "S&P 500" and the "S&P 100." What are they, anyway? They are stock index futures. Also like options, they are based on a strike price and an expiration date. An S&P 500 June 1200 call is worth money if the index closes at 1250 on the third Friday of June. Do they dump 50/1250th's of the market basket on you? No. The settlement is always in cash.

Stock indices are based on a basket of stocks. The S&P 500 and NASDAQ 100 broadly represent the market as a whole. (The NASDAQ 100, naturally, represents only the NASDAQ.) There are also several industry-based indices for semiconductors, technology, health care, now even an index which takes into account the current prices for Internet stocks.

These index futures are generally liquid, easy to trade, and some (like the Internet or technology index) with decent price movement. Many day traders consider these indices key information. These traders don't actually trade these indices though, but rather use them as leading indicators of market direction or as a possible hedge against individual stock trade.

We Pick Stocks. Why?

So which of these is best suited to day trading? The short answer is: stocks. Stocks—at least the more popular ones, seem to have everything we need for fast day trading: liquidity, volume, movement, breadth of ownership, access to information, trading access. Stocks are easier to understand. There is more professional advice available and more services for the small investor. With stocks it is easier to limit exposure. And unlike the options world there are no expirations to worry about—stocks never expire (until you sell them, that is).

To Infinity, and Beyond

As you get more familiar with day trading (or any kind of trading, for that matter) you might want to venture into some of these financial instruments. Training courses for futures and options occur almost nightly in most major cities, and there are the usual video and Net-based self-paced training programs available. Browse your *Investor's Business Daily* or *Wall Street Journal*. Or check out Jake Bernstein's book *The Compleat Day Trader* for more about futures trading or "Day Traders of Orange County" (www.worldwidetraders.com) for more about trading equity options. The CBOE and CBOT also maintain useful Web sites (www.cboe.com, www.cbot.com) for investors of all flavors.

Stay seated please, class. In Chapter 5, "Why All the Fuss?", we will take a closer look at why so many people—from the head of the SEC to several members of Congress—have their knickers in a twist over day trading. Why all the fuss?

Daily Specials

Day trading sounds pretty lonely, isn't there a clubhouse you can hang out in? Actually, there are several. Day Traders of Orange County has a chat room open 24 hours a day where you can swap ideas, methods, and strategies after hours. Check out their Web site at www.worldwidetraders.com.

The Least You Need to Know

➤ Day traders look for action—liquidity, volume, and price movement—in whatever they trade.

➤ For most day-trading strategies a good stock should trade at least 100,000 shares a day, and move at least four or five times the trading unit—the more the better.

➤ Not all stocks bounce the same way, it is important to study how a particular stock moves in relationship to the market, other stocks, and company news.

➤ Options have limitations for day trading (high spread, dampened price movement) but can be used to hedge other trades.

➤ Commodity futures trading requires specialized knowledge that few ordinary day traders have.

Why All the Fuss?

In This Chapter

➤ Why doesn't everyone approve of day trading?

➤ Who doesn't approve—and why?

➤ What do traditional and online brokers think?

➤ Tales of the formerly rich and famous

For four cheerful chapters we've led you through this brave new world of day trading. But in Chapter 5, we'd like to take a different course. It is time to confront the fact that not everyone thinks day trading is such a hot idea. In fact, quite a few folks out there think day trading represents the end of civilization as we know it. All right, so maybe that is a bit of an exaggeration. What some folks fear, in fact, is that day trading means the end of the civilized stock-trading business as *they* know it.

Who's Making Such a Stink?

Here's a short list of the folks who aren't such big fans of day trading:

➤ The Securities and Exchange Commission (the SEC)

➤ The National Association of Securities Dealers (NASD)

➤ Full-service stockbrokers

➤ A handful of members of Congress

Alarm Bells

Complaints to the SEC have risen by an astonishing 330 percent in the last year (early 1998 to early 1999). Ranging from difficulty in accessing accounts and executing trades to mishandling trades and unexpected margin calls, many of the complaints are from online traders. But the SEC isn't blaming the online brokers, it is advising online traders to understand the risks.

And many stock-market players are, at best, lukewarm to the idea, knowing full well that it has great potential to harm their businesses. Among the folks who are more than a little wary are:

➤ Market makers

➤ Online brokerage houses

➤ The financial press

Let's wander down these lists one at a time to see who doesn't like what and why.

The Disapproving Parents

The Securities and Exchange Commission, responsible for enforcing the nation's securities laws and known as Wall Street's "Top Cop," would like to say this to online traders—you're on your own, pal. Responding to the rise in complaints to the SEC over system delays and mishandled orders, SEC Chairman Arthur Levitt Jr. places the responsibility squarely with the trader, not the broker.

Behind the Screen

Arthur Levitt Jr., chairman of the Securities and Exchange Commission, was named to the post by President Clinton after a long and successful career on Wall Street. He must be sympathetic toward brokers and big traders, right? Wrong. According to *The* Wall Street Journal *Guide to Who's Who and What's What on Wall Street,* many of his initiatives as SEC chairman have been designed to stamp out practices that once were integral parts of Mr. Levitt's life in the securities industry. "When you come to a job like this, your mind changes about so many issues that, before, you had kind of a proprietary interest in," Levitt explained.

Levitt believes that traders need to recognize the following:

➤ The limitations of online trading technology: Things can go wrong; have a backup option.

➤ The risks associated with fast-moving stocks: Some stocks move up and down so quickly that prices online brokers quote may no longer be accurate by the time the order is executed.

➤ The risks associated with buying on margin: Be aware of both what is expected of you, and your potential for loss.

These statements offer little comfort to frustrated customers trying to make a buck.

Badges? We Don't Need No Stinking Badges!

The National Association of Securities Dealers, on the other hand, is more directly involved with some of the day-trading issues that have been getting the most press. One of the most unusual situations involves the Philadelphia Stock Exchange:

The Philadelphia Stock Exchange began to notice that many of the newly opened day-trading firms were flocking to join the exchange, making it their regulator, rather than the NASD. Why? It appears to be because the PSE does not require its off-floor traders to pass the NASD's Series 7 exam. A Series 7 license is what stockbrokers must have before they can sell stock. It is a difficult test that requires knowledge of a wide variety of investments, securities law, the proper way to figure margin requirements, and other investment-related financial matters. This multiple-choice exam is also called the General Securities Registered Representative Examination.

On March 10, 1999, the Philadelphia Stock Exchange proposed a rule change that henceforth would require any trader associated with a member firm would have to pass a Series 7 exam. The chairman and chief executive of the exchange, Meyer S. Frucher, hopes that this will address the worry that many day traders don't know enough about investing: "We felt that people who did not have sufficient background as traders were being enticed to come in and risk large sums of money without education. People need to be protected from themselves."

Behind the Screen

Walter Hamilton, a financial writer for the *Los Angeles Times*, sums up the general feeling toward day traders like this: "In every great bull run on Wall Street, someone or something comes to symbolize what's wrong with the market—'wrong' usually meaning excessive profits earned at others' expense. From the "go-go" mutual-fund managers of the late 1960s to penny-oil stock investors of the late 1970s to takeover-traders in the mid 1980s—Hollywood's Gordon Gekko—the villains have uniformly been accused of unbridled greed. We cheered when they finally crashed and burned. Today, the personification of late 1990s bull-market greed is the 'day trader.'"

And if this rule change passes, what does that mean to day traders? That those day-trading firms affiliated with the PSE would no longer be able to offer a seat at the computer to just anyone with the required minimum trading balance. That day traders who wanted to trade from a day-trading office would first have to sit down with a number 2 pencil and pass a rigorous test.

Trading Terms

Rule 405 requires full-service brokerage houses to obtain significant facts from customers who are opening new accounts: to "Know your customer." Armed with this knowledge, the broker is required to only make stock recommendations that would be appropriate for that customer's financial situation and long-term financial goals.

This same feeling of protectiveness has also sprung up in several members of Congress. On February 11, 1999, four members of Congress asked the General Accounting Office to conduct a probe of the day-trading industry. Only time will tell if their efforts bring about any rules changes.

"Know Your Customer"

Are big, full-service brokerage houses in favor of day trading? Heavens no. The basic problem is that the idea of buying a stock and selling it seconds, minutes, or hours later, goes against every tenet that they hold dear. For decades, investment houses have been building up images of slow and steady growth, of financial success in the long run rather than an overnight windfall. And these same investment houses have been building this fatherly image of solid advice so that they could do one thing and one thing only—charge their customers a hefty commission.

Behind the Screen

Many day-trading firms that operate trading rooms around the country are under the spotlight, and they're crying foul. Regulators are asking trading rooms for information regarding their clients' success rates. But hey, the firms respond, why should they have to prove that a majority of their clients make money when Merrill Lynch and other full-service brokerage houses don't have to meet a requirement like that?

Full-service stockbrokers operate under the "Know Your Customer" rule. This is a real rule, rule number 405 of the New York Stock Exchange. Actually, stockbrokers are required to know their customers (and their customers' financial situation, risk tolerance, and long-term financial goals) well enough to discourage their clients from making any kind of nutty, wild move that might jeopardize the client's portfolio. If a client who has long been a conservative investor in gas and electric stocks phone up and announce that he'd like to buy 1,000 shares of Amazon.com on margin, the stockbroker would at least have to discuss it with someone higher up in his company before placing the trade.

Online Threats

Net stocks are soaring…and most of the big brokerage houses are frowning at the sight: "Overvalued! The bubble will soon burst! It can't go on like this!" Many of the big brokers' analysts spout gloom and doom as the forecast for these rapidly rising stocks. And who is trading these stocks, pumping the prices up ever higher? The answer, class, is…day traders! So here we have conservative firms taking a conservative stance with regard to a renegade part of the market. Net stocks—they just don't trust 'em. And day traders who trade net stocks? Even worse.

So don't look for the old-line firms to come out in favor of day trading. And chances are, they won't make any effort to develop products that will interest or assist day traders.

But the online brokers must be loving this day-trading thing, right? Well…not so fast. Yes, commissions and profits are way up as a result of increased trading. So are their own companies' stock prices (as of this writing, anyway). But does the practice of day trading have a dark side where the online brokerage houses are concerned? Absolutely.

But aren't the online brokerage houses really cleaning up on this movement? Sure, but they're also having to pay out every so often. Why? Because they're getting *sued* every so often. System delays, system overloads, system breakdowns—you see, the system is not perfect. As we were writing this very chapter (on April 21, 1999), we couldn't access our own trading accounts on Charles Schwab because the system was down for a few hours. No doubt a few disgruntled customers will file over that one, claiming that they lost big sums of money as a result. In February 1999, an E*Trade customer sued them for damages for lost financial opportunities after the company's trading system crashed four times in one week.

There is also greater potential for a major margin headache. We will cover margin in a later chapter, but suffice it to say that the more margin that is

Alarm Bells

Frank Zarb, the chairman of the National Association of Securities Dealers, has this to say about day trading: "Investors must be properly warned about the risks they may be taking in this environment with unprecedented levels of day trading." He is particularly concerned about the vulnerability of potential traders with insufficient capital and investment knowledge.

extended on fast market stocks, the greater financial exposure that the houses open themselves up to in a major market downturn. Sure, they'll make margin calls. The problem is, will enough customers have the money to cover the margin? Or will the brokerage house take a tumble?

Behind the Screen

Day traders rule. OK, maybe not, but they certainly have a big presence—on the NASDAQ, that is. Day traders make up 12 to 15 percent of average trading volume of NASDAQ, and the figure is rising. And, according to the *Los Angeles Times,* when you add in the "millions of online investors [who] account for another 20 percent of the NASDAQ volume and often mimic day-trading strategies, trigger-happy small investors may now control one third of NASDAQ activity."

So day-trading is a bit of a two-edged sword for the online brokerage houses. More action, more profit, but much more potential for serious business headaches.

Who's Making the Market?

More active trading is normally a bonanza for the professional market makers who make a living buying and selling—dealing, really—in stocks. But day traders have learned to grab some of the profits previously enjoyed exclusively by this elite club. And day traders often create wild price swings in stocks they trade, resulting in greater exposure. So it's common for NASDAQ market makers and NYSE specialists (whose roles we'll define in the next two chapters) to consider day traders as adversaries. They will resist any rule or technology that gives more power to day traders.

Planners Pan it

All across America, folks have hung out their shingles as financial planners. Not stock-brokers per se, but folks with a variety of credentials who'd like to help you with your investment portfolio, insurance needs, taxes, trusts, and other aspects of long-range financial planning. What do these folks think about day trading? Let's check in with one.

Jack W. Everett, CFP, AIMC, of Granite Bay, California, has been a financial planner for 26 years. In his monthly newsletter, *Financial Focus,* he tells the following story:

> Recently a tax client came to me with a major concern. He was excited about this wonderful way to get rich quick that he had discovered. Day trading was the

pathway to riches. In fact, he had just made a six-figure profit in one trade, trip-ling his money in a matter of a couple of days. The only problem was that he didn't have enough money to pay the taxes. Right there is a clue that there could be more to it than instant riches. As it turns out, he really doesn't have a tax problem. The rest of his trades solved it for him!

Flat, Busted, Broke

Who else is pretty down on the idea of day trading? More than a handful of folks who gave it a whirl and lost their shirts. Here are just a few hard-luck stories we were able to find in the media:

➤ In the *Los Angeles Times*: A woman who "raised cash to day trade by taking out a second mortgage on her home … recently dropped out [of coming to the trading room] after losing most of her $50,000."

➤ On *60 Minutes*: A liberal arts major lost the bulk of a $200,000 inheritance in less than a year.

➤ In the *New York Times*: A widower tried several times to make money day trading only to say "in terms of making a profit, I would have been better off putting the money in a mutual fund."

You should be acutely aware that day trading has been unsuccessful for a great many people who have tried it. For every person who shows up in the pages of a newspaper, there are more than a handful who keep quiet about their losses.

Changing the Rules

So, is anyone really going to do anything to make it tougher for the general public to day trade? No one really knows what the future will hold. But in the meantime, the NASD has proposed a rule change requiring members to disclose the risks in jumping in and out of stocks. The proposed rules will require member firms to assess their clients' suitability to day trade by looking closely at their financial situation and level of trading experience. Member firms would also give clients a disclosure statement with the following grim points about day trading:

➤ Investors should be prepared to lose all their money and should not day trade with retirement savings, student loans, or second mortgages. They should be wary of advertisements emphasizing large profits.

➤ Day trading requires in-depth knowledge of the securities markets and trading techniques. Investors are competing with professional, licensed traders.

➤ Investors should be familiar with the securities firm's business practices, includ-ing the operation of order-execution systems and procedures, and should confirm that a firm has adequate systems capacity to permit customers to engage in day trading.

The Electronic Traders Association (an association of day trading firms) welcomes the guidelines. James Lee, who is both the head of the Electronic Traders Association as well as president of Momentum Securities Management in Houston, had this to say: "This is almost verbatim...[the] risk-disclosure document we voluntarily proposed in January of 1999. We support it."

The Least You Need to Know

➤ Day trading has more than a handful of foes—the SEC, NASD, and full-service brokers to name just a few.

➤ Complaints to the SEC have risen dramatically in the past year, but in cases involving online trading the SEC generally blames the trader, not the broker.

➤ Full-service brokers won't be cultivating day traders anytime soon; the practice goes against the very investing principles they hold dear.

➤ The chairman of the National Association of Securities Dealers believes that investors should be properly warned about the potential risks of day trading.

➤ Online brokerage houses have profited from day trading, but they have also been the target of lawsuits brought by unhappy traders.

Part 2
A Trip to the Markets

Before you can really understand day trading, you need to understand just how the stock markets function (the NYSE, the NASDAQ...). Not only do you have to understand how the markets function, you need to know what the critical players do—specialists, market makers, ECNs and the like.

Only by thoroughly understanding what these folks do and how they do it will you begin to see how day trading works.

And a thorough understanding will also help you home in on just what you might want to trade—because you want to trade something that moves, *and the more you understand how to spot what is about to move, the better.*

Trading Places: The NYSE

Once we know *what's* traded, the next logical step is to understand *how* it's traded. But we can't go far in this direction without discussing how the markets themselves work. It would be like designing a lightbulb without understanding electricity. It might work, but only through sheer luck.

In this chapter we'll take apart the New York Stock Exchange and see what's inside.

Wall and Broad

In 1792, on a street corner in lowest Manhattan, a group of 24 traders got together to trade a few shares in two emerging companies. Strictly *al fresca*—no limestone and marble buildings, no majestic columns. No IBM, no Xerox, not even Procter & Gamble or Coke. These "name" companies were still 70 years or more away. The companies whose stock was traded were small, nameless, local companies, long since faded into the mists of time. But that's where it all started, at least as far as we're concerned in the here and now.

A Star Is Born

What started in 1792 not only still exists, it continues to thrive. Now it is housed in a grand classical shrine, with all the Corinithian columns and carved marble trimmings of the stateliest statehouses: the New York Stock Exchange, or NYSE. Somebody way back named it the "Big Board" and that name has stuck through the years for good reason. It is a grand old building with a venerable trading floor, on which the passionate dance of market activity continues throughout the 6^1/$_2$-hour trading day.

A Little More History

The history of the NYSE is phenomenal when taken in perspective. Through these advances we can see the growing strength of the engine that drives the U.S.—business.

Here are just a few early Big Board milestones:

➤ In 1865, the average daily volume was just above 34 *thousand* shares traded for 141 companies.

➤ By 1900, the volume had grown to 505,000 per day for 369 companies.

➤ By 1920, 825,000 per day on 689 companies.

➤ Then it was *down* to 750,000 per day on 862 companies in 1940.

Then it really took off:

➤ By 1960, the average daily volume rose to 3 *million* on 1143 issues.

➤ In 1980, 44 million per day, 1,570 issues.

➤ In 1990, 157 million per day, 1,774 issues.

➤ In 1997, 525 million per day, 3,028 issues.

➤ And the all-time record is 1.2 *billion* shares, traded on the mini-crash day of October 27, 1997.

A few technology breakthroughs helped along the way:

➤ In 1878, the first telephone was installed.

➤ In 1978 the first electronic linkage to other exchanges was installed.

➤ In 1984, orders were electronically routed to the floor using SuperDot.

➤ In 1995, hundreds of old TV-style monitors were replaced with modern flat-panel displays in the world's largest installation of this technology to date.

➤ In 1996, floor brokers started using handheld wireless information tools.

Trading Terms

Listed stocks are stocks listed and traded on the NYSE trading floor. This term is still widely used and once contrasted with **unlisted** stocks, or **over the counter** stocks once dealt by individual securities dealers over the phone. The trading platform for most of the bigger unlisted stocks evolved into NASDAQ, an exchange of its own. Others still trade OTC, but these are generally off the day trader's radar screen.

What do all of these advances mean to the day trader?

➤ Growth in trading volume and public interest, fed by trading technology improvements, is obvious.

➤ The unsuccessful or uncommitted day trader can use this information, if not for day trading, to at least score better on *Jeopardy!*

Big and Small, but Mostly Big

The NYSE is mostly a playground for big, "large-cap" companies in American industry—sometimes overseas industry, too. Large cap means with a total market capitalization (price times total shares outstanding) of $100 million or more. There are about 3,000 companies currently listed. It's an elite club, with the most stringent listing rules of any market, it's for the most part a quality club. Facts and figures abound, but we won't go into them here—check out www.nyse.com for more.

The NYSE Web site.

Behind the Screen

Security at the New York Stock Exchange is tight, very tight. All visitors pass through airport-like metal detectors before being admitted. And packages? Parked outside the back-alley visitors' entrance to the NYSE is a mobile security truck with a conveyor belt that passes all packages through an x-ray machine. *All* packages, including every bagel, every cup of coffee, every takeout pizza that is headed inside the building.

Making the Day Trader's List

These older, well-established firms mostly found on the NYSE may sound a little too placid and set in their ways for the day trader. We get plenty of liquidity and volume, information, and easy trading access. But what about movement?

True, many old-line NYSE companies are less volatile than their NASDAQ "upstart" counterparts. But for every 3M or Archer-Daniels-Midland "dud," there is a young momentum-driven answer: America Online, Micron, Seagate to name a few. Whether it's listed or not isn't the criteria; it's the stock and especially its trading pattern that count.

Behind The Screen

Day trading *can* work on "quiet" NYSE stocks. In Chapter 21, we'll explore a trading strategy that actually takes advantage of low volume and volatility.

The Big Apple Auction

The NYSE is an *auction* market. If you don't remember anything else, remember that.

What do we mean? An auction market, like the one you once saw at the state fair for all those prize winning 4-H cows, is a place where buyers and sellers get together to buy and sell. The auctioneer plays traffic cop, trying to match the buyers and the sellers. As with any true auction, side deals mostly aren't allowed. And price is determined purely by supply and demand.

Enter the Auctioneer

The auctioneer has total control over the auction because of the rapid-fire (and largely unintelligible) identification of the audience's bids. At the state fair, there is one cow for sale at a time. Bidders bid and the auctioneer sells to the highest bidder. Such a scenario wouldn't be practical for a nationwide market where people all over are trying to sell stocks, so the NYSE auctioneer deals with both bids (offers to buy) and asks (offers to sell) at once. Here, a little more than a traffic cop, the auctioneer is sort of a matchmaker. The auctioneer looks at the list of bids and offers, and matches them together according to price and quantity.

Front-Row Seats

Part of the fun of attending an auction is the ability to see what's going on. How the sellers behave, how the buyer behaves. The size of the buying and selling crowd. Visibility counts for even more if you're actually trading in the market. The NYSE gives you some information about the traders at the party, but not as much as does the NASDAQ (through Level II screens, more later). This fact gives a slight edge to NASDAQ for the really serious trader.

In the case of the NYSE, the auctioneer sees the traders, you see the results. Exception: The NYSE does disclose the order *size,* or number of shares available at the current bid and ask price. The rest of the order book is viewable only to the auctioneer.

An Auction Specialist

The NYSE "auctioneer" is known as a *specialist.* Let's talk more about this special person…

The Specialist's Specialty

Understanding what the specialist does in a day's work will give the insight you need to successfully trade with him and be up to the minute with the Exchange floor.

Who He (She) Is, What He (She) Does

A specialist specializes in making markets for one or more securities and is normally awarded the privilege by the NYSE for doing so. The specialist keeps an order book and spends the day looking at and matching existing and incoming orders. What does the order book look like? You guessed it—a computer screen! Usually a big one, too.

Sometimes the specialist gets the order in person from a member firm's floor broker. Sometimes, it just shows up electronically through DOT or SuperDot, the electronic routing system. By volume it's about half and half, but by number of orders, the vast majority, 80 percent, are electronic.

Behind the Screen

Who are all those people down there with colored vests on? School crossing guards who forgot to change before showing up on the floor of the exchange? No. Because of the hectic pace during trading hours, a system developed in which to quickly identify who worked for whom. Floor traders wear colored jackets that identify the firm they represent. Clerks and messengers wear colored vests that also signify a firm association. Neither look will ever win a fashion award, but the system serves its purpose.

Trading Terms

An **order imbalance** is an excess of buy or sell orders that makes it impossible to match up orders evenly. This may cause trading to be temporarily suspended. An **opening delay** is when a stock doesn't begin to trade when the market opens due to news events or an extreme imbalance of orders. The specialist has 15 minutes from the opening bell to indicate a price range at which the stock will begin trading.

A Question of Balance

The specialist is required to provide liquidity for the NYSE's public customers. If there aren't enough buy and sell orders, the specialist must still provide a fair market. This can mean trading from his firm's own account, or it can mean delaying an opening or halting trading until the proper balance of buyers and sellers is achieved (often at a much different price!). The specialist is usually reluctant to take these actions because it can exacerbate the situation already causing the imbalance.

The Reward System

The main reward for the specialist is the opportunity to pocket the spread—the difference between the bid and ask price, for every normal market-order transaction performed. Specialists are also rewarded for creating fair markets with orderly price executions. A good specialist can get specialist status for more stocks. Specialists may also trade for their own firm's accounts, buying low and selling high, within the rules, to make a profit.

Electronic SuperDots

SuperDot stands for Super Designated-Order Turnaround System. No need to memorize this name, it was probably invented by some computer geek anyway. What you *do* need to know is that SuperDot is the electronic routing system used by the NYSE to route orders to the exchange floor.

Why SuperDot?

SuperDot, like most other computer-automated processes, replaced a cumbersome people-paper system. Well, not entirely. People and paper are still used to guide large and special orders to the trading floor for special negotiation and handling.

But for the average order from the average investor, it is simply faster and more efficient to electronically deposit the order right into the specialist's order book. Eighty percent of NYSE's orders come in this way. SuperDot can be used for up to 2,099 shares per order. (We're not sure how they picked that number!)

Behind the Screen

Ever seen those old black-and-white photos of the floor of the stock exchange piled ankle-deep with small scraps of paper at the close of a trading day? Every transaction involved multiple pieces of paper—scribbled on, crumpled up, and tossed on the floor before moving on to the next transaction. But visitors who stand in the gallery nowadays gazing down on the floor action will see a much tidier scene. Are the traders of today less prone to littering than their predecessors? Nah. Although you will still see some paper on the floor, more and more trades are paperless.

What This Means to You

Chances are, as a day trader your orders will be delivered through SuperDot from your online or direct-access broker's systems. SuperDot is fast and reliable, both for order entry and trade reporting. Under most conditions, entry occurs within seconds of placing the order. Exceptions to this only occur on the very busiest days.

Keep in mind that SuperDot is *not* a trading or automate-execution system. Trades are still executed by specialists. If there is an order imbalance, or if you have placed a limit (fixed-price) order, SuperDot will only get it there; it won't guarantee fast execution (or any execution at all).

For all intents and purposes, SuperDot makes day trading on the NYSE possible.

Anatomy of a Trade

OK, all of this background is nice, but how does it all work? Good question. Here's a little three-act play that should help illuminate the issue:

Cast of Characters

There are two main characters in each and every trade:

➤ **The specialist:** We already introduced him. He/she matches the orders and actually executes the trade.

➤ **The specialist's clerk:** Always found sitting inside the trading station right next to the specialist, the clerk, as you can imagine, speedily and dutifully maintains the order book and reports executions. The order book contains buy and sell orders at all different prices, including the current market price.

Supporting cast includes:

➤ **Floor brokers:** Usually representing big-name brokerage firms, these brokers specially handle large or sensitive orders. They deliver them to the specialist and may negotiate with the specialist or other floor brokers in the presence of the specialist.

➤ **Your member firm:** Again usually a big, well-known name, a firm that has a "seat," or membership on the NYSE, and thus can trade stocks there. You, as a retail customer, normally deal with the NYSE through a member firm, although in some cases your firm, especially if not a member, will pass your order to another member firm. The member firm provides you with access tools (such as online ordering tools) to place orders through the firm.

Behind the Screen

"Take a seat..." Seats are so useful: a place to sit at the dinner table, somewhere to toss your jacket at the end of the day. The price of a seat can range from 20 bucks for a crummy folding chair to something much costlier, like a genuine Stickley, Eames, or Mattson. But the costliest seat of all is a seat on the New York Stock Exchange. This "seat" allows you to wander the floor and trade directly with specialists—like a floor broker. The most recent selling price of a seat was two million dollars. And it takes more than just the two million bucks to get the seat—you must be approved by the NYSE board of governors. Stick with the Stickley!

➤ **The other guy's member firm:** Same concept, but for the trader "on the other side" (buying what you sell, selling what you buy) of your trade. Can be the same firm as your "member firm," but the order is supposed to go through the NYSE anyway. There are a few exceptions to this.

➤ **You, the customer:** You know who you are. You place the order, buy or sell, market (at the market price) or limit (at a specified price).

➤ **The other guy:** Someone, large institution or another guy (or gal) like you, who happened to place an order, probably at about the same time, that matches yours.

Setting the Stage

Let's suppose that both you and the other guy are trading online, so for the moment we can bypass laborious descriptions of the broker's offices and all that. Let's talk about the NYSE floor.

There are 17 *trading posts* or stations spread evenly throughout the trading floor, which itself is the size of an indoor sports arena. Each trading post is roughly circular and 15 or so feet across. There are open windows all around the post. Each post trades on average 150 or so different securities. Some windows are very busy, others look like a bank window on Christmas night. The specialists sit *outside* the posts in spots designated to them and the stocks they trade. The clerks sit *inside* the post window at whisper-distance to the specialist. The clerk and specialist can see a small flat panel display cantilevered out from the post, so they can look at a customer (floor broker) and the order book simultaneously. A series of large flat-panel displays adorns the post above the windows, each showing quotes of the securities traded at that window by that specialist and clerk. A series of conduits big enough to carry Alaskan crude rise up from the trading post, carrying myriad data lines to exchange computers.

Act One

You decide to go for it. It's time to buy 100 shares of American Online (AOL) at the market price. The market as quoted is Bid 115, Ask 115$^1/_8$, last trade at 115$^1/_8$. You enter the order. Your order is routed electronically by your broker directly to the trading floor by SuperDot. It ends up on the order book as an offer to buy along with all other market orders, at the "ask" price of 115$^1/_8$, since the market is 115 to 115$^1/_8$.

The order book tracks all orders, whether placed as market orders at the current bid/ask or *away* from the market as limit orders. Your nextdoor neighbor may also have ordered 100 shares of AOL, but specified a limit price of 114$^3/_4$; that is, the maximum she would pay is 114$^3/_4$. This order is in the electronic book, but is not at the current market and won't be executed. (We'll cover limits and other fixed-price orders later in Chapter 12—don't worry.) All limit orders placed at 115$^1/_8$ will be shown as "size" at the current ask price of 115$^1/_8$. (At the time this book is being written, "size" is hard to find in many of the home-based trader's information tools. We expect this to change eventually)

Act Two

The other guy just bought a new BMW and needs to cash out of his AOL stock. So he too places a market order, he wants to sell instead of buy. This sell market order "hits the bid" of 115, the current "bid" price, and is transacted at that price assuming that 100 shares of "size" were available.

The Beemer guy gets 115 and you pay $115\frac{1}{8}$ for the same shares. What happened to the $\frac{1}{8}$-point difference? The specialist keeps it. Twelve dollars and 50 cents ($\frac{1}{8} \times 100$) reward for his/her split-second of effort.

Act Three

The trade is completed and entered by the clerk. It is routed back to NYSE computers and directly to your member firm and to your trading screen. We've seen this whole process take as little as 5 or 10 seconds using a typical online broker.

Epilogue

So long as there are sufficient market and limit orders at the current bid/ask of 115 to $115\frac{1}{8}$, the price will stay there. As the orders on one side or the other dry up, the price will start to move. First, booked limit orders will be picked up at the higher or lower prices. But the price movement will also trigger other market orders from other customers eager to get in on the action. For an active stock, there is a steady stream of new orders at all prices, at and away from the market. Day trading becomes more fun—and more productive.

We're getting ahead of ourselves, but you can see that "size" is a good indicator of direction. While size only shows you shares offered or bid for at the current market (not away from the market—a distinct advantage offered by NASDAQ Level II), you can plainly see when buying or selling pressure is drying up. Size bid is the number of shares limit order bidders or the specialist will buy. Size offer is the number of shares for sale at the ask price from limit order sellers or the specialist. So a more complete quote:

AOL	Bid 115	Offer $115\frac{1}{8}$	Size 5,000 × 10,000

...indicates orders for 10,000 shares for sale at $115\frac{1}{8}$ but buy orders for only 5,000 at 115. If there are more for sale than are being bought, a price drop is indicated. If the quote changes to:

AOL	Bid 115	Offer $115\frac{1}{8}$	Size 1,000 × 50,000

Daily Specials

AOL closed at $115\frac{1}{2}$ on Tuesday, so first thing Wednesday morning it will open at $115\frac{1}{2}$, right? Wrong. Before trading begins each day the specialist looks to see what kinds of orders he has waiting and ready to go. Kind of like a food stall in a bazaar—if you look out and see hungry people waiting to buy fresh-baked bread, you might raise the price a tiny bit. Nobody outside your stall waiting when you open? Then maybe you will lower your price a tiny bit.... Stock prices work the same way at the opening of the market.

...then downward price movement is even more clearly indicated. Once the 1,000 shares bid are taken out, the bid price will drop to the next level, maybe $114^7/8$. Market players or the specialist will then reduce their "offers," or ask prices to 115 to try to attract more buyers. Otherwise they are likely to be left out of the inside market, and thus out of the action.

Notes:

➤ Once the price changes, size changes automatically. Size quotes are for a given bid and ask price.

➤ Occasionally specialists may over- or understate size by taking positions themselves. Reason: To purposely drive traders into or out of the market.

Other Dance Floors

Eighty-three percent of listed-stock orders go through the process we just described—to the trading floor in New York and back to you. This figure includes orders delivered both by SuperDot and "manually" by floor brokers.

The other 17 percent may or may not be important to day traders. About 9 percent go through "regional" exchanges—Philadelphia, Cincinnati, Pacific, Boston. Why? Maybe the NYSE is busy, or there's a better chance for a member firm to obtain a slightly more favorable execution. For all intents and purposes, prices are the same as NYSE, and for the day trader, these smaller exchanges aren't very important, nor even accessible. At least, not today.

The other 8 percent go through *electronic communications networks*, or ECNs. ECNs started out as sort-of wire services for big institutional shareholders to trade directly with each other, avoiding broker and market maker commissions and markups. They also provide some after-hours trading capability. ECNs have gradually become more available to the average investor seeking fast executions at the best prices. The use of ECNs and the ECN concept is growing and will likely become more important for listed stocks, as it already has for most NASDAQ stocks. Today, the only ECN set up for listed stocks is "Instinet," but that may change. You'll read more about ECNs in the next chapter. The day trader should be familiar with them.

Our lecture on the New York Stock Exchange has ended. And now let's turn our attention to the NASDAQ.

The Least You Need to Know

➤ Price movement results from actual customer orders placed onto the specialist's book. Occasionally the specialist may trade from his own account.

➤ Only the specialist has visibility to the order book. The only order book clue is the "size" quoted at the current bid and ask.

➤ Size is based on actual limit, or fixed price, orders plus stock the specialist is willing to buy or sell from his own account.

➤ Specialists make most of their money by pocketing the spread on market orders and by trading for their firm's own account.

➤ Specialists can halt trading if they determine an imbalance of orders.

Chapter 7

Trading Places: The NASDAQ

In This Chapter

➤ A short history of NASDAQ

➤ NASDAQ: the virtual, electronic market

➤ What—and who—is a market maker?

➤ The story behind SOES

➤ What an ECN is—and why you should care

In Chapter 6 you learned about the Big Board and its true-to-life marketplace in lower Manhattan. Quite a tourist destination. People from all over the world stand in line (and clear an extreme security check) just to see it work. Hustle and bustle, hundreds of screens and tickers laced with colorful numbers, people in suits and colorful smocks running around with little slips of paper or hand-held devices. Paper all over the floor. A low background din not unlike an old crowded train station. Excitement in the air. An awesome exhibition of power and order.

After this tour, what's next on the itinerary? Do we jump back on the bus and head over to NASDAQ? Nope. You can't get there by bus.

Why not? Isn't NASDAQ also a stock exchange? Doesn't it actually trade more volume than the NYSE for a greater number of different securities? Don't they sponsor football games? Yes. But you can't get there on a bus! You can only get there by computer!

Cyberfloor

NASDAQ stands for National Association of Securities Dealers and Automated Quotations. *Automated* is the key word here. NASDAQ is a computer-based system linking securities dealers ("market makers") together in a tight, high-speed, state-of-the-art computer network. We suppose your bus could take you to Rockville, Maryland, home of NASDAQ's central computer hub, but unless you're really a technogeek in disguise, this probably won't hold much interest. And they probably won't let you in anyway!

A Negotiated Market

In Chapter 6 we learned that the NYSE is an auction market. That is, buyers and sellers send orders to an auctioneer, the specialist, who matches them together to make trades. The specialist determines prices by the orders themselves: Whatever price it takes to match the most orders is the price of the day.

NASDAQ is different. NASDAQ is known as a *negotiated* market. But think of it as an open-air market with lots of buyers and sellers and *no* auctioneer. All of the buyers and sellers of a particular commodity post their bids (what they'll pay you) and ask or offer (what they'll charge you) prices. The buyer paying the best (highest) price will get filled by sellers first. Likewise, the seller offering the best (lowest) price will attract the most buyer attention. In a "real" marketplace, you would see a bunch of people gathered around a small space yelling out or displaying their prices to other dealers, who would in turn buy and sell to meet their needs.

Behind the Screen

"Today on the trading floor of the New York Stock Exchange..." drones the blow-dried financial reporter announcing the latest stock prices. But you won't hear a report on the day's NASDAQ action start that way because, hey, there's no floor! "Today in the bowels of the NASDAQ computer system..." just doesn't have the same dramatic sound, does it?

Enter the Computer

This doesn't work very well on a national (or international) scale. Geography is a problem, as is the sheer number of traders and securities involved. Up until the 1970s, trading on "over-the-counter" securities was limited to smaller companies, usually with a handful of dealers who were trading them. The market—that is, the aggregate of buy and sell orders and their prices—could be had with a simple phone call or two to a market maker in a stock. The National Association of Securities Dealers (NASD) and its member dealers saw great opportunity to expand this trading approach by computerizing it, which they did with great foresight in 1971.

Now, instead of being yelled out on a market floor, all dealer or market-maker bids and offers are displayed simultaneously on a computer screen. The equivalent of the NYSE's venerated order book is available and accessible online to all dealers in a stock. Dealers can see each other's bid and offer prices, and can post their own. As we will see, with Level II access to the NASDAQ computer network, you, too, can see all the bid and offer prices, at and away from the market.

Maker's Market

Market makers are the "dealers" who make the NASDAQ market work. They buy and sell stocks in the open NASDAQ market, providing liquidity and a conduit for their customers (including you) to buy and sell shares.

Market Makers Are People, Too

"Gosh, I always liked to wheel and deal, so why can't I be a market maker?" you might ask. Just who are these folks, anyway?

Market makers are actually securities firms, large and small, who register to buy and sell a particular security. They follow NASDAQ rules to make a market. Large investment banks such as Goldman, Sachs & Co. and Morgan Stanley are market makers. But many smaller firms and securities wholesalers can also be market makers. There are literally thousands of market-maker firms. Specially assigned employees in these firms actually do the job of making markets. As we will see, they're professional day traders, too!

Market makers don't do their job on a public exchange floor. Rather, they sit deep in the bowels of their firms' headquarters, far from any audience, armed with an array of computer screens and telephones. You may never see a market maker, but it is possible to see his bid and ask quotes—his intentions—in the NASDAQ computerized market. A single human market maker may operate in one, a handful, or as many as 20 or 30 stocks at a time.

There are 60 or so prominent market maker firms trading the 6,000 or so securities on NASDAQ. Some lower volume or "thinly traded" securities may only have three or four market makers. Other big names—Dell, Microsoft, Intel—may have 40 or more firms making a market in the stock.

What Does a Market Maker Do?

Uh, they make markets. Not a good enough answer for you? Oh alright, here is a slightly more pedantic one:

Market makers are essentially dealers. They are there to try to execute buy and sell orders for their firms' customers: you. But as dealers, they are trying to make money themselves (for their firm) by capturing spreads (remember, the difference between the bid and ask price). And according to NASDAQ rules, market makers are supposed to create a "two-sided market," that is, always post a bid price, or price they will buy at, and an ask price, a price they will sell at.

Trading Terms

The **inside price** is the best bid and best offer price currently available in the market. **Inside bid** refers to the best, or *highest* bid price, while **inside offer** refers to the best, or *lowest* offer price.

Trading Terms

A **Level II screen** is an exclusive, real-time screen showing the whole NASDAQ market—all posted bids and offers.

Suppose you trade with ABC brokerage, and you want to buy 100 shares of Starbucks. But ABC isn't a market maker in Starbucks, so how does the purchase get made? What happens? ABC will place an order into the NASDAQ electronic marketplace. A market maker, usually the next in line at the inside, or best-offer, price, will fill it if it is a market order. Limit, or fixed-price, orders, are often also filled by market makers after being advertised in the market through an electronic communications network or ECN (more in a minute).

Market makers create markets by posting their bid and ask prices into the NASDAQ computer system. They look at their own customers' orders as well as the rest of the market in deciding what price to post at. Market makers essentially bargain with each other, and the public, through their postings.

You can see these bid/ask postings as a high-performance day trader through the NASDAQ Level II screen. Each posting has the market maker's four letter code, a price and number of shares that are represented by the bid or offer. It is often possible to figure out a market maker's "hand"—his intentions—by watching the sequence of bids and offers placed on NASDAQ.

You might hear about a NASDAQ Level III screen—this is what market makers use to post their bid and ask prices. Alas, this high-level screen is only available to the market makers themselves.

Market Makers Under the Microscope

Market makers at one time made quite a bit of money trading for their own accounts. Some of this was through retail commissions from their own customer's orders, but the majority was through the capture of the spread. A quarter of a point on several million shares a day adds up to serious cash!

There was quite a fuss about this in the mid 1990s. Market makers were accused of colluding to keep spreads artificially high. Customer orders between the spread (say, one sixteenth better than the current bid price) simply weren't posted! The SEC came calling, and since 1997 the limit order protection rule now forbids this practice.

Market makers can still trade with each other by phone, like the good old days, and bypass public view on the computer screen. But to keep things fair, the SEC tapes many of these calls, again to prevent price fixing and excessive spreads.

Market Makers Play Rugby

Rugby players? No, we're not trying to portray the market maker as a gritty, unyielding athlete. Rather, the analogy is used to make a point: Unlike the NYSE, where the specialist can stop trading if there is an imbalance of orders (more buys than sells, and vice versa), in NASDAQ, no market maker can stop trading. Even if there is a flood of orders, play never stops. A particular market maker may not choose to trade at or close to the current price, or inside price, but another market maker more determined to make a trade will. By definition, there is always an inside, or best bid and ask price, and so there is always a market.

The Rumor Mill Grinds On...

Until very recently, NASDAQ would only shut down trading in extraordinary circumstances, such as a major corporate announcement. Specific news from the company was required. On March 26, 1999, the NASD (NASDAQ's governing body) implemented a new rule allowing NASDAQ to shut down trading in response to market news or rumors (in contrast to news submitted by the company). But it stopped short of allowing trading to be stopped due to volatility or severe price movements alone. The result? In most conditions of extreme volatility or price movement, market makers are left to play it out, often with drastic one-day effects on stock prices. If a high-flying high-tech company misses an earnings forecast, look out below!

Behind the Screen

The action on the stock market is always fast-paced, but lately the governing rules have been changing at a rapid clip as well! Due to the NASDAQ's amazing volatility lately, a recent rule change allows NASDAQ to halt trading in a stock in response to market news or rumor. Used to be they had to hear from the head of the company before they would halt trading, but who's got time these days?

Electronic Everything

With the exception of the few phone transactions that occur on NASDAQ, everything is electronic. The market itself, a collection of bid and ask price postings from all market makers, is all computerized. Order execution is also electronic.

No Yelling on This Floor

A NASDAQ computerized market is maintained on each NASDAQ stock. The market posts bids and offers from all market makers in that stock. Seen on a Level II computer screen, a market might look like this:

INTC   115×115$^1/_4$

Name	Bid	Size	Name	Ask	Size
GSCO	115	10	MONT	115$^1/_4$	10
PWJC	115	8	NITE	115$^3/_8$	10
OLDE	115	10	TSCO	115$^3/_8$	10
ISLD	114$^7/_8$	10	GSCO	115$^1/_2$	10
SUTR	114$^7/_8$	8	ISLD	115$^5/_8$	5

What have we here? The market for Intel (symbol INTC). Shown are five bid quotes and five ask quotes on NASDAQ. The four-letter symbols (GSCO, PWJC) represent different market makers. ISLD is an electronic communications network; we'll cover that in a minute. The prices on the left are bid prices, or prices those market makers are willing to pay for stock. The prices on the right are ask prices, or prices at which the market makers are willing to sell stock.

The inside, or best, bid, is 115. The inside ask is 115$^1/_4$. These inside prices are what you would see on any normal Level I quote, such as Yahoo!Finance. The *size* represents the number of shares available at each price. We'll spend a lot more time later on interpreting what is going on here. For now, you have a snapshot of a market.

The market maker doesn't post all shares available or desired to buy. He/she posts just what he wants to display, buy, or sell in the market at that given time.

Swift, Silent Execution

As the market floor is electronic, one would expect actual order transactions to be electronic too. Right again. Bids or offers displayed on NASDAQ can be "taken out" by other market makers, or with today's new trading tools, by traders directly. These electronic "takeouts" are usually done through an automated system called *SOES*, or small order execution system.

As we mentioned above, not all inventory or demand is posted directly on the NASDAQ screen. Market makers have to post at least one bid and ask, but not every-thing. Some shares are traded through this open marketplace, others are traded directly between market makers, traders, or institutions through electronic communications networks, where buyers, sellers, and sometimes market makers trade with each other directly.

Hot SOES

SOES allows individual traders to trade directly and automatically with the market. A market order placed for 1,000 shares or less will automatically "SOES" the lead market maker at the best, or inside, price. Most individual online trades for 1,000 shares or less are filled through SOES automatically and invisibly through a broker's software. SOES orders are usually filled in seconds. Very few take longer than 60 seconds.

SOES becomes a special weapon for the high-performance day trader, who can spot quotes through Level II screens and nail them with orders almost instantaneously.

Why SOES?

SOES—installed in the early 1980s—became important after the 1987 crash. At that time market makers had to be contacted, often by phone, to arrange a trade. When the market began to sink on that fateful October day, panicked market makers simply backed away from trade requests and refused to answer their phones. SOES provides customers with greater liquidity—a market maker must post a bid and an ask, and he/she must honor a SOES order with a few exceptions made clear in the rules.

SOES rules

SOES is a very handy tool, but there are some rules you need to understand:

➤ SOES trades can only be executed in lots up to 1,000 shares. (Not really a problem for most of us small-trading fry!) The limit may be set lower on some smaller stocks.

➤ There is a five-minute rule. The same trader is prevented from trading on the same side (that is, the buy side or the sell side) of the same stock within a five-minute period. Otherwise, a trader could swamp the market with orders and take liquidity away from other traders.

➤ SOES is for customers only—no dealers or member-firm registered representatives (brokers).

➤ SOES is mandatory—a market maker can't back away from an advertised price.

The Infamous SOES Bandit

SOES gave rise to the first wave of new day traders, the so-called SOES bandits. SOES bandits took advantage of the almost instantaneous direct execution power to perform the first real rapid-fire electronic trading with market makers. Often the strategy was simple: In a rapidly moving market, the SOES bandit would simply pick up outdated (by seconds, sometimes) market-maker quotes. The totally focused day trader could beat many a market maker, who often was watching more than one stock at a time. Another tactic: An SOES bandit might take out the last offer at the inside ask price, often forcing the stock price up unless the market maker quickly renewed the previous offer.

Market makers and their firms soon responded to these tactics with protests to the SEC. A few new rules have been put in place, including a new 100-share minimum advertised quote, to reduce the effectiveness of SOES bandits. Nevertheless, SOES remains one of the important tools of the day trader, but certainly not the only weapon in the arsenal. ECNs have emerged as the tool of choice for many day traders.

Trading Terms

ECNs, or electronic communications networks, are an alternative trading path allowing NASDAQ customers to trade directly with each other or to place orders directly into the market.

ECN: A New Network

So far we've described the "mainstream" NASDAQ market: a computerized marketplace of quotations displayed by market makers for trading with each other and the buying public. But just to make things a little more complicated, another trading path opened up 30 years ago and has gradually become a serious competitor to the regular NASDAQ market and even the NYSE. This trading path is the *ECN*, or *electronic communications network*. There are several of these networks.

ECNs—Why and What?

ECNs were originally set up for institutional traders, brokers, and other traders of large blocks of stock. Imagine how disruptive the sudden arrival of a 100,000-share order would be in a computerized market trading bids and asks normally of 1,000 shares. Entire quote boards would be wiped out! The ECN provides an alternative.

Some ECNs also provide a means to trade "after hours." Most attentive investors have seen stories about after-hours trading (usually on your stock that just tanked from an earnings report!) on Instinet. Instinet, started by Reuters in 1969, provides a liquid after-hours market for big institutions. It isn't yet available for individuals, but it's being discussed.

ECN customers, who must be members of the network, simply enter their buy or sell order. Anyone else on the network can see the order and fill it, or contact the originator to negotiate. Some networks match orders electronically. Some networks pass orders to the regular NASDAQ market if no fill is found inside the network. You can see these orders in the NASDAQ market Level II as four letter symbols: "ISLD" for the Island network, "INCA" for Instinet, for example.

ECNs are used most to trade NASDAQ stocks but in the case of Instinet, can also be used to trade NYSE stocks.

Finding the ECN Channel

ECNs were usually limited to an exclusive few customers—big financial institutions, mutual funds, big traders. But now many more individuals have access through some forward-thinking online brokers such as Datek.

What has happened? You guessed it—a dramatic rise in volume. ECN volume has risen from less than 10 percent to almost 25 percent of share volume for NASDAQ stocks.

Keeping the Ratings Up

Why are ECNs so popular? Three reasons: anonymity, automation, and economy. Whereas normal NASDAQ orders are "transparent," that is, in full view of the marketplace and Level II public, the identity of ECN buyers and sellers is visible only to other ECN members. No impact on the open market or its prices, no 800-pound-gorilla orders hitting the market and drying up demand or supply (big traders and market makers actually use ECNs to hide their identity and motivations). Everything is taken care of on a semi-private computer network.

ECNs are also economical: Customers don't pay the market maker's spread. Spread is important especially in large-share transactions! ECNs only charge a small per-share handling fee, from less than a penny to a few cents per share.

Where ECNs fail: The smaller number of traders may mean less liquidity, especially for smaller stocks. A big thing to keep in mind about ECNs: Order execution is not mandatory as it is for SOES. An order placed may never be executed.

Last but not least, ECNs are the major means for day traders to put fixed-price (limit) orders into the market.

Pause for Station Identification

There are several ECNs. The two most important for the day trader to understand are Instinet and Island. Day traders don't have Instinet access, but Instinet after-hours quotes can indicate where a stock is going the next trading day. Island, on the other hand, is becoming much more accessible to the day-trading public and offers what is almost becoming a new trading market. Island provides the individual online trader with access to the markets resembling that of the market maker. That is, the individual trader's fixed-price orders entered on Island will be displayed directly on NASDAQ (as ISLD) alongside market maker quotes.

Behind the Screen

Just like the instant fortunes being created by really young guys like the founders of Internet businesses like Amazon.com or Yahoo!, the founders of ECNs have made a pretty penny. Gerald D. Putnam founded ECN Archipelago just a scant two years ago. In March 1999, both E*Trade and Goldman Sachs put up $25 million dollars each to buy stakes in his company.

Other smaller ECNs include

➤ B-Trade (Bloomberg, BTRD)

➤ Archipelago (or Teranova, TNTO)

➤ RediBook (Speer, Leeds & Kellogg, REDI)

➤ Attain (AllTech, ATTN)

Finally, NASDAQ also provides an electronic order-routing system known as SelectNet. SelectNet isn't really an ECN but functions a little like one. It allows quotes to be displayed and orders placed to market makers. SelectNet quotes don't show up in the NASDAQ market and executions aren't mandatory. SelectNet is often used by market makers trading with each other. For the day trader, SelectNet works like an ECN except that orders are shown only to market makers, not other traders.

Anatomy of a Trade

With ECNs, there are a lot of paths through which an order can travel. In the interest of simplicity, we will refrain from describing them all!

Act One

Daily Specials

NASDAQ Level II visibility helps you time order placement and decide whether to try for a better price. If lots of offers are stacked up at 115¹/₄, that price is likely to remain in effect for a while or even go down, as a market maker in the pack gets more anxious to unload shares. If only one market maker is offering shares at that price, the price is likely to rise once that offer is "taken out."

You decide it's time to buy 100 shares of Intel. Since you are now part of the Internet generation, we'll assume that you place the order through an online broker.

But first, you check the quote. It gives a "last trade," of 115, with a bid of 115 and an ask of 115¹/₄. What you see are the inside bids and offers. There are stacks of other bids and offers away from the market at poorer prices. The best price offered is 115¹/₄. If this is OK, you simply enter a market order. If you want to try for a better price, you enter a limit order. (You'll read more about the different kinds of orders in Chapter 12, "May We Take Your Order?")

Act Two

Your order is transmitted electronically by your broker to NASDAQ (or it will go directly if you have high-performance direct-access trading). A market order to buy 100 shares of INTC will normally be filled by one of the market makers offering shares at the "inside" ask price.

Normally, you don't know or care who filled the order. But high-performance trading systems allow you to "preference" market makers or route orders to an ECN, (usually Island) first, then automatically to NASDAQ and its market makers if an Island fill is unavailable.

Act Three

The market maker, once your order is filled, has the option maintain his/her offer price or take it down and post a new one. Market makers normally have 20 seconds to report your trade and to make a decision to retain or adjust their quote. The execution is reported back to your broker and is updated in your account.

Had enough of this talk about the two different stock markets, the NYSE and the NASDAQ? Sorry, but its not over yet. Chapter 8, "On the Move," adds more to the picture to help you sharpen your knowledge of how it all works—and how to make it work for you.

The Least You Need to Know

➤ The NASDAQ is a truly virtual market: It is computer-based and has no trading floor.

➤ On NASDAQ, all market-maker bids and offers are displayed simultaneously on a computer screen. You can see these quotes on the Level II screen.

➤ The small order execution system (SOES) provides automatic execution with a market maker at the inside bid or offer price for 1,000 shares or less.

➤ Electronic communications networks (ECNs) can be used to trade NASDAQ stocks with market makers or other traders, always at a fixed "limit" price.

➤ ECNs are becoming more important as more individual traders seek direct access to markets.

Chapter 8

On the Move

> ### In This Chapter
>
> ➤ Comparing the NASDAQ and the NYSE
>
> ➤ Going inside the indexes
>
> ➤ Fundamental and technical trading
>
> ➤ What's in a quote?
>
> ➤ What makes a stock price move up or down

Chapters 4–7 discussed some of day trading's "body parts"—what's traded and how it's traded on the important exchanges. In this chapter, we'll start putting arms, legs, brains, and livers together into a body form. But be advised in advance that Frankenstein won't come alive until Parts 5 and 6, when we take all we know to create a day-trading strategy and lifestyle. Remember, patience is one of the qualities of a successful day trader!

Comparing NASDAQ and NYSE

For the day trader there are important differences between the NYSE and NASDAQ. Before discussing them, let's review the workings of these markets:

30-Second Review—NYSE

The NYSE is an auction market maintained by specialists. In Chapter 6, you learned how orders flow to the specialist, who in turn executes them by matching with other orders or occasionally with inventory from his own account. The specialist quotes bid, ask, and "size" at the current bid and ask. Other than that, the NYSE order book is invisible to the day trader. Orders flow to the specialist electronically through SuperDot and only rarely for most day traders through a "manual" floor broker.

Price movement is said to be *order driven*, that is, specialists peg bid and ask from orders on the book. A movement in orders from one side to the other (e.g., sell to buy) creates movement in the price of the stock.

NYSE—"listed"— stocks traditionally represent more established, stable companies than NASDAQ. Specialists try to maintain an orderly flow of executions and prices, and may halt trading if order flow gets especially out of whack. As a result, NYSE stocks tend to be less volatile. Besides the trading floor, there are alternatives to trading with a specialist, but for the average day trader these are probably not important.

NYSE order flow.

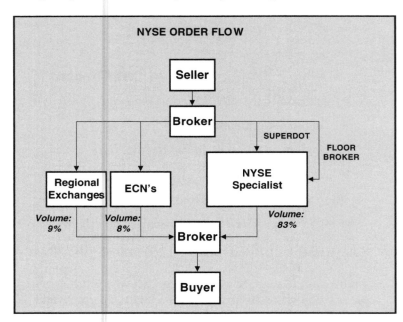

30-Second Review—NASDAQ

NASDAQ is a negotiated market, sort of a free-for-all with no leadership or direction set by a specialist or "auctioneer." A number of market makers participate interactively and competitively to quote prices, which may or may not reflect actual orders behind them at the sponsoring firm.

The entire system is computer driven. Instead of an order book (like the NYSE), we have a nationwide computer bulletin board listing all available quotes. Market makers must display quotes in the stocks for which they make a market. Electronic SOES ordering automates order execution against a market maker for under-1,000 share orders, while the ECNs provide an alternative path around the market-maker market or sometimes into the market-maker market. NASDAQ stocks tend to be smaller and/or higher growth companies. This, with the relative lack of central leadership or order from a specialist often results in greater volatility.

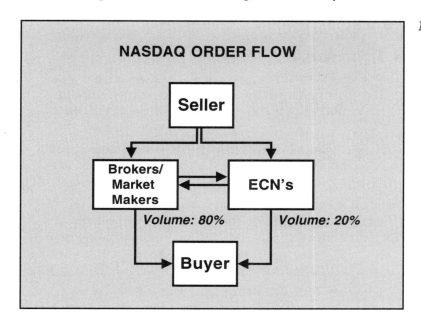

NASDAQ order flow.

So What's the Big Difference?

Both markets provide good opportunities for the day trader. In aggregate, the NASDAQ is probably better suited for day trading. NASDAQ stocks tend to be more volatile and driven by momentum. These are features most day traders look for, but they come with additional risk.

The NASDAQ, through Level II screens, also gives a glimpse into the future by showing bid and ask activity behind the current "inside" price. This "transparency" is a key element of advanced or "high-performance" day trading but is expensive to acquire and can take extraordinary skill to interpret. We don't think Level II access is essential for the beginning day trader. Repeating: Both markets provide good opportunity.

Indexing the Market

In the late 1800s, Messrs. Dow and Jones invented the series of indices for which their names are forever remembered: The Dow Jones Industrial,

Daily Specials

Is a Level II screen essential for day trading? We don't think so. Particularly not for the beginning day trader. But it helps—and like most things that help, it costs money and you have to learn how to use it!

Transportation (then, Rail) and Utilities averages. What did we get? Single-number indicators representing underlying activity in the markets. What are these averages? Mathematically derived composites which are calculated, now in real time, from individual prices of a chosen group of stocks.

Can 30 Represent Thousands?

The Dow Jones Industrial Average (DJIA) is the most popular of them all. But it includes only 30 stocks! Can we get a reading of the market based on this indicator alone? Does Kodak's clunker earnings report and resulting swoon mean the whole market is tanking?

Answer: Not really. And creative financial minds recognized this some time ago and began to provide more broadly based indices to hang your hat on. Among the most popular:

➤ **S&P 500:** This is Standard & Poor's catch-all index, bagging 500 stocks (NYSE, AMEX and NASDAQ) into a single number. These are chosen by capitalization, or total market value. It is a large (big cap) and medium (mid cap) composite, made up of about 80% industrial, 10% utility, and 10% financial firms.

➤ **S&P 100:** Baby brother of the 500, the 100 is the top 100 of the S&P 500, a more elite selection of firms.

➤ **NASDAQ 100:** Like the S&P 100 but only NASDAQ stocks. This one is increasingly valuable to the day trader specializing in NASDAQ stocks.

➤ **Sector indices:** As the name implies, these are groups of chosen stocks, usually 50 or less, that represent a sector. For example, the CBOE Telecommunications Index has 22 stocks representing that industry.

Daily Specials

"I've been taught to keep an eye on the opening futures every day," a day trader who has attended two different seminars told us. "That wherever the futures are at the opening bell, that is where the market is going to go."

Fine, but How Do I Use?

Indices are good indicators of overall market direction. That was probably fairly obvious. More to the point, for the day trader day trading Lucent Technologies, it might be useful to look at the S&P 100 and even the CBOE Telecom to see which way the current is flowing. Vast amounts of contrarian money have been made in the market's history paddling against the current, but more often it's a good indicator of which direction you should be paddling. Or if you should be in the river at all.

As we mentioned in Chapter 4, many of these indices have futures contracts associated with them. Some of these contracts trade 24 hours a day. A look at the S&P 500 contract at 6 A.M. will give you an idea of what's in store for the day. Don't ignore these indicators.

Behind the Screen

Watching index futures trading is really important. They are a leading indicator, a composite indicator of what all the pros think. Big money and big research analysis from all over the world is behind their action. We don't always recommend playing "follow the leader," but here it probably isn't a bad idea.

So Quoth the Market

We've danced on this floor some in preceding chapters. Here's a bit more about price quotes and what they mean. For illustration we'll use the model and format of quote delivered by Yahoo!Finance but the same will apply to almost all normal or "free" quote services.

What's in a Quote?

Quotes contain the following:

➤ **Last price**   The last price at which a stock traded.

➤ **Bid price**   "Best" price the market maker (NASDAQ) or booked orders (NYSE) are willing to pay for shares you sell to them. Their buy price. The "inside" bid is the *highest* bid price amongst all bidders. This is the price shown in summarized bid quotes on most quote services.

➤ **Ask price**   Price the market maker or specialist is willing to sell you stock. Their "offer" price. The "inside" ask is the *lowest* offer price.

➤ **Volume**   Shows the number of shares traded during that trading day. Most detailed quote views show average daily trading volume. The observant trader can see if a stock is getting more or less interest than usual during that day.

➤ **Day high**   Displays the highest price traded during the day.

➤ **Day low**   The lowest transaction price of the day.

➤ **Year high, year low**   Refers to the highest or lowest price for the year, sometimes referred to as the 52-week high and low. Most quotes are for 52 weeks, not the calendar year, for those of you looking at these numbers on January 3!

➤ **Size bid**   (NYSE only) Represents the number of shares attempting to be bought in the market (corresponding to buy orders placed by other traders) at the current price. Size quotes are generally hard to find online but may be available in some detailed quote screens (which are too slow to really use). They are available at brokerage offices and their lobby screens and on high performance trading platforms.

➤ **Size ask**   (NYSE only) Represents the number of shares for sale at the current market price.

Behind the Screen

At the time of this writing, most "free" quote services in Web portals don't show the NYSE bid and ask price, while most brokerage firms do. The NYSE is evaluating how much data to feed to whom, including parts of the order book away from the inside price. It is a question of what to charge (exchanges make a lot of money by furnishing quote data) and how much of the specialist's "business" to make public. The NYSE realizes that these possible choices put some of their customers at a disadvantage, and these customers might defect to NASDAQ stocks. (Yes, the major exchanges *do* compete!) Watch for changes in the amount of information available and where it shows up for what charge.

Who Pays for Quotes?

Exchanges make a lot of money from quotes, and recently there's been a lot of debate as to whether they should. Most free quote feeds are delayed. NYSE quotes are delayed 20 minutes and NASDAQ quotes are delayed for 15 minutes. This was done primarily to give the markets a premium real-time product they could sell, which they do. When you get a real time quote from your online broker, that broker pays the exchange a fee (usually only a penny or two) for that quote. They may or may not pass this charge to you depending on your status as a customer.

Now, with the advent of day trading and other morphings of rapid-fire online investing, and with a larger investing public growing ever more accustomed to fast, up-to-the-minute information, there's talk that any delay should become history. Real-time quotes *should* be cheaper, or even free. Time will tell....

Fundamental Changes

Day traders—like all other traders—make no money if a stock doesn't move. We'll spend a few minutes on why stocks do and don't move.

Behind the Scenes

Stocks moving on fundamentals are moving on information underlying the company's financial health and performance. Now, we don't plan for this book to be a course in finance or reading balance sheets, so we'll skip the business basics. Essentially, a stock should move up if revenues and earnings are growing, and down if they aren't.

Fundamental business performance takes longer than a day to change (for most companies, anyway, until the emergence of Internet companies!). So why is it important to the day trader?

All a Matter of Time

Mostly, it's a matter of timing and gauging market perceptions. Earnings announcements provide interesting opportunities for day traders, who may want to capitalize on the expectations or "hype" of an upcoming earnings report. If the market expectation is extremely high on a company's performance, the day trader will try to capitalize on the pre-announcement hysteria. The day trader may also try to capitalize on the post-announcement reality, which works in two ways: *disappointment* if the number is missed or *realization* that the price is ahead of the performance. (So many times we see a stock down even after a good report.)

The day trader can trade with the flow or against it, if he/she feels the event is overdone and due to reverse course quickly.

Technical Changes

Many feel that prices behave more as a function of technical factors than fundamentals. A market is an aggregate of thousands of very specific trading events. These may appear random, but technicians believe natural patterns occur within the chaos. A stock nearing the high point of a trading range, for example, will naturally draw sellers. If it "breaks through," it naturally attracts buyers. The technician doesn't try to predict individual trader decisions, but rather the pattern of the aggregate "trading mind."

Trading Terms

A stock that's been hovering for a long time just under a milestone price, say, $100, is said to have a **breakthrough** when it finally blasts through that price.

Sense of the Action

There are hundreds of technical indicators. Almost all of them work some of the time, but none of them work all of the time. If they did, then everyone would use them, and the underlying pattern they predicted would change! Different indicators work on different stocks or even different industries. We'll take a tour through technical analysis in Part 5, "Reading the Tea Leaves."

Trading Terms

Shorting stock is selling stock borrowed from your broker anticipating a downward price move.

Trading Terms

A **downtick** refers to any sale price (or in the case of NASDAQ, bid price) that is lower than the previous price. The stock in this condition is said to be in a downtick. Downtick rules also apply to a stock where the last sale was at the *same* price, but the most recent previous *change* was to a lower price.

For the day trader, it's useful to be aware of technical factors and use those that seem to work and be understandable. Technical indicators add a lot of new instruments to the instrument panel, but the day trader still needs to look out the window!

Up, Down—Cash in Either Way

Most of us are naturally programmed to be optimists, particularly when it comes to money. We expect things to go up, and it's our nature to try to capitalize on things going up. Most traders trade this way, but it's important to the day trader to cash in on moves in both directions. In a sense, the opportunity for gain is doubled for the day trader who looks at both sides.

Sell Me Short

A short sale is a sale of stock that a trader doesn't own. The stock is borrowed from the broker, who makes it available at prevailing margin (interest rates). The trader simply declares in a sell order that it is a short sale, and bingo, it happens. The short seller is, of course, planning to buy the shares back at a lower price later on. The day trader wants to do that by the end of the day.

Rules, Rules, Rules

One thing that dampens the short seller's enthusiasm is a protective legacy left over from the 1929 crash: It's against the rules to sell short on a *downtick*.

Why is this prohibited? To prevent markets from snowballing downhill as they did in '29. For the day trader, this removes some of the ammunition from the arsenal, for he/she can only sell short when a stock is going up. This makes timing especially critical—if a down move is anticipated, the day trader must make a move while the stock is still going up. Tricky! This is one reason why Level II access is useful—a trader can see demand drying up before prices start to be affected.

Day Trader's Armaggedon

Did we scare you with this heading? Well, maybe a little? There's a point to be made about day trading and its future.

Last time we looked, we were in the midst of a 17-year "bull market," the greatest of all time. Some would say we're *not* in the midst, we're near the end.

Because of the short-sale rule, day trading doesn't work so well in a "bear" or down market. Sure, very little besides the guy who jumps out the window goes *straight* down. There are usually upticks along the way, and put options can be played. But if you're an aspiring day trader who's never experienced a down market and quits a day-job to day trade, remember that profits can be harder to come by in a down market.

The Least You Need to Know

➤ For day trading, NASDAQ stocks tend to be more suitable as they are more volatile and momentum driven.

➤ NASDAQ is the more "transparent" of the two major markets, with Level II screens available (at a price) to ordinary traders.

➤ Market indices like the S&P 500, the NASDAQ 100, and sector indices are often good indicators of overall market direction.

➤ Technicians believe that composite actions of all traders form patterns, and these patterns can predict stock price movement.

➤ Shorting stock captures profits on down moves, but can't be done on a downtick.

Part 3
Tools to Keep You Informed

Information is the grist for the day-trading mill. Information on who is doing what and when. Information on what to do when and why. Information...for information's sake!

Day traders have their own favorite sources of information and we will show you where to find them. General financial information as well as specialized sources of "power" information tailor-made for the needs of day traders.

Alas, much of this specialized information is not free. To save your time and your money, we've identified the best sources available.

Chapter 9

Watching the World Go 'Round

In This Chapter

➤ The investment-information boom

➤ Financial papers day traders like

➤ Financial TV shows traders can't live without

➤ Great Internet sites

➤ Great financial and technology newsletters

Congratulations, you've made it a third of the way through this book and towards becoming a knowledgeable day trader! Keep reading—we'll introduce a few more puzzle pieces, then show how it all fits together.

Part 2 began to describe pieces and parts of the day trader's world—the inner workings of the market—that are all-important to the day trader. But the world of trading means nothing without access to information about market events and trading activity. This information comes packaged in so many ways! In Part 3, we will explore some of the different information packages and give solid leads on where to find the good stuff.

A Window Seat

The rapid growth of all forms of online trading, including day trading, has fortunately led to a boom in the availability of new types of information services. Venerable stand-bys like the *Wall Street Journal* are now complemented by (not to mention competing with) a plethora of new Web sites and information feeds.

Behind the Screen

So, which came first—increased investor activity or increased investor information? A classic chicken-and-egg scenario if there ever was one. Never before have so many sophisticated sources of information been available to the ordinary investor: online investor newsletters like TheStreet.com that arrive in your e-mail box several times a day; up-to-the-minute company press releases about pending deals and company earnings; centralized Web sites like investorama.com that can link you to thousands of other financial sites.

Why wasn't this kind of stuff available before? Perhaps there weren't that many people outside the investing profession interested in such high-level detail and analysis. But in our information-soaked and numbers-obsessed society, we just can't get enough of it nowadays! And trust us—more is coming!

Amazingly, these new electronic "newstands" contain information that is mostly free. Most have banner ads, and some require signups that may put you in the bull's-eye of someone's marketing target. It may not be precisely real time, and you'll have to find it yourself instead of having it pushed to you (that's high-tech marketing talk for having something delivered continuously without requesting it a page at a time). But for the price—nada—it's pretty doggone good. While it may not be *all* you need to be a high-performance day trader, it provides a good foundation, and it may be all the "casual" day trader needs.

Behind the Screen

Why is all of this great information now free? It's expensive to produce and provide all this research. Who pays? ADVERTISERS.

So Many Forms

Not too many years ago, the only investment information available outside a trip to the broker's office was your morning paper! Yesterday's closing prices, and if you really had a good paper, maybe high, low, volume, and a few news stories. There was no way to keep track of price changes or news events as they happened, so day trading in today's style wasn't really possible.

Now there are so many forms of information that you can't even keep track! Basic tools are mostly free or available with a modest subscription. In this chapter we will take a look at these tools:

➤ Newspapers

➤ Broadcast and cable TV

➤ Internet portals and news feeds

➤ Research and commentary sites on the net

➤ Net newsletters

➤ Chat rooms

Advanced tools are mostly paid for and maybe specifically designed for day traders. You'll find out more about these cool tools in upcoming chapters:

➤ "Push" market data and newswires

➤ Technical analysis tools

➤ Day-trading bulletins

➤ Day-trading training and simulation sites

➤ Day-trading chat rooms

➤ Integrated data and trading platforms

Smart News

Not only do we get more information from more sources nowadays, it's starting to get smart. No day trader, nor any other human, can possibly keep track of everything that is going on. Increasingly sophisticated news and data feeds set off buzzers or alerts when certain news stories come out or when certain price events occur. And the wireless world is evolving so that you don't *always* have to be glued to the PC. Some services ring your pager or even a cell phone if the right (or wrong!) things happen. Real bells and whistles! We'll talk some more about this "smart" info in the next chapter, but the *basic* information described in this chapter—you'll just have to go out and get it yourself.

The Whole Point Is Advantage

Whether you settle for what we refer to as "the basics" or go for the whole information enchilada, always keep in mind the *reason* you need market information. A successful day trader needs to:

➤ Know *more* than most.

➤ Know it *sooner* than most.

If you settle for less, you'll find yourself at the end of the whip. This is an expensive place to hang out. You want to be the one cracking the whip, making the easy money as a smart trader, getting there before the masses, right?

Remember: *Knowledge is power.*

Daily Fishwraps

We might be a little old fashioned, but we still like the morning paper. Good financial papers can tell a heckuva lot about what's going in the marketplace on both Wall Street and Main Street. For those of us who like to see "where the puck is going," these are important reads.

A Financial Paper

When we say a *financial* paper, we really mean it. For the most part, you should read the local newspaper for sports scores, gardening tips, and garage sales. Financial sections are weak, and what little information they have is usually old, stale, and known to everybody.

Daily Specials

One source of indicators for the stock day trader is the equity options page. Here you can see for yourself the "heavy" option trade volumes. If you're day trading a stock that had big call–buying activity yesterday, it could be preparing for an "up" move. Someone knows something you don't. Works for the downside, too, with put volume. We usually look at the option page before even opening the stock page (We? Well, Peter does. Jennifer doesn't.)

The Journal

The venerable *grande dame* of financial papers, the *Wall Street Journal* provides the best combination of good investment data and good Main Street marketing gems in the "Marketplace" section. Good, complete stock quotes are included, but there isn't a whole lot of "behind the scenes" information or stock-price analysis.

The *Journal* is also useful for monitoring trends and rule changes that may affect day trading. That's a very popular topic these days.

Investing in IBD

The '80s gave us renewed interest in money, greed, and the financial markets. It also gave us *Investor's Business Daily*. IBD is more focused on the true trader than the WSJ. IBD has quotes, but adds a lot more analysis behind its quote presentation. There are detailed graphics of "stocks in the news." IBD also reports key trend and momentum information, some of which is proprietary.

Here's an example:

Investors Business Daily Stock Data.

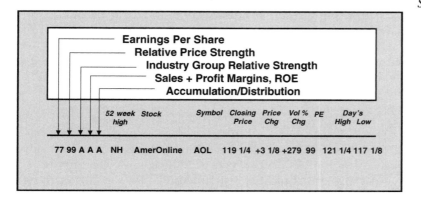

Some of the things we like:

➤ **Relative Strength:** Relative strength is a "what-have-you-done-for-me-lately" indicator of strength of a particular stock or industry versus the market at large. Relative price strength shows the performance of a company versus all other stocks. A "99" is darned good.

Relative industry strength shows the performance of a company's industry against other industries. Relative price strength scores are presented as a percentile. (90% means a stock outperformed 90% of the market during the last 12 months.) Relative industry strength gets grade letters. Upward momentum is evident for a stock with an RPS of 99 and a RIS of "A."

➤ **Accumulation/Distribution:** IBD's "proprietary" measure, A/D measures the volume trading on the ask price compared with volume on the bid price. If most of the volume is trading on the ask, then the stock is said to be *accumulating*, then most of the trades (and thus most of the pressure) are on the buy side, often by institutional customers. The "A" grade is another good momentum indicator.

The only thing we don't like about these indicators is that the time period they analyze is an entire year. Momentum over an entire year may not mean as much to a day trader as that over a few days, weeks, or months.

➤ **Volume % Change:** Show stocks with large volume changes that might be "in play" when trading begins. "+279%" for AOL shows big time momentum. Also worth a look: "Greatest Volume % Changes" listing in IBD.

IBD also has the most ads we've seen for products and services useful to the day trader. It is the closest thing we've seen to a true day trader's rag.

Get with the Times

The *New York Times* has a surprisingly useful business section. In fact many of the topics that the *Times* covers and the articles they produce don't appear elsewhere. The *Times* probably does the best job summarizing the key movers, up and down, from the day before, and a bit of theorizing as to why they moved. The *Times* also does a good job keeping up with trends in the brokerage industry (they are in New York, after all!) and regulations that affect day traders.

The Squawk Box

Of course, now we're talking about TV! Amongst all the 500 channels or so of junk on cable TV, there are actually a few good shows that give good, live, up-to-the-minute news and commentary, especially at that most critical juncture of the day: the opening.

Behind the Screen

Television doesn't interest you. You gave it up years ago for more intellectual pursuits, eh? Well, if you're going to day trade, you're going to watch television. All the time. From sunup to sundown. Why? Because all the other day traders are watching television too, and trading on what they see and hear. Is CNBC reporting on a particular stock this morning? Watch it move!

See NBC

The most developed financial news channel of all, CNBC does a pretty good job. It's good to have on in the background, anyway, as you watch what concerns you most on your computer. We like CNBC.

CNBC gives a continuous ticker feed with delayed individual stock prices. It also shows real-time indices and market indicators (such as TICK, ARMS, PREM, to be discussed later).

Also important: the market commentary, especially at the beginning of the day. As the market opens, "Squawk Box" and "Maria's Check List" bring us right to the trading floor, where Maria Bartiromo (a.k.a. The Money Honey) tells us where the action is; what's up, what's down, where the trading-floor ruckus is. Ron Insana and Joe Kernan give regular reports on active or volatile issues, along with insights into what's really happening behind the scenes. Interviews with key market analysts and strategists occur through the day. The astute trader can see and use the commentaries to time day trades; often they cause the very move being predicted.

Behind the Screen

From *People* magazine we learn of Maria Bartiromo's June 1999 wedding to *Individual Investor* publisher Jonathan "Jono" Steinberg, son of financier Saul Steinberg. Two high-profile financial-information providers to keep an eye on. Who would have thought a magazine devoted to West Coast celebrities would now turn its sights on figures from the financial world? Shows how far things have come for investors in the 1990s.

Mountains in Bloom

Bloomberg Financial, a rapidly rising star in all forms of financial news services (to the chagrin of old standbys Dow Jones and Standard & Poors), is dabbling with morning cable programming. Bloomberg runs a program from 5 A.M. to 8 A.M. (local time) each day. Against a backdrop of numbers and news blurbs on a fancy, high-tech screen, Bloomberg shows the latest information and interviews. But it ends at 8 A.M., so is really only good for a market opening. We've found it on the USA network, but can't really tell you where to find it in the rest of the country. Sorry.

Nighttime TV

We can't discuss financial media without mentioning the venerable favorites (at our house, anyway) *Wall Street Week with Louis Rukeyser* and *Nightly Business Report*, both broadcast by PBS. These shows provide valuable insight into the moods and underpinnings of the market. They also bring in folks with years of experience and perspective trading in all kinds of markets.

In the fast-paced business world in which we live and trade, does a show like Louis Rukeyser's, filled with old Wall Street codgers, still apply? Should what these grey beards have to say about the market still matter to a trigger-happy day trader? We think so. We think it's a valuable resource for younger day traders raised exclusively in the era of the bull. Not to mention that we could all learn a thing or two about turning a witty phrase from listening to Lou's opening commentary.

Behind the Screen

Louis Rukeyser is famed for his witty commentary on what's happening in the markets. And he can be ruthlessly snide about fads, trends, net stocks, and other bubbles. So what has he said about the day-trading phenomenon? Well, we're not sure.... Although we count ourselves among Lou's Friday faithful, our efforts to catch him making fun of day traders (so that we could report it to you) were thwarted by our local PBS affiliate. First they changed the years-old time slot of 7:30 to a time just past our bedtime, then he was bumped for endless weeks of pledge drives featuring *Riverdance*. So we gave up.

The Others

Coming on strong, but not quite as good as those mentioned above, are cable channels MSNBC and CNNfn. These networks present more of a "main street" view of Wall Street and lack the strong commentary and behind-the-scenes scoops presented by the others. We wouldn't be surprised to see these improve over time.

And on the Radio

We shouldn't neglect the venerable radio. Public radio stations—National Public Radio—carry a series of "Marketplace" reports in the morning and evening, providing market summaries and insightful in-depth reports on current happenings in the business and investment world. A good listen while preparing for (or wrapping up) the day, and one of the few day-trading activities you can do while driving to work, getting the kids ready for school, or taking a shower.

A Net Full of News

Now that you've read the morning paper and taken in a little (or a lotta) TV, it's time to get serious and start looking at what's happening in the marketplace. Right now. As it happens. Stock by stock, trade by trade, story by story.

Quote and news services come in three basic forms:

➤ Free

➤ Semi-Free

➤ Paid For

You might suspect that what you get gets better as you move from "free" to "paid for," and yes, your hunch is right on the money, as it were.

Really Free

You can get a stock quote almost anywhere these days. The major portals—Yahoo!, Excite, @Home, Snap.com all have stock-quote sections, usually right on the front page or on a finance page. Why, we wouldn't be surprised to see stock quotes available on Marthastewart.com or Disneyadventures.com!

These quotes are really free, and really pretty good, for informational purposes. "Detailed" quotes actually show a lot about trading ranges and volumes. Quote pages link to a host of other useful information sites, some within the portal, some outside. News stories almost up to the minute are available from the major business news feeds. And the charting capabilities are good to spectacular for the price. However, these quotes are delayed, which both dilutes and diminishes their usefulness to the day trader. We think free quote services are good to keep a general eye on what's going on and to spot emerging trends and events. But they're a little underpowered for the high-performance day trader.

So where are these "supersites?"

Daily Specials

If you're in the Yahoo!Finance site and want to see if there is any recent news on a company, first type in the stock symbol. When the quote comes up, scroll down the page and you will see a list of articles and press releases that concern the company, with the most recent info at the top of the list. Click on the story to read the whole thing.

➤ **Yahoo!Finance Quotes:** Delayed quotes, summary or detail; good, quick daily, weekly, longer-term charts; newswire feeds from most of the majors; links to research; and fundamental analysis. Great performance and layout, great all-around site. (quote.yahoo.com)

➤ **Excite Finance:** Similar to Yahoo. Not quite as fast in our experience. (www.excite.com/finance)

➤ **CBS Marketwatch:** Probably the most complete "free" package of all. Delayed quotes, press releases, and original content and analysis; good columns and reports on specific industries; good links to fundamental analysis and a fantastic free charting utility (subject of Chapter 18); real-time quotes available for a fee. Complete service and more sophisticated than Yahoo!, and free. Our only gripe: it's a bit pokey on a 56K modem. (cbs.marketwatch.com)

➤ **Reuters Moneynet:** Good wire service, including international. Quotes too, wire story search tool. (www.moneynet.com)

➤ **Altavista Finance:** Biggest search engine of all, plus the normal quote machine. (altavista.wallst.com)

Yahoo!Finance detailed quote screen with chart.

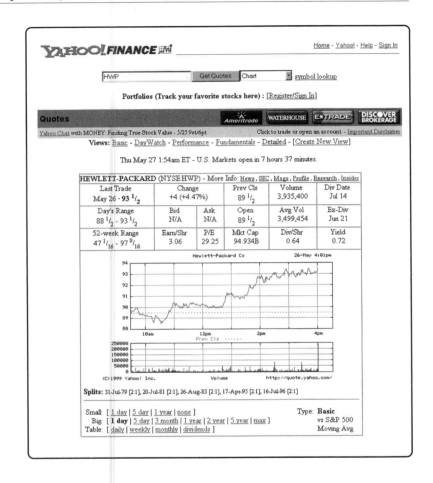

We've heard of some free real-time quote services that defray the cost with advertising. Haven't checked them out but it seems like a good idea. Lack of real-time quotes does limit the value of the free sites for "close-up" day trading. And again, the user must "pull" information. But their value outweighs their shortcomings, and day traders should actively follow them to stay in tune with what's going on.

And all for free. Isn't the Internet wonderful?

Semi-Free

All online brokerages offer some form of free quotes. Normally delayed quotes, like those found in the portals, are furnished for free. To get a real-time quote normally you need an account with the brokerage. Some of the more "ambitious" online brokerages give free unlimited quotes, while others give a "quote bank" that is replenished every time a trade is made.

Broker quotes are real time but most lack Level II NASDAQ detail or NYSE size. Most broker quotes do provide NYSE bid and ask. Another obvious advantage of broker quotes is that you are right there on your broker's Internet facility, ready to trade.

We'll get into what other services these brokers offer in Chapter 14, "Getting It Online." Semi-free quotes aren't the only thing involved in choosing a broker!

Paid For

Like the rest of life, you get what you pay for. There are paid-for quote services that'll knock your socks off, both in the type and amount of data delivered and the technology used to deliver it. We'll save these for the next chapter.

Research Like a Fool

Sites that provide "raw" quote information and news feed are valuable, but wouldn't it be nice to have some insightful research and commentary to go with it? Well, Internet-for-free has fortunately provided here, too. It's truly amazing what's free or available for the low, low cost of looking at a few unobtrusive ads.

Zack's Fifth Avenue

Research sites package and deliver research usually done somewhere else. They collect research releases from brokerage firms or other investment information filed with the SEC or elsewhere. Sorted and summarized, it's there for the taking.

➤ **Briefing.com** brings frequently updated market commentaries. It also summarizes brokerage upgrades, downgrades, and "coverage(s) initiated" each day and over time. (By the way—the daily summary is usually available on Yahoo!Finance, too.) For a small fee, you can get a more high-performance, up-to-the-minute feed. (www.briefing.com)

➤ **Zack's Investment Research** provides all sorts of free (and some paid-for) stock evaluations and research. There is also an excellent paid-for service adding such things as stock screening tools (you enter the parameters, it finds the stocks). This costs a bit, though. (www.ultra.zacks.com)

➤ **Rapid Research** provides stock screening and selection tools with customized or "stock" searches. (www.rapidresearch.com)

➤ **FreeEdgar** provides a source of company SEC filings—annual and quarterly reports. Good for fundamental research and understanding

Trading Terms

When a stock is tracked and analyzed by a brokerage house, it is said to be **covered**. Some big stocks are covered by all of the firms, some smaller stocks are only covered by a few. When a firm announces that they will henceforth be covering a new stock, a press release is sent out and it is taken as an endorsement of some sort.

the business, especially detailed "10-K" reports. Many of these Edgar-sourced reports are also found in Yahoo!Finance. (www.freeedgar.com)

Fool's Commentary

The Internet provides access to an amazing assortment of factual data. But more and more insightful commentary shows up all the time. Content prepared and written for the Net is well packaged, easy to read and grasp, and often about topics related to technology and the Net by people who understand the technology. Result: Lots of good stuff for day traders, and many a fun read.

➤ **The Motley Fool:** King of the commentary hill, the Fool provides opinions and daily commentary that is crisp, colorful, understandable, and well thought out. Daily "Ups and Downs" summaries tell you what's going where and, more important, *why*. The "Lunchtime News" and "Fool Plate Special" round out the day. There are more complete detailed company or industry commentaries. The Fool staff aren't afraid to point an accusing finger at stocks that should be accused, nor to laud the laudable. They are authors of a refreshing, eclectic, slightly contrarian investment style (read *The Motley Fool Investment Guide*) and apply this same refreshing look at the daily investment world. If nothing else, the Fool is a lot of fun! (www.fool.com)

The Motley Fool.

➤ **TheStreet.com** provides intraday newsletters and commentary primarily from the desk of James J. Cramer, a professional hedge fund manager who seems to have embarked on another career path as a journalist and trading insider. Insightful commentary often tells what's going on in the trading pits and in the minds of traders, brokers, and major investors. A bit bitchy sometimes, but a good read (www.thestreet.com)

Behind the Screen

Had you ever heard of James J. Cramer before? And now you see his name and his face *everywhere*! Who is this guy and where did he come from? A Harvard graduate, he's been described as a better reporter and writer than a money manager, and a better money manager than any writer. And with all of the writing he does, when the heck does he have time to trade?! Cramer crams his writing in wherever he can, to the delight of his friends and the distress of his detractors.

Tech Talk

No treatise on day-trading information would be complete without a trip through the ever-growing list of technology newsletters. Techies use the Net to provide and keep up on all kinds of information, and investment info is no exception. Why do we care? Tech stocks as a group have been the day trader's greenest pasture so far. There's a lot of good stuff out there:

➤ **Silicon Investor** is really a tech-laden chat room loaded with all kinds of stuff ranging from sophisticated professional analysis and prognostication to pure junk. It's a lot of fun, and often useful, too. Lots of inside dope on key tech companies. Free unless you want to post messages.

Silicon Investor.

➤ **News.com** provides tech-only news from a variety of sources including Bloomberg. Big gainers and losers are dissected each day. (www.news.com)

➤ **Red Herring Online** is tied to a "business of technology" magazine of the same name. Honest, insightful commentary on the technology business and technology finance. New industries, new companies, new IPO's before and after debut. (www.herring.com)

➤ **The Internet Stock Report** is focused on, well, you know. Produced by internet information provider Mecklermedia and offers commentary on business and trading patterns of Internet stocks. Good place to get more info about new IPO's. (www.internetnews.com/stocks)

Now that you have a taste for available "basic" free or low-cost information sources, we can go forward into more specialized information services designed for and used by the pros. Chapter 10, "More Information, Please," covers professional information for traders and investors of all types; Chapter 11, "For a Day Trader's Eyes Only," covers information sources created especially for the day trader.

The Least You Need to Know

➤ Many basic information tools are either free or reasonably priced—cable TV, online research sites, Net newsletters, and chat rooms, to name just a few.

➤ Even in this fast-paced market, the *Wall Street Journal* is still worth reading, and *Wall Street Week with Louis Rukeyser* is still worth watching.

➤ *Investors Business Daily* is the closest thing to a day trader's newspaper.

➤ With stock quotes, you get what you pay for. Real-time quotes will cost you, free quotes are time delayed.

➤ Online research sites are invaluable to day traders, the information is sorted and summarized and there for the taking.

Chapter 10

More Information, Please

If day traders are gold miners rushing to a new mother lode of prosperity, emerging information providers of all flavors are selling picks and shovels to their enthusiastic (not to mention hopeful) customers. New services are coming out practically every day. Let's put on our dungarees and see what's out there.

A Bigger Radar Screen

Wanna know everything? Sure. High-performance information services, once strictly the domain of the true pro, now bring all kinds of information to all of us. They also organize it and alert the trader to its arrival and importance.

Kinds of Radar Screens

Many types of high-performance market information are available. These information platforms are helpful to any investor, *including* the day trader:

➤ Power-market data and news feeds spew out tons of real-time market data and news on stocks, markets, business, and world events

➤ Technical-analysis tools help traders decipher patterns in prices and other trading data

➤ Less technical, but important—reference sites set up by NASD, NYSE, and the SEC to keep you up to date on the latest rules, who's who, trading performance, and problem resolution

We'll cover these in this chapter. In Chapter 11, "For a Day Trader's Eyes Only," we'll dig into services that are *specifically* set up for day traders:

➤ Specialized, Internet-based day-trading information sources providing day-trading ideas, analysis, training, and chat

➤ Integrated "direct-access" day-trading systems providing information and direct-trading access in a single bundle

As you might guess, these tools come with all sorts of bells and whistles.

What's It Gonna Cost?

As you might also guess, none of this (save a few chat rooms) is free! Cost can vary from a few bucks to north of $300 a month, depending on how many and which feeds are "bolted on" to a basic service. Although free samples abound, these packages are designed for the serious professional and are priced accordingly.

> **Alarm Bells**
>
> This stuff can add up. Don't lose track of your fixed monthly costs with all of these add-ons. First ask yourself how much you will have to make as a day trader to justify all of this.

You will note, however, that a lot of packages are available. It's competitive out there! Provider firms are only profitable if they achieve a certain level of subscribers and *keep* them. (As much of the business world is realizing, it costs a lot less to retain a customer than to find a new one.) Upshot: Pricing is getting more competitive, and good deals are to be had for longer term (i.e., one-year) subscriptions.

Learning Your Lesson

These data feeds and systems are very complex, and yes, full of numbers and statistics. If the goal is to master them before you lose all your money, and you weren't born a multi-millionaire, what do you do?

Decent training packages are available for many of these tools. They take the form of self-paced videos, practice screens, online help and "FAQs," and seminars. Toll-free support lines are, thankfully, fairly common. We think the training offerings are time well spent, sometimes even before buying a package. Always check it out thoroughly before using it to invest your money!

Power Push

In the old days, the day trader's only tool to keep up with the pulse of the market was the venerable stock ticker. In the *old,* old days, this was a teletype machine hammering out trade prices and volumes nearly as they happened on miles and miles of paper. They evolved to electronic passby screens proudly displayed in easy window view of most brokerages and also showing up at the bottom of most financial cable news shows. Then, time and work permitting, you could trot down to your broker's office for juicy up-to-the-minute data and graphic tools. Have you always wished you had one of those for your home? Now, at least if you're fairly serious about this, you can!

Behind the Screen

Here's a powerful thought—you can now access stock info that only really, really rich guys used to have access to. Ever seen those shots of tycoons from early in the century, posed at their desks next to a private ticker tape machine in a glass bell with the narrow paper tape winding down the side and piling up on the floor? And where do you think the term "ticker–tape parade" came from? That's right: Folks would rip up all that used ticker tape and toss it out the windows at returning heroes. Hmmm... what do they do now to honor paraders—hoist PCs out the window?

The World at Your Fingertips

You *can* have it all. All at once, real time, without lifting a finger. Customized to your individual needs to follow what you want to follow. End of commercial.

Modern technology and a small flock of companies have teamed up to offer such a service, once available only to professionals, right from your computer. With a reasonably fast computer, 56K modem, and a phone line, you can know anything about any market, any stock, or any news item, as it happens, from anywhere. And this is the real thing, eh? The same data the professionals use.

Power-feed services package together a wide array of direct data and news feeds. These are combined with tools to help you get the most out of it.

Just the Features, Please

Most market data services provide the following:

➤ Real-time quotes
➤ Real-time ticker
➤ Time and sales screen to track stock transactions
➤ Real-time market averages and indices

➤ One or many scrolling news headline feeds

➤ Full news stories available

➤ Color-enhanced NASDAQ Level II screens

➤ Customized charting

➤ Price alerts for last trade, bid, ask, or volume

➤ News alerts

Also nice to know:

➤ These are "push" feeds. You set it up and let it roll. Scrolling is automatic.

➤ News and quotes are direct from the source. No middlemen or editing.

➤ Most provide easy download to local PC programs for more analysis or record keeping.

➤ Many are integrated with direct-access trading services; more sophisticated analysis or charting; and research, bulletins, expert opinion, and chat rooms.

➤ Most have dedicated customer support.

Double Half-Caf Light Foam No-Cal...

American life has certainly changed in this century—from the early decades when cars only came in one color (black) to the bewildering array of choices now offered to us for the simplest things, like a cup of coffee. How you want your information (and how much information you want) is up to you. Customization is one of the really cool things about these packages. You can set up a screen literally any way you want, with several windows each monitoring just the data you want to monitor. You choose the size, you choose the colors. Excellent color options draw your eyes to what's really important. You set your own bells and whistles—alarms and alerts to tell you when the things you're tracking reach certain price or volume levels. They also ring up any news item crossing the wires involving a company you're following.

Behind the Screen

While trolling the Internet in search of information on stocks, should you worry that someone is watching? SEC Commissioner Laura S. Unger recently observed, "If you check out a stock quote in the newspaper, no one knows that you are interested in buying that security. If you check out that same stock online, your broker—whether discount or full-service—has the technological capability to know that you are interested in that stock." Kinda creepy.

Let's Take a Closer Look

The size, format, and lack of color here on the pages of this book make it impossible to examine one of these screens in detail. But we'll furnish a shot just as an example. You can see better views and even simulations by visiting provider sites. This shot is from Signal Online, a service of Data Broadcasting Company.

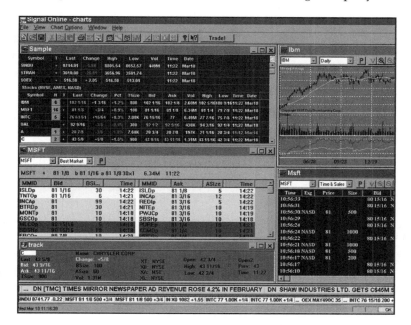

Sample power information feed: Signal Online.

Whoa! Who's going to profit here? You or your eye doctor? Lots of tiny numbers, all flashing and moving at the pulse of business. These screens *do* take some getting used to (and a big monitor helps), but you'll learn what to look for and how to set up your screen to best fit your needs (and the limitations of your corrective lenses).

Map, Please

To make it easier to figure out what you just looked at, we've provided a little road map to help out:

Again, you can set up these windows any way you like. Which windows, how big, what colors, which stocks—it's entirely up to you. Power at your fingertips. *You're in control.* We'll travel a little further into how these tools are *used* in the next few chapters.

*Road map for the sample
Signal Online screen.*

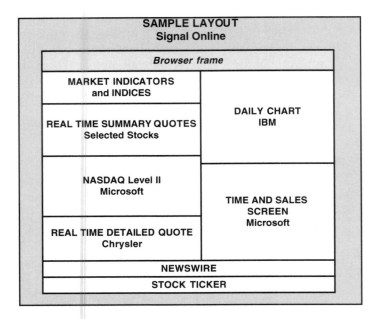

```
                    SAMPLE LAYOUT
                     Signal Online

┌──────────────────────────────────────────────┐
│                 Browser frame                  │
├──────────────────────┬─────────────────────────┤
│   MARKET INDICATORS   │                         │
│     and INDICES       │                         │
│                       │      DAILY CHART        │
├──────────────────────┤         IBM             │
│ REAL TIME SUMMARY     │                         │
│      QUOTES           │                         │
│   Selected Stocks     │                         │
├──────────────────────┼─────────────────────────┤
│                       │                         │
│   NASDAQ Level II     │                         │
│     Microsoft         │    TIME AND SALES       │
│                       │       SCREEN            │
├──────────────────────┤      Microsoft          │
│ REAL TIME DETAILED    │                         │
│      QUOTE            │                         │
│     Chrysler          │                         │
├──────────────────────┴─────────────────────────┤
│                   NEWSWIRE                       │
├──────────────────────────────────────────────── ┤
│                 STOCK TICKER                     │
└──────────────────────────────────────────────── ┘
```

A Look at the Sticker

As we said earlier, these services aren't cheap. Certainly they're in a different league from the free or nominal-fee services we described in the last chapter.

Alarm Bells

It's tempting to sign up for the yearly deal, but make sure you consider two things. First, it's a non-refundable ticket, so make certain of your plans as a day trader. Second, verify the financial viability of the provider. It's not a great deal if the company goes out of business in three months. Some of these services are provided by small firms lacking in tested longevity.

Most providers show a rather detailed fee schedule, starting with a basic quote feed that runs anywhere from under $100 to $175 per month. For this, you get standard and customizable real-time tickers, wire-feed scrolling headlines and news stories, charting, and market-summary information.

At this writing, most also offer a "special deal" that provides free NASDAQ Level II if you sign up and pay for a year in advance. (Remember the annual prepayment discounts—take advantage.) Most offer a free 30- or 60-day trial. We recommend you sign up for this, then the prepaid NASDAQ Level II if you can—lots more power for free.

Just like when you're looking for a new car, you'll be tempted with options. All services offer "bolt-on" additional news feeds, analysis tools, and research access. Access to other exchanges (options, commodities, foreign), news wires (Dow Jones or AP real time), and paid-for research from Zack's, Instant Advisor, and others cost more. Your $175/mo. Taurus can quickly turn into a luxury Town Car costing several hundred dollars a month. Start simple and build, and make sure the two to five-thousand dollars a year is well spent and within your budget.

Getting Wired

Turbo access—when the Internet isn't fast enough. You can get connected in a variety of ways. ISDN lines cost $50 to $100/month plus a hefty installation charge, but are today the most-used consumer high-performance network service. You can go all the way up to corporate-style T1 data lines and shared T1 frame relay lines costing $325 to $500 per month. DSL is another option for those of you close to a provider (major metro areas only, at this writing). DSL service is only $40/mo. Cable broadband service is spreading too—same price. These "wide pipe" services provide direct connect and fast Internet service at 4 to 10 times (or more) the speed of a smooth-running 56K phone line. This landscape is rapidly evolving, and not all services are available everywhere. But they're coming on fast.

Where Do I Sign Up?

A number of companies are providing power-feed services. Some are brand new, some evolved from services previously aimed at the professional. As with any business on the Net, changes can occur all the time, so we won't go into extreme detail on each company here. This is such a competitive business, the prices might have fallen by the time you read this! Here is a short snapshot of the majors:

➤ **eSignal** (formerly StockEdge/Signal Online—Data Broadcasting Company): Consumer friendly with nice brochures and training materials, and helpful sales people. Complete package, including wireless alerts and technical charting. The new release provides real-time stock quotes starting at $79, but it quickly gets more expensive from there. Includes options, futures and foreign markets. (www.dbc.com)

➤ **PC Quote Online:** PC Quote offers services very similar in description and price to StockEdge/Signal. (www.pcquote.com)

➤ **S&P Comstock:** One of the grand old dames of the business, carrying a professional product into the consumer world. Effective screens, easier to read than some. Appears to be a good product with all the features but a little more costly. No worries about the future of this company. (www.spcomstock.com)

➤ **Quote.com:** Quote data plus a lot of market analysis, commentary, and company data. Less expensive than the others and appears a good value. (www.quote.com)

➤ **DTNiQ:** The price leader. Their product contains much of the same stuff as the others but no wireless feeds; Internet-only. Not as many newswire or research/commentary bells and whistles. But baseline power data needs can be met for under $1,500/year, prepaid. (www.dtniq.com)

➤ **CBS MarketWatch:** A "basic" free service but it adds in a menu of for-fee services for power users. These come from a joint venture with Data Broadcasting (StockEdge/Signal). Worth a look, especially with so much free information available. (cbs.marketwatch.com)

eSignal, from Data Broadcasting Company.

Look Ma, No Wires!

Wanna watch your investments from the 10th green? From the back of a 38-foot yacht cruising the San Francisco Bay? From behind the wheel while travelling to your next sales appointment? From the gym? While commuting to and fro?

FM—No Static at All

Technology, of course, makes it possible. As if real-time direct and Internet access weren't good enough, now you can even keep an eye on things without being connected at all!

Several firms provide a host of wireless quote services. These services transmit data via FM signals or through pager and cell-phone networks at near real-time speed. You get a small, handheld receiver not unlike a large pager, walkie-talkie, or handheld computer. Enter a stock symbol, get a real-time quote. Or set "alerts" to notify you when price targets are reached, or when news events come across the wires concerning stocks or markets you're interested in.

These quote services give stock quotes for the major equity markets. Many go farther to provide option and commodity-market quotes, and almost all track major market indices.

Downsides: 1) No NASDAQ Level II quotes (that we've seen so far), and 2) You can't enter trades. Your trusty cell phone, your broker, and perhaps touch-tone trading will have to suffice.

Cool Gadgets Aren't Free

While you'll no doubt win lots of points with your friends for carrying one of these things around, they do have a price. Most companies sell you the receiver ($200-$400), then charge a monthly subscription, plus add-ons for optional quote feeds, plus (sometimes) exchange fees for real-time quotes, plus, plus, plus.... Some services provide the device free with an advance-paid subscription, sort of a razors and blades thing.

Expect to pay a few hundred dollars to start, and between $1,000 and $2,000 a year to use one of these services. But if you can't sit at a screen all day, these products are indispensable. It doesn't take long to recoup the cost if it truly enables you to watch what you're doing when "on the go."

And—we almost forgot—there are extra goodies sure to ice the cake. You can get sports scores, and with some you can even send wireless messages, faxes, and pages. We expect these services eventually to be bundled into laptop PCs with trading platforms, so you'll be able to do the day-trading thing anywhere, anytime.

The Store Window

There are several providers of wireless market information services. We'll mention two here; for others, pick up any edition of *Investor's Business Daily* and read the ads.

➤ **Quotrek** is another Data Broadcasting Company service. Quotrek uses the FM band with a device resembling a walkie talkie, with an LCD display. You can customize quote feeds to give you a personal real-time ticker for stocks you watch. Alerts and alarms of all sorts can be set. The battery lasts 8 hours. The one-time receiver charge is $295 plus a $125 setup and connect fee. The basic monthly charge is $90. (www.dbc.com or 1-800-287-9519)

Behind the Screen

Researching a book is an arduous task. We're not trying to play on your sympathy, we just want to take a second to thank some folks for their help. Whereas we sent out umpteen messages and made umpteen more phone calls to various folks in the creation of this book, the fastest help we got was from the folks who sell these financial pager systems. We had our info faxed in minutes. So thank you both, Bruno from Mobeo and Mark from Quotrek!

➤ **Mobeo** provides a service using a pager network. The form factor of the receiver is more like a large pager unit (still fits in your pocket) with a full keyboard. Mobeo claims better geographic coverage and faster response using the wireless pager network. You can send and receive e-mail, pages, and faxes, making this more of a multi-purpose device. Cost is $399 + $25 to get started, plus $125 a month and modest exchange fees. Mobeo waives the initial $399 charge if you buy a 2-year subscription. (www.mobeo.com or 1-800-328-0870)

Create the Perfect Chart

Power-market data feeds deluge the day trader with all kinds of information, but most have only basic charting tools. These tools draw nice charts providing a good start towards visual interpretation. But many high-performance day traders look for stronger analytic tools that can help predict future price movement or provide clear buy or sell signals from sophisticated statistical algorithms.

Omigosh, Statistics?

Complex statistical analysis? We won't go too far here, and we'll dabble a bit more in Part 5, "Reading the Tea Leaves." Essentially what the technician does is look for repeatable price patterns or correlation between stock movements and:

1. Market movement

2. Other stock movement

3. Factors outside the market

4. A combination of any of these

The technician looks backward at what happened, and uses it to predict what will happen. Artificial intelligence (egad!) may be applied. It's much the same process used to forecast the weather, and then some. And we hope that, for you, it's more accurate!

Tech Tools

There have always been more statisticians than jobs. Although the '80s produced a bit of a "Total Quality Control"-driven job boom, there were still plenty of statisticians to develop and implement a wide array of technical tools. (We're being a little facetious; many of these tools existed long before the age of TQC.) These tools print out nice graphs but also give buy-and-sell "signals," target prices, support and resistance levels, breakouts, and so on. Again, we'll dig into these a bit later.

Most of these tools are packaged as client software for your PC. But some are available through the Net, and some are set up to hook into power data feeds like eSignal.

Net-Based Tools

These tools are server-based and run for fees in the $50/month range:

➤ **MarketEdge** provides basic technical analysis of more than 5000 stocks with a proprietary analysis system. Available through many online brokers more cheaply than the $49.95/mo advertised price. (www.stkwtch.com)

➤ **Gears** is similar to MarketEdge. Some services are free. The site advertisements focus on *sell* signals. (Remember, selling is one of the hardest things for investors to do!) (www.the-gears.com)

➤ **Market Radar** predicts "break-out" points, a nice focus and especially useful for the day trader. $150/year. (www.marketradar.com)

Market Radar.

Software Packages

These tools are client based (installed on your PC). You won't find them at CompUSA, however! They are powerful and specialized for use by the trained pro (or day trader).

➤ **MetaStock** claims to be the "world's most popular technical analysis software." We have no reason to dispute that. Metastock works with DBC (Signal) feeds and a training video is available. (www.equis.com)

➤ **Omega Research** claims to be the "world leader in strategy backtesting," a backbone of statistical analysis. You can acquire the package as part of a suite that includes direct-access stock and option trading—an "integrated" trading platform. (www.omegaresearch.com)

➤ **TeleChart 2000** provides an inexpensive ($39) client-software package and supports it with paid-for data and trading tip feeds ($29/mo). Appears to be a good value. (800-776-4940. No Web address provided)

Remember, if you feel a little lost in this forest of tools, we're only trying to introduce them here. When and how to use them, if we do our job right, will become a little more obvious in Chapter 16, "A High-Performance Trading Jet." Even so, it will take greater exposure and practice to get it right.

The Rules Committee

Someone's gotta make the rules, and someone's gotta enforce them. Someone has to keep track of all data deemed to be in the public interest. A thankless task, no doubt. But the NYSE, NASD, and SEC (Securities and Exchange Commission) have not only taken this job to heart, they've also done us all a favor in providing useful, well-designed Web sites.

These sites provide all sorts of educational, trading, public relations, and company information. You can learn more about the "specialist" system or "SelectNet." The SEC site provides links to all annual reports and company filings, and keeps you advised of rulings and inquiries. You can learn who NASDAQ market makers are, and what they have to do to become market makers. You can find out how to resolve problems with your broker and what to do if you think you've been "had." You can also get historical data on a variety of things.

Daily Specials

Visit the SEC website at www.sec.gov for all manner of interesting information. You can even read speeches made by Chairman Arthur Levitt and the other SEC commissioners. It's a good way to keep up with what the SEC is thinking about, and nowadays, they're thinking *a lot* about online trading and day trading.

Securities and Exchange Commission Web site.

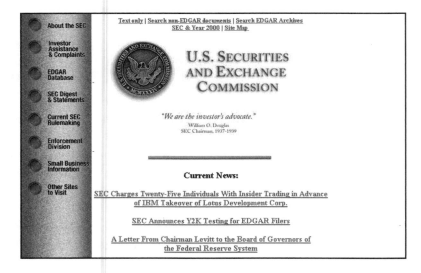

A Couple of Favorites

NASD has a "community" of Web sites (www.nasd.com, www.nasdaqtrader.com) catering to all desires—the individual investor, brokers, financial journalists. Especially useful for the day trader is the Nasdaq Trader site, providing information on market makers and tools to identify who they are from their four-letter Exchange code.

NASDAQ TRADER Web site.

The SEC site (www.sec.gov) is very well done and offers the latest rulings and statements on such things as the regulation of day trading and increased scrutiny of firms offering day-trading services. Good stuff to keep abreast of. (See Appendix C for a recent Arthur Levitt speech discussing investor and broker responsibilities in the electronic age). "Scam" warnings are available. You can submit complaints or keep track of results of other complaints. Finally, you can acquire all publicly submitted corporate reports.

The Least You Need to Know

➤ Day traders now have access to up-to-the-minute news and stock information, which can be "push" delivered throughout the day.

➤ These services provide a variety of useful and valuable information. However, costs add up. Be mindful of the cost and make sure the value of the data *to you* is proportionate to the cost.

➤ Traders can customize an information package so that it tracks the price and volume levels of chosen stocks and provides alerts when certain levels are reached.

➤ Technical-analysis tools can help a trader visualize price movement. They also provide buy and sell signals.

➤ SEC, NYSE, and NASD all maintain excellent sites designed to inform and protect you. Check them out.

Chapter 11

For a Day Trader's Eyes Only

In This Chapter

➤ Internet sites exclusively for day traders

➤ Practice first—sites with simulated trading

➤ The rumor mill—online chat rooms and hyped stock

➤ One-stop shopping—high-performance trading platforms combine information and access

The explosion of interest in day trading across the country has brought a bloom of information specifically aimed at the day trader. Information tools discussed in Chapters 9 and 10 help the day trader but weren't specifically designed for him/her. Now we cross that bridge.

Day-trading information tools include full-service sites, bulletins and "daily pick" newsletters, training tools, and simulators. It's hard to find a site that is *purely* any one of these. Mostly you'll find sites that combine several of these features with real-time quotes, charting, chat rooms, bookstores, links to brokerages, or their own "bundled" high-performance trading platform. Just the sheer number of them gives an idea of how big this day trading thing really is.

The Virtual Coffee Pot

You want the best of both worlds. On one hand, stay at home, work independently for as many hours as you wish. Use the Net or direct connections to get all the important data and trading platforms. Your commute is the distance between your bed and your keyboard. But are you missing out on the benefits of working in cahoots with others? Never thought you'd say it, but maybe.

Other people can provide insights and ideas on what worked, what didn't, and why. Hearing the stories and ideas of others can broaden your radar screen. Not that we recommend trading on tips—we don't go that far. But the experiences and insights of others can be very valuable.

And, don't forget, day trading can be rather lonely—just having some company can be good for you. A good laugh at a bum trade, the latest Monica Lewinsky joke, or your favorite sports scores can relieve the tension faster than a bottle of Tylenol. It's *not* like working for a big company all over again. You don't have to go to meetings, make presentations, review stuff with your boss and co-workers. These sites don't provide co-workers, they provide *friends*: other traders, and a selection of good trading information and tools.

If you're fortunate enough to live in a locale that has a trading room (a specialized brokerage providing terminals and access to day traders), you'll get all this, live and in person, each trading day (if you feel like extending your commute beyond your den).

Behind the Screen

Can you day trade from anywhere? Technology seems to be heading that way. Here is an observation from SEC commissioner Laura S. Unger: "Recently I met an individual who had spent the last six months deep in the Congo filming a documentary on elephants. She could not access fresh food (and was forced to eat canned goods), but she could access the rest of the world via her e-mail. Twice a week, she used a car battery, some wires, and a satellite dish to log on to her computer to receive and send e-mails. She assured me that individuals who shoot documentaries about elephants in the Congo do not have brokerage accounts, but if she did, she would be able to access it." Wow. And all we really want is to be able to do this from the beach in Hawaii....

Cream and Sugar

We'd like to make you aware of four complete sites providing services aimed exclusively at the day trader. These Internet-based services range up to $150/month.

➤ **Tradehard.com** is an aptly named newcomer, providing a complete set of resources for the day trader. Quotes, indicators, market analysis, strategies, tactics, advanced strategies, learning tools, chat, interviews, articles, tips, charts, and news. This site seems to have it all. Daily lists of stocks show momentum, breakouts, or other high potential opportunities. You can sign up for a 3-day trial and stay on for a modest monthly fee. (www.tradehard.com)

TRADEHARD.COM
Web site.

➤ **Avid Trading Company** provides a nicely designed, navigable site that includes stock picks, narratives, market-indicator commentary, and even short-sale ideas. Links take you to other tools, a chat room and even a recreation "room." We like their slogan: "Combining the prowess of the trader with the power of the Web." Definitely aimed at sharpening the skills and success of the day trader. Many but not all services are free. (www.avidinfo.com)

➤ **Pristine Day Traders** is another full-service day-trading site. The site has four main services and offers training, a bookstore, and a reading list. The services include daily bulletins and a "real-time trading room" which provides real-time commentary and bulletins through the day (limited to 500 subscribers). A "lite" bulletin provides a daily morning look at day-trading opportunities tuned to the needs of the less experienced trader. The flagship bulletin, "Pristine Day Trader," aims at the swing (2-5 day) trader, a niche "overlooked by many active investors" and day-trading services as well. Most services require subscriptions. (www.pristine.com)

➤ **Day Trading International** provides subscription daily-pick and newsletter services. Daily picks are based on technical analysis run the night before and are e-mailed to each member prior to the market opening. Many of these picks, like Pristine, are aimed at the swing trader. (www.daytradingintl.com)

➤ **Day Traders of Orange County** (California) is actually an investment club! The club meets twice a month (if you happen to live in

Daily Specials

The Web site run by Day Traders of Orange County is well worth a visit. You can find their site at www.worldwidetraders.com.

Disneyland country), but also puts up a lot of good stuff on the Web. How-to's, chat, training, and trading resources are also available. This site devotes more than most to non-equity trading platforms: equity options, futures, commodities, and currencies. (www.worldwidetraders.com)

Day Traders of Orange County Web site.

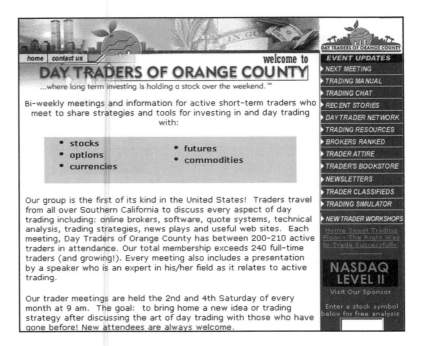

Don't Skip Batting Practice

A few sites specialize in training and making day traders aware of the latest products and services. Some provide traditional educational materials, and some actually go so far as to provide a simulated day-trading experience.

A few places provide a veritable "batting cage" to give you some practice at day trading. However you decide to do it, this sort of "paper trading" is a very important step. We've said it before: It's important to take a few practice swings, either on paper or on the Net, before stepping to the plate in the big game.

The Short List

There are others, but here are a few sites (mostly) dedicated to training and practice:

Trading Terms

The **paper trade** simulates stock trading by identifying and recording hypothetical trades, keeping track of all trades and daily profit and loss. This can be done by recording trades literally "on paper" or by using special software simulators.

➤ **Elite Trader** provides a variety of services including news and chat. But they specialize in training, offering a complete training course and free and paid tutorials. There is a bookstore and a reference list of brokers and software available for the day trader. You can also evaluate and buy computer hardware. (www.elitetrader.com)

Elite Trader Web site.

➤ **Teachdaq** offers itself as the "school of stock-market training." Courses are designed for all types of investing, including day trading. A complete, three-course series takes you through "Day Trading 301," including terms, tools, and techniques taught by ex-brokers and traders, and hands-on, instructor-guided simulation. Plan on spending five days and $1,000 for the whole series (and a trip to New York). (www.teachdaq.com)

➤ **SyeNet** offers "an online community for active stock day traders and investors." It's a good assortment of information, training, and links. There is a Toolbox and a Day Trader's Information Center. Notable is the Virtual Trading Room, a tutorial and market-simulation facility. There is also a Best Practices reference. (www.dtrade.com)

➤ **The E-Trade Game** isn't necessarily aimed at day traders but nevertheless can provide valuable experience. You get $100K in funny money to invest (and if you're extremely successful, you'll win one of two $1,000 prizes—in *real* money). You can practice Internet-based day trading and option trading at no charge or risk. (www.etrade.com)

On the Local Scene

If you have a local day-trading firm, it probably offers training, or at least an opportunity to simulate trading or paper trade using their systems. The local hands-on approach can be preferable to heavy classroom-type study, especially for the knowledgeable investor. But what you'll see is complex, it moves fast, and it can be overwhelming. If your investing experience is limited to mutual funds in an IRA, stick with the classroom (and this book) before showing up in your local trading room.

And like everything else in the day-trading arena, shop carefully before you sign up!

The Rumor Mill

Here's where day trading gets a little wild. The mystique of the latest rumor, the latest idea pulls hard on your heart (and purse) strings. They all sound so good!

Markets have always been driven by rumors. People want to believe what they hear, especially if it sounds like a great profit opportunity nobody else knows about. The Internet provides an excellent forum for this sort of informal "information." Because the audience has grown so much larger than the corner barbershop, the effect, and the *potential* effect, on markets has grown dramatically.

Behind the Screen

One of our favorite financial columns is Christopher Byron's "The Back of the Envelope" in the *New York Observer*. He wields a sharp knife, slashing away the puffery that surrounds so much dealmaking nowadays. And day-trading chat rooms have certainly felt the blade. A recent headline read: "Internet Lemmings Gather in Chatrooms and Drive Up Stocks." Here are a few piquant observations from the column:

Want to know how to make a bazillion dollars in a minute? It's easy. All you need is a $2 stock and a press release. If you put the press release out at, oh, say, 8:30 A.M., and you make sure to get the suffix ".com" in it somewhere, you could be looking at a $12 stock by lunchtime...news that the stock has suddenly acquired "mo" spreads through the Web like a late-summer grass fire across Manitoba...all the traders in the game, including the moderators [of the chat rooms], are busy simultaneously watching the advice being put out in all the other chat rooms, creating a kind of non-stop, self-reinforcing public-opinion poll among thousands of people trading billions of dollars daily—all of them trying to second guess each other regarding which way they think hundreds of different stocks will move in the next two minutes.

Stockhouse.com has identified "9 Red Flags That Identify Online Message Board Scammers." (Visit their Web site to see the whole handy list.) Here are two of the red flags they identify:

➤ Be on the lookout for someone who repeatedly attacks or belittles others on a stock's message boards.

➤ Look for a poster with a short history on their profile who suddenly shows up during a stock run and appears to know "all about" the company.

Several sites specialize in providing chat space, and a host of sites dedicated to other purposes also have chat rooms. Seems like the whole world is chatting in cyberspace!

The Day Trader's Buzz

Two sites provide "hot" day-trading chat:

➤ **The Momentum Trader** has an active chat room monitored by founder Ken Wolff. Real-time recommendations and calls for bottoms and tops are entered for traders to see and discuss. Access costs, but there's a lot of free training to go with it. (www.mtrader.com)

➤ **Day Traders On-Line** provides a research service and what is probably the largest chat room at the time of this writing. The Trading Desk is hosted by the firm's staff. The Web site gives especially lucid commentary on how to make the best use of the site. They recommend watching the Desk for a while before using it. There are morning e-mail dispatches containing daily tips. Tips through the day are broadcast directly into the Trading Desk to avoid "the delay of 3 to 6 seconds." This site is for the serious day trader (www.daytraders.com).

Alarm Bells

You can sure do a lot these days with a good graphics program, and one enterprising fellow tried recently to put out a phony press release that looked like it had come from the depths of the Bloomberg Financial juggernaut. It worked for a while, running up the company stock (he happened to work at the company, naturally) until the hoax was discovered. Cast a jaundiced eye toward all you see, no matter how official it looks.

Day Traders On-line Web site.

Re-Enter the Fool

Almost every portal and financial Web site has a chat room. But we'd be remiss if we didn't mention the Motley Fool again here. The Fool (www.fool.com) has continuous chat organized stock by stock. We've found this chat in many cases to be very insightful, posted by folks who 1) May know a lot, and 2) Don't think like all the rest. MF editors occasionally chime in. There's a lot of commentary on "momentum" stocks or stock in play. Of course, as with any chat room, there are the usual morons and loudmouths who clutter the space from time to time. But worth a look.

Book 'Em, Danno

There are a rapidly growing assortment of day-trading books (besides this one). Most are written by professional traders, and many originate from trading firms that offer trading platforms and training. For the most part, these books are designed for someone who already has extensive investment knowledge and some familiarity with day trading. We recommend these books *after* you read this one (of course!), and better yet, after you see some "live" day trading if possible. These books talk to you as if you've seen it all before and are now in the process of sharpening your skills and strategies.

A short list:

➤ *The Electronic Day Trader* (Friedfertig/West, McGraw-Hill, 1998) provides detailed coverage of inner market dynamics, rules, and day-trading strategies.

➤ *Electronic Day Trader's Secrets* (also Friedfertig/West, McGraw-Hill, 1999) provides anecdotes and stories from actual day traders. Good for learning styles, strategies, and pitfalls.

➤ *How To Get Started In Electronic Day Trading* (David Nassar, McGraw-Hill, 1999) gives another angle into market dynamics and insight on how to use some the tools.

➤ *Day Trade Online* (Christopher Farrell, Wiley, 1999) gives insight on how to day-trade the NYSE.

➤ *The Compleat Day Trader* (Jake Bernstein, McGraw-Hill, 1995) is mostly technical analysis, focusing on the commodities markets, but is a good source for advancing day traders.

Daily Specials

You've read the book, now take the course! Coming soon to a bookstore near you—for a mere $299 you'll be able to buy a copy of the *How to Get Started in Electronic Day Trading Home Study Course.* Based on the best-selling book, it includes an interactive CD-ROM, audiotapes, and a workbook.

Integration Without a Bus

So far we've talked only about day-trading *information* (maybe information *overload* by now). But perhaps you're wondering, with all the great information available, why hasn't someone integrated it with a trading platform into a single package? One that provides execution convenience and speed alongside the information feeds? All in a single product from a single firm?

A One-Stop Shop

It's been done. Several services provide full data feeds, news feeds, chat, and the works, bundled together with high-performance trading access for home use. You can put your buy/sell buttons right below the ticker or Level II screen, offering the benefits of quickness and, in some cases, avoiding a second PC and data connection. Some incorporate regular Internet brokers such as Datek. Many use direct high-speed connections bypassing the Internet.

These high-performance systems are designed for the serious high-performance trader. No surprise. And they cost money. Again, no surprise. We'll take a closer look at the world of high-performance trading platforms such as S&P Comstock, Watcher, Castle Online, Edgetrade, and others in Chapter 16, "A High-Performance Trading Jet."

This concludes (thankfully, you say?) our discussion of day-trading information. But access to information is only part of the day-trading story. In the five chapters in Part 4, "Tools of the Trade," we talk about trading access—trading tools themselves and the firms that provide them.

The Least You Need to Know

➤ Day trading can be a lonely enterprise requiring intense concentration. A little "community" with other day traders goes a long way.

➤ "Full-service" day-trading Web sites provide a complete selection of trading information, training, chat, tips, quotes, charts, trader stories, interviews, strategies, and tactics.

➤ If you have one in your area, a visit to a local day-trading broker or trading room is a good way to get started and get "hands on" exposure.

➤ Day-trading "chat" is widely available, but be sure you take it for what it is— chat.

➤ High-performance integrated trading platforms combine real-time information with real-time trading access, or execution capability.

Part 4
Tools of the Trade

Day trading stock involves more than just clicking the "buy" button. Buy how many, and at what price? There are myriad ways to launch orders and specify your price, and you'll need to familiarize yourself with all of them.

And when you buy, what will you pay with? Meet your new best friend (or perhaps your newest enemy), Mr. Margin. We'll examine what margin is, how it works, and when to use it.

Aside from which hot stock to buy, there are all those other choices you'll have to make, too: How do you choose the right online broker? What does a Level II screen do for you? And for those who really love their high-tech tools, you'll learn just how high-performance you can go with this!

Chapter 12

May We Take Your Order?

In This Chapter

➤ The different types of buy and sell orders

➤ What if you cancel or change your mind?

➤ Fixing your price with limit orders

➤ Using stop orders to hit price points

➤ Buying long and selling short

Consider yourself informed about information. All the colors and flavors, for free or for fee, available to satisfy every craving of the day and short-term trader. Fast, real-time, and easy. The information has always been there for pros, but now it's available to you. Where you want it and when you want it, which for the day trader means *right now.*

So now the obvious question: What are we supposed to *do* with it all?

Well, we *trade*, right? Bulls-eye. Access to information isn't much good unless we have fast, real-time access to trading. So the next five chapters will focus on the trading tools and platforms that make day trading possible. We'll talk about specific tools such as ordering tools, margin, and the oft-mentioned NASDAQ Level II screen, which all come together to form the backbone of a day-trading system. We'll also cover electronic brokerages and direct trading platforms built *just for day traders.* These service providers offer the trading access, often bundled with day-trading information, that makes it all work. Think you better read this? You bet.

In this chapter, we'll take a look at the different types of orders. It isn't just a simple matter of "buy and sell"—you'll be amazed at the things you can do! The discussion wouldn't be complete without a little on how and when to *use* these order types, so we'll touch on that too. Read on!

Mark It "Market," "Day," or "Good Till Cancelled"

There are two major ingredients in any order: *timing* and *price*. Here we'll deal with timing; in the following two sections we'll talk about price. Then, comes *direction*, "long" versus "short," betting on either an increase or a decrease in the price of the stock.

Trading Terms

Slippage is the movement of the actual trade price away from the price at the time the order is placed. It is a function of volatility and speed of order transmission and execution.

Timing really refers to the length of time an order is left open. This can be used strategically in a lot of ways. You can leave orders open for only an instant, trying to pick up (or dispose of) shares right away at a particular price, either away from or at the market. Or you can leave orders open for a day or longer, hoping to catch a low (or high) or protect yourself against an adverse move when you can't watch closely. You'll begin to see that the possibilities are endless. The nice thing is that you have the flexibility to choose what's best to meet your objectives.

Make Mine Market, Please

The simplest, most basic form of order is the market order. Simply, a market order must be executed at the best price available when the order reaches the market maker or trading floor. So your order is simply:

Buy 500 shares INTC at the market.

Alarm Bells

Trades placed after the market closes won't necessarily go through the next morning at the closing price from the day before. If market makers see a "line" outside their "stall," they'll open the price higher. Jennifer forgot this the day she placed an order for shares of IVIL not long after it went public. It closed that day at 93, but gap-opened the next morning at 100. Lesson learned, thank you very much.

Notice that no price is specified. The market order says, "Just execute me now, I don't care about the price." What you're trying to do is get (or sell) stock *now*. While price is important, it's secondary. Presumably you've looked over quoted bid and ask price and think it's OK or at least close enough to meet your objectives.

The pitfall, of course, is that the stock could very easily move away from your price before it's executed! The order gets filled and you get the stock. That's the only thing that's guaranteed. But you don't control price, and surprises can and do happen. Particularly if the stock is very volatile, and *particularly* if your trading system isn't very fast. A minute can cost a lot of money in a fast-moving stock!

High-performance momentum day traders often use market orders. They can watch price movement very closely in real time. High-performance trading systems, in conjunction with SOES and SUPERDOT, are fast enough to reduce the risk of slippage.

But what if you want to control price? You aren't fast enough (or your information and trading system isn't) to fire SOES market orders and get the prices you want? Miss your targets a lot? Or just have more things to attend to than watching every little pulse?

Good news! You can set fixed-price orders as well. These are the limit and stop orders. But we won't talk about them quite yet.

Once placed, a market order is good for the duration of the trading day. At the end of the day, they expire. No ifs ands, or buts! An order placed after the end of trading is assumed to be good for all of the next trading day. It's good for housekeeping; orders don't pile up on the desks and computers of brokers, market makers, and specialists, which keeps them in a better mood.

A Day at a Time

The day or short-term trader normally doesn't want anything open longer than a day. The longer the order is open, the greater the risk of unfavorable timing on the execution. A buy-limit order (be patient, we'll cover this) placed when a stock is on the way up could be executed when a stock is headed for the Deep South! That's not what you want, is it? For most day traders, even a day is a long, long time.

> **Daily Specials**
>
> Day traders buy and sell the same stock on the same day. But if for some reason a day trader still owns the stock at the end of the day, he's said to be "taking it home with him," in trader's parlance.

Good Till What?

This type of order is even less attractive to the day trader: *good till cancelled*, or GTC. Good till cancelled means forever: The order stays on the books until it's executed. You might forget about it, but the market won't. Best not to be unpleasantly surprised by a fill on a forgotten order—you have *enough* to worry about!

Fill or Kill

You thought this was another flippant Idiot's Guide heading? Nope, not this time. This is what the order is actually called, and it's pretty descriptive. What happens is easy to guess—the order is transmitted to the exchange. If it isn't filled immediately through a market maker's quote or an order on the specialist's book, it is cancelled. This minimizes the exposure to slippage, although it's kind of a moot point with market orders, which in theory are filled instantly anyway. Not every online broker, we've noticed, has a "fill or kill" option.

Canceling the Flight

You changed your mind. Don't want to go there, never did. But the order's been placed. Whaddya do? Can you cancel? Is the ticket non-refundable? What are the cancellation penalties? Unlike plane tickets, canceling or changing stock trades isn't really too bad, but there are a few pitfalls.

Alarm Bells

If a cancellation arrives after a transaction is complete, is it reversed? *No!* You must place another order to close out the position (sell, if the original transaction was to buy). By the time all of this transpires, the market may have changed a lot and you might face large losses. Be careful!

Backing Out

All brokerages and trading systems allow order cancellation. Simply identify the order and hit the Cancel button. You made a mistake. Things changed. No one will ever know! You won't have to stand in line, but there may be a small fee charged by your broker. Normally this is less than $10 but is higher than the 25-cent fee charged by NASDAQ.

Cancellation normally works just as fast as the original order placement. Orders reaching an exchange in seconds can be cancelled in seconds—when things are working right. But when markets and electronic trading systems become extremely busy, cancellations can be painfully slow. Your cancellation may arrive after the order is filled. It's nobody's fault—just the nature of the beast. Your broker will (or should) warn you when trading activity is heavy and things are moving slowly.

Catching an Earlier Flight

Often you'll just want to change, not cancel, an order. It doesn't make sense with a market order, which will have executed by the time you change it. But you can change limit or stop prices or the timing of an order. Again, it should be a simple series of mouse clicks. Done.

Know Your Limits

Market orders guarantee an execution but not a price. Is there another choice? Of course. The limit order guarantees a price but not an execution. With a limit order you place a limit on either:

➤ The amount you are willing to pay for a stock.

➤ The amount you are willing to accept to sell the stock.

The limit isn't absolute—if the price is *better* (lower for a buy limit, higher for a sell limit) you'll get filled at that better price.

Buy Limit Orders

You might think a stock is headed higher, but might "dip" between now and when it finally does so. You want to catch the dip. You place a buy limit order.

The buy limit order is an order to buy shares at a limit price, usually (unless you're nuts) lower than the current market, or "away" from the market. When (and if!) the stock hits that lower price the order is executed. "Lower price" is based on last trade on NYSE, ask on NASDAQ, or bid on an ECN (no spread). Computerized order books keep those orders waiting for the specialists and market makers to attempt to execute when the time is right (or it's done automatically on the ECN), when the price target is reached.

So your order might look like this:

> **Buy 500 shares INTC limit 117^1/$_2$**

Alarm Bells

Why do we say "eligible for execution" instead of just "executed"? There is a risk that a limit order may not execute even if the price target is reached. The reason is simple: There may be orders ahead of yours at the same price. (This is called "stock ahead.") If the supply of stock dries up at that price before your order is executed, and it heads back up again, your order gets left out, at least until the next trip down.

Which means your order will become eligible for execution when the "inside" ask price is 117^1/$_2$. This order might be placed, for example, when the stock is trading at 118.

Sell Limit Orders

Sell limit orders are similar to buy limit orders, except that they set a sell-price target instead of a buy-price target. Naturally, a sell-price target will be higher than the current trading price. So…

> **Sell 500 shares INTC limit 120**

…instructs the market maker to execute your 500 shares when the *bid* price is at or better than 120.

Using Your Limits

Limit orders are used to:

➤ Improve buy or sell prices

➤ Manage positions that can't be followed in "real time"

Without looking at every possible instant, you could potentially "catch" a buy of Intel at 117^1/$_2$ or get a more lucrative 120 on a sale. Again, there is a risk of not entering or exiting the position *at all*. You can follow the action up to the second and zap your price with a market order (with guaranteed fill at or very near your price) or you can take the more hands-off limit order approach. You have the choice, and now you know the tradeoffs.

Stop Me Before I Fall Again!

Combining the best features of market orders and limit orders, *stop* orders provide yet another tool for the active trader and day trader's kit. Stop orders say, in effect, when the market hits a certain price, "stop here" and enter a market order. The market order, as above, executes right now at the best available price. So now we have a guaranteed fill. With liquidity and all but the wildest markets, you sort of have a guaranteed price.

Buy Stop Orders

A buy stop is simply a buy order that becomes an active market order when the stock rises to a specified "stop" price. Suppose Intel is trading at 119 and you're mildly interested in owning it but only if it takes off (or if you're already short at 125). You might place the following:

Buy 500 INTC at 120 stop

Nothing will happen until Intel hits 120. Then your order becomes an active market order. Fill is guaranteed, but price isn't—it could be at 120, higher, or even lower.

Alarm Bells

We see a problem with stop losses repeatedly, especially on NASDAQ stocks. To market makers, the stop loss order represents cheap stock—a veritable bargain at 118. (Remember, the market maker is on the buy side in this deal.) What do they do? They try to get it. Then what? Prevailing supply/demand that existed before the contrived "dip" drives the price right back up. We've seen enough stop orders turn into "low for the day" prices to recommend staying away.

Buy stops are used to protect against a price rise. As long as a stock is trading quietly in a narrow range, you'd rather use the money for something else. But if it makes a move, you want to be there. So you place a buy stop. When the stock finally "breaks out," you get your fill. Even if you don't get the exact stop price, you expect momentum behind the move, so a quarter or a half above, what's the big deal? The point is, you're in!

Buy stops are probably most used by day traders to protect short positions. You sold short at 125, now you want to make sure to lock in at least some profit and not let it get away. So long as INTC dawdles at 119 you're happy and will get happier if it goes lower. But just in case they announce that earnings will double in the upcoming quarter, you set a stop to avoid being wiped out. The buy stop order on a short sale is a safety net.

Sell Stop

Sell stops, often called stop loss orders, are set to safety net a long position. You bought Intel at 115 and now it's gone to 119. You place the following to "lock in" the profit:

Sell 500 INTC at 118 stop

So what happens if the stock goes to 122? Nothing! Your profit grows. Conversely, a hiccup sending the stock down to 116 will trigger your stop and you'll be executed at (or near, hopefully) 118, saving two bucks. Free insurance, sounds like a no brainer, eh? Well, it's almost without pitfalls....

Putting a Limit to a Stop

Seems like we're done with limit and stop orders. We've discussed limit and stop, buy and sell. Guess what? We're not. There is a shade of gray in this black-or-white world called the stop limit order. You guessed right! It's a combination of a stop order and a limit order.

When a stop limit order is used, a limit order is triggered when a stop price is reached. The handle on this one's a bit slippery, but it's easier to grasp with an example of an order and the strategy behind it:

Buy 500 INTC stop 120, limit 120$^1/_4$

Intel is still at 119. What are you trying to do with this order? You're saying, in effect: "If Intel 'breaks resistance' (or makes a move through 120), then I'm a buyer at 120$^1/_4$ or better (meaning a lower price)." It's a buy stop order with more closure. You're not exposing yourself to the total whim of a market order. It's a good tool for a day trader playing a stock with big burst potential. Of course, the same risk applies as with other limit orders—you may not get the stock at all! A day trader able to watch every pulse of the market for a stock may not need this but it's a good tool to know about.

Paying the Freight

A short footnote for the day trader considering the use of limit and stop orders: A few firms, notably the deep-discount retail online brokers, will charge a little extra. We've seen $5 charges added for fixed-price orders—to a rock-bottom $7 to $12 commission. Not a big issue, but something to be aware of.

The Long and Short of It

Most of the time when we talk about buying and selling stocks, we're talking about buying stock with money, holding it, and selling it back for money. This is what we call "going long." Successful long trading requires the stock price to go *up*. But what if we think a stock is headed lower? We can't take our money and buy "negative" stock, or can we?

Selling Yourself Short

Not really. But the markets and brokerages have provided a mechanism to play the down move, too. (It would be a pity for them to miss out on all of these potential trades, wouldn't it?) The mechanism they set up is called the *short sale*. In a short sale, you borrow the stock from your broker (or clearing firm if you have direct access) and sell it into the market. You receive cash but pay interest (margin) on the shares you borrow. You are hoping to buy the stock back later at a lower price. When you do, you "repay" the stock back to the broker.

But You've Gotta Know the Rules

There are a few key rules governing short sales, which all traders, day and otherwise, must know:

➤ **Uptick rule**   We brought it up earlier, but once again, as a reminder, short sales can only be "opened" when the market is on an "uptick" or "plus tick." That is, the last sale price or inside bid price must be above the previous one.

Trading Terms

A **zero-plus tick** is a minor exception to the "uptick" rule: It occurs when the last trade was made at the same price as the previous one, but the previous one was higher than the trade two or more trades ago.

Why do we have an uptick rule? It's a leftover from the '29 crash. Very simple—the major exchanges, in the interest of security and stability, wanted to prevent a selling "snowball, or "dogpile" as some traders call it."

The upshot: The stock must be going up, even if very briefly, for the short sale to be executed. Some trading systems won't even accept a short sale order on a down tick. Moreover, you want to play your shorts while the stock is ascending— don't wait too long to find a top, because you'll be boxed out by the uptick rule.

➤ **Minimum price**   To short a stock it must be above $5 in price.

➤ **30-day rule**   New issues can't be shorted during the first 30 days of public trading

➤ **Availability**   Not a rule so much as a fact of life. In order to short a stock, there must be stock available to borrow. Shorting doesn't work or may be barred from very thinly traded or illiquid stocks. It's up to your broker or trading firm.

Daily Specials

One little goody to remember: Brokers often won't charge margin interest on a short trade unless the position is held overnight. So true day shorting can be free (of interest anyway). Every little bit helps.

Putting Your Shorts On

Short sale orders can be entered on all electronic trading systems provided the rules are met. Instead of entering a "sell" order, a "sell short" order is entered. To close out a short sale, the "buy" or "buy to cover" button is the one to use.

Shorting at the Margin

A short sale is always handled as a margin transaction. Shares are borrowed. The current margin-interest rate is applied for however long the short position is open. The margin maintenance requirement (details coming next chapter) is a little higher—a slightly greater account-equity percentage is required to borrow stocks for shorting than to borrow cash to buy long.

What's important to remember is that bad trades (that is, the stock goes up) can cause you to be automatically "bought in" if margin requirements aren't satisfied. This can be disastrous if the stock is in a short squeeze.

What if the lender (of shares) wants them back? This causes a curious little short-selling trap. The owner of borrowed shares can recall them at any time. Often your broker simply replaces them with other borrowed shares and your position is maintained. But what if there are no more shares to borrow? Your position gets closed automatically, regardless of your position and margin. Recently we've seen this happen with hot Internet stocks. There simply aren't enough shares to go around, and traders get closed out of short positions at awkward times and prices. Which simply leads to higher prices and even a short squeeze.

Trading Terms

Short squeezes occur when a sizable number of short traders get pushed to the exits all at once. A modest up-move in a volatile, heavily shorted stock can get it started. Then it's like a herd trapped in a fire—orders fly in, some automatic margin buy-ins, and just add fuel to the fire. It's a bad place to be.

Losing Your Shorts

You've seen a few of the short trader's risks. Aside from these corner cases, the pervasive risk of short trading is the possibility of infinite loss. Going long means risking the price of the stock: Buy a stock at $30 and you can lose all $30, but that's it, and it's unlikely you'll lose that much unless the thing goes completely belly up. The short seller, on the other hand, who shorts a stock at $30, risks any and all loss as the price climbs higher. It can be hundreds of dollars. It happens: Many short sellers have come to grief on the Internet stocks.

Shorting as a Strategy

Most of us stock traders are incurable optimists: Anything we buy is sure to go up. It's just in our nature to think that way. But the astute day trader balances long trades with a few short ones. Not all markets go up all the time. A balanced approach makes the income stream more consistent while avoiding being caught on one side of the market. It's a little harder to deploy short trading with the uptick rule, but it's a club that every day trader should have in his bag.

The Least You Need to Know

➤ In addition to simply buying and selling stock at the market price, there are several ways to determine the price at which you'd like to buy or the price at which you'd like to sell.

➤ Limit orders are used to either improve buy or sell prices, or to manage positions that can't be followed in real time.

➤ Sell limit orders are used to set a price target at which your stock will automatically be sold without you requesting it.

➤ Stop orders become market orders at the "stop" price.

➤ In a short sale, you borrow stock from your broker and sell it into the market, hoping to buy it back later (to repay your broker) at a lower price.

Chapter 13

Living at the Margin

In This Chapter

➤ All about using margin funds

➤ Margin terms and rules

➤ What does margin really cost?

➤ Dealing with a margin call

➤ When should you use margin?

"Well," you may be thinking, "maybe I'll try this day-trading thing after all. But if I don't mortgage my house, hock my grandma's jewelry, or raid my kid's savings accounts, I'll only have a few grand to play with." Are you out of the game before you even begin? Not necessarily....

Maybe you can go to your banker and ask him for a loan. Tell him you want to try a fast, speculative, moneymaking idea, then watch him laugh as he shows you the door.

Is there anyone else you could approach to loan you the money to put into a fast, speculative, moneymaking idea? Yes, there is. It's your broker.

At the Margin

The idea behind margin funds is simple: It is a form of credit. Your brokerage house or clearing firm is willing to loan you money to buy stock because they want to increase profits they make beyond charging commissions. They also want to collect interest on money they loan you to invest with.

Margin comes with some complex rules, however. In order to protect you, the broker, and, yes, the economy (remember 1929?), the Federal Reserve Board, the exchanges (NYSE and NASD), and the brokers themselves have established rules to regulate the amount you can borrow. Reason: to reduce their exposure.

Terms, Conditions, and a Few More Terms

Let's examine some of the rules, terms, and variables involved with using margin funds.

Current Market Value

The current market value is the total value of the shares you have in your account as of the last trading date. The value is updated at the close of the market each market day. This process is known in the industry as "mark to the market."

Initial Margin Requirement

The initial margin requirement is the amount that you must deposit when purchasing marginable stocks. This requirement is set by the Federal Reserve Board and is called "Regulation T." These requirements can and will change as the market conditions change.

There are two parts to the initial margin requirement. First is a minimum initial deposit required. As of this writing, the initial deposit required by the Feds to establish a margin account is $2,000. Don't worry, you don't actually give this money to the government, you deposit it in your brokerage account.

The second part is a minimum equity percentage. Currently, this is 50 percent. This means for any securities purchased, the equity percentage must be 50 percent. (At least in the eyes of the Fed. Your broker may have a different idea—we'll get to that.) So if you deposit $2,000, you can buy $4,000 worth of stock.

Debit Balance

The debit balance is the amount loaned to you by your broker. This is the amount you owe your broker plus accumulated interest on the loan. If you put down $2,000 and buy $4,000 worth of stock, your debit balance would start at $2,000 and rise daily or monthly as interest is charged.

Equity

Equity is the difference between the current market value of your stock and the debit balance of your account. This figure can rise and fall along with the value of your stock. In the original example this figure is also $2,000 ($4,000 - $2,000 = $2,000 for those who didn't make it through 8th-grade algebra).

As the stock moves (and as interest accrues) the equity percent will change.

Behind the Screen

So far, all of this margin talk has to do with stock you keep in your account. But what does this mean to a day trader who sells all stocks at the end of the day and only keeps cash in the account? Answer: Regulation T, and your broker's rules, still apply. These rules put a cap on your "buying power"—the total value of the securities you can control.

Excess Equity

This sounds like something we'd all want, doesn't it? You bet! Excess equity occurs when your stock goes up! Suppose your $4,000 stock becomes $5,000 worth of stock. Your "debit balance" remains $2,000 (we'll forgo the accrued interest for simplicity). So your equity is $3,000, up $1,000 from where you started. Is it all excess? Can you take it all out and go buy a new mountain bike?

Answer: No, not necessarily. You must still maintain a minimum equity position in the account. That position, or amount, is known as a minimum maintenance requirement. We'll get to that in a minute.

Or, can you buy more stock? The answer is "yes," in fact $2,000 worth (your newly acquired $1,000 excess equity turns into $2,000 of buying power because of the Regulation T 50-percent rule. But you can't use it to repay the debit. That still remains at $2,000. The only thing that repays the debit is cash—either from selling stock or directly from you.

Minimum Maintenance Requirement

So far we've been talking about initial margin requirements and "buying power" limitations. To enter a position, you must start with 50 percent, and if the stock stays at the same price, your debit and equity stay the same, and everybody's happy. If the stock goes up, the debit stays the same, your equity increases, and everybody's happier. But what if the stock goes down?

Brokers and clearing houses, sometimes with help from exchange guidelines, set rules to cover the minimum equity percent that you're allowed to maintain after the initial purchase. If you drop below this minimum, your broker will come after you to repay the loan. (We'll get to *that* sordid scenario in a minute.)

The minimum equity is known as a minimum maintenance requirement. Many Internet brokers have a 35-percent minimum maintenance requirement for normal marginable securities. Some go down to 25 percent, and, as we'll see, some raise that requirement quite a bit when volatile highflying Internet stocks are involved!

What does this mean? It means that if your equity falls below 35 percent, you get a call from your broker. So if your $4,000 worth of stock becomes $2,500, and you still owe your debit of $2,000, your equity is $500. That's only 20 percent equity, and you're below your minimum maintenance requirement. You can choose not to answer your phone for a few days, but that isn't such a good idea. We'll get to that, too.

Trading Terms

Marginable securities are securities that your broker (with the help of the SEC) deems appropriate for margin buying—stocks with a decent track record. Generally this excludes shares under $5 (no penny stocks, please) and many IPO shares. If your latest whim isn't marginable, you'll have to pay 100 percent cash.

Why is there a "minimum maintenance requirement," and why is it different from the initial 50-percent mandated requirement? It is to give the investor some cushion—imagine if you buy 100 shares of stock on 50 percent margin, then it goes down an eighth—you have to come up with another $6.25 (50% of an eighth, times 100 shares) to settle! What a headache! So brokers give margin positions some room to move.

Oh, yes, what about the mountain biker who made $1,000 and wants to take it all out to buy the new bike? Well, it works out. The position is now $5,000, and the minimum maintenance requirement at 35% is $1,750. The equity position is $3,000, so the answer is *yes*. There's enough available to get a backpack, too!

The Margin Hit List

Every rule has its exceptions. Yada, yada, yada. And so do the minimum maintenance requirement rules. In fact, these exceptions have been in the news lately.

With all of the breathtaking ups and downs that the Internet stocks have gone through, it should come as no great surprise that these stocks are considered risks. Risks to the brokers who are loaning you the funds, that is. And so the houses have targeted stocks that will not meet their standard margin criteria. Meaning—too much of a gamble for them to loan you so much money! Instead of a 35 percent "MMR," you'll need to maintain anywhere from 40- to 100-percent equity. Here are just a few of the stocks on the hot list:

AOL, AMZN, LCOS, SEEK, SIEB, AWEB, MALL, EBAY, XCIT, GEEK, EGGS, BAMM, WAVO, MZON, COOL, ESOL, IDS, CNET, ATRX, CDE, EXAP, NAVR, TSRI, UBID, GERN, MINE, OMKT, CIEN, MKTW, PCOR

Each broker has its list, and it's updated frequently.

Gee, those look like some of the hottest day-trading stocks. You can put a ".com" after most of those company names. Why do the brokers consider them risky? Because if the Internet market tanks (a scenario that is predicted on a daily basis), many of these stocks would lose a great percentage of their value.

For those of you "short" people who like to sell stock short (to capitalize on down moves), brokers typically make it more difficult for you pessimists by requiring 40 percent or more MMR instead of 35 percent. Again, these rules vary.

What's the Point?

Why do we care about margin? Is it so you can impress all your friends by saying you control $100,000 in securities, when all you had to begin with was 50 grand? Maybe. But the bigger reason is *leverage*. Leverage is the expansion of the earning power of your capital. Afterburners, in a manner of speaking.

If you buy that $4,000 in stock and pay $4,000 in cash, and it goes up $1,000, you've made $1,000 on $4,000 invested, or a 25-percent return. Not bad. But if you used the maximum 50-percent initial margin, you invested only $2,000 in your own capital. You still earned $1,000 in profit. Which equates to a return of 50 percent. Even less bad.

Of course, the power of the lever works both ways. Suppose the stock goes *down* $2,000. In the first scenario, you lose 50 percent. Bad. If you used margin, guess what? You lose 100 percent. Worse. What's more, your broker will be calling you.

What Does Margin Cost?

Just like with the rest of the credit industry, interest on margin funds can vary from brokerage house to brokerage house. As of this writing, the current industry norm is from 7 to 9 percent. This is fairly cheap money, considering the broker's risk.

The Daily Numbers

Interest is figured daily. (Or *nightly*, in reality—important for the day trader!) It compounds. Some brokers "hit" your account with it monthly, others might raise your debits daily.

Daily Specials

Free money! Doesn't that have a great sound to it? Don't laugh, some brokerage houses really will give you free money. If you're day trading with margin funds and go in and out of a trade on the same day, you won't have to pay interest on the margin funds used to make the purchase, because you didn't hold the position overnight. Check with your brokerage house to see if intraday trades incur interest charges. Regardless of whether you're charged or not, initial margin requirement and margin maintenance rules still apply, even for your day trades.

"Dear, Your Broker Is on the Phone..."

Egads, your broker is on the phone. A margin call! How'd that happen? Simply put, the value of your account no longer supports the loan. Your account is in the toilet. "Those Net stocks got clobbered yesterday," and now you pay.

How Much Do I Need?

Your equity is $500 on a now-$2,500 portfolio. Your minimum maintenance requirement (let's keep it simple) is 35 percent for all the stocks in your portfolio.

So you need 35 percent of $2,500, or $875 minimum equity to reach 35 percent. What does your broker ask for? $875 less your $500 existing equity, or $375. If you have a lot of Net stocks in your account, with 50, 60, 70 percent MMRs, your broker will be asking for more. Each broker has a margin "department" that makes the call (decision), then makes the call (on the phone).

There are two ways to meet a margin call:

➤ Depositing more funds

➤ Liquidating stocks

Let's see how each of these works. Which is better? You'll have to decide that one yourself when the situation arises.

Behind the Screen

Why are these brokers so skittish? Look at what happened with theglobe.com: The offering price was to be a mere $9 a share. Some investors went to sleep the night before it went public, secure in the knowledge that their opening order of 1,000 shares at the market price was certain to net them riches. Hmmm...but what really happened the next morning? The stock opened at $87 a share! It reached a high that day of $97 before ending the day at $63.50. Anyone who placed a market order at the opening (thinking they were spending only $9,000) against a 50–percent margin would have purchased $87,000 worth of shares—$43,500 of that with his broker's money. The shares would have only been worth $63,500. Can you say "margin call"?

Will You Take a Check?

You can bring your account back up to the minimum maintenance level by depositing more money into it. And sadly, if the value of your stock continues to sink, by depositing even more money into it. And more. And still more.

Lock, Stock, and Barrel

Your account can also be brought back into compliance by selling stock to generate cash. You will need to sell enough shares to bring your equity back up to minimum requirements. You can sell stock, but be warned—the brokerage house can also chose to sell your stock. This is called a "sell out."

And the sell out is often at ridiculously low prices—often the bottom of a down move. Reason? Lots of other margin traders are out there doing the same thing, with the same result, as you. They're all forced to the exits at the same time. Too much stock trying to get through the exit door at once—well, you know the rest. It's a margin "squeeze." (And if you're not among the unfortunate, it can be a great buying opportunity!)

> **Alarm Bells**
>
> Remember, when stocks are going up (and when haven't they in the last 17 years?), margin is a good thing. Return rates on your precious invested capital can double. But this powerful "lever" works the other way. You can end up with nothing but debt. Margin calls are ominous and scary.

> **Behind the Screen**
>
> Internet stocks tanked on April 20, 1999. Day traders' chat rooms were filled with comments from traders who were just beginning to learn what a bad day felt like. The *Wall Street Journal* found these poignant quotes from traders:
>
> "I feel like I'm on the [back] end of the *Titanic* as it is sinking. 'Hold on. This is it.'"
>
> "This day trading isn't panning out the way it's supposed to."
>
> So the phones must have been ringing in those households...a margin call on line one, a margin call on line two. Oddly enough, when polling the industry, the *Journal* found that there were no more margin calls than on an ordinary day.

Should You Use Margin?

So how do you make the decision as to whether using margin funds is right for you? On the one hand, it can help you buy more stock and make more money. On the other hand, it can help you buy more stock and *lose* more money.

Margin is a tool, like all the other investing and day-trading tools we'll talk about. It can help you be a bigger, more flexible, more successful day trader—if used properly.

The Least You Need to Know

➤ Margin is a form of credit extended by your broker, who will charge interest accordingly. It can double your purchasing power.

➤ In order to use margin funds, your account must meet an initial margin requirement of 50 percent, minimum of $2,000. Then account equity must remain above a minimum maintenance requirement, often 35 percent but sometimes higher.

➤ Should your account fall below the minimum maintenance requirement, you will receive a margin call from your broker asking you to bring the account back in compliance.

➤ You can bring your account back into compliance either by depositing the required funds or selling stock. The broker may also choose to sell out your stock.

➤ Margin can help you buy more stock, but it can also help you lose more money.

Chapter 14

Getting It Online

In This Chapter

➤ Online trading

➤ Checking out the online brokerages

➤ Evaluating features and services

➤ Finding your best deal

Now that you're familiar with some of the necessary day-trading tools, "where to buy it" becomes the big question. The day or short-term trader needs to select a trading platform that meets his/her needs at the best price.

And the answer isn't as simple as running out to the closest store with the best price. There are dozens of trading platforms offering a trading "product," and no two are alike. When shopping for access, you have to choose among several combinations of services and pricing structures, keeping in mind key attributes such as performance and ease of use.

It's like buying a car: a complex package with all kinds of features and attributes—some you like, and some you wish you could change. And you'll have an ongoing relation-ship with your purchase (although it might be easier to switch online brokers than to switch cars). You're looking for features and performance. Thank goodness we don't really care about styling. But on the other hand, you're buying something you can't really see....

In this chapter, we'll explore some of the services available and what to look for in an online platform. But since these services evolve faster than we can write, we'll refrain from comparing specific platforms and firms—it's all on their Web sites. We'll also "turn you on" to a few sites that compare and rate online services. "Do it yourself" is a key theme in this chapter (and this book!), so we'll put you in the driver's seat for online trading-platform shopping!

Trading at the Speed of Light

The whole idea, remember, is to get access to the markets as quickly and easily as possible. It's the Internet Age, and information travels at the speed of light. Shouldn't trading work at the speed of light, too? Of course. Not to worry… for the history buffs an old vacuum-tube system will be available for view in the Smithsonian.

One of the important changes of the Internet Age is the ability—and willingness—to do it yourself. Data once only available to the professional is now available at the click of the mouse. That same click can create an automatic execution that once required several intermediate hands to perform. We're seeing a tremendous disintermediation occurring in all forms of online commerce and communication.

Behind the Screen

Never heard the word *disintermediation* before? It's a marketing term that simply means the removal of middlemen once necessary to perform a transaction or distribute a product. When Dell sells you a PC directly, they've "disintermediated" distributors and retailers. Through online trading you "disintermediate" some parts of the traditional retail brokerage, including the broker "person" him/herself. As commerce expands on the Web, more and more traditional businesses and functions may well find themselves disintermediated!

The result is a massive increase in the speed of business, customer knowledge, customer control, and options available to the customer. This is felt in few places more than in the brokerage industry, where scores of customers (like you) have put aside the traditional broker/customer relationship in favor of doing it yourselves. Speed, knowledge, control.

But that's not all…its *cheaper*! Ah, the magic word. Online trading costs can be a minute fraction of the cost of a traditional "intermediated" trade. Literally hundreds of dollars cheaper.

Cost, speed, knowledge, control…what's the net effect? (Pardon the pun.) It is to level the playing field. Online investors now have access to most of the same tools used by the professionals. Where once you would've had to work for a Wall Street firm to access these tools, you can now have them as an individual—in your home. It's light years ahead of where we were even as the '90s began.

Sedan or Performance Machine?

Life's full of choices, and we know we didn't need to tell you that. But in the online trading platform "showroom," you can choose among a myriad of basic Internet-based transportation choices. Or you can head off to the high-performance corner of integrated direct-access systems if speed's really your thing.

The Internet Chevy

Internet services offer online trading through normal Internet access tools—56K modem, ISP, Web site. Companies provide a range of services, including traditional brokerages and newer Internet-only ventures. There are many choices, but a few broad comments:

➤ Internet brokerages often still use middlemen. An online broker can take your order but not actually execute it; instead they give it (or sell it, remember "paid for order flow"?) to another trading firm. Upshot: You may not get the best price or the best speed.

➤ Internet brokerage performance is tied directly to the performance of the Internet itself. Your ISP and traffic levels in general will affect performance. Some brokers may have older systems in place that handle orders essentially as e-mail. Ask questions and pay attention to performance.

We feel that these services are at least a good place to start. They're a lot cheaper and, for some types of trading, may be all you need.

The Direct-Access Corvette

Direct-access trading systems offer direct linkage to the markets and market makers themselves, usually through a "clearinghouse" that presents and records the trades. Your order shows up exactly as placed. It's essentially what the pros, including your broker, use to place orders.

These systems often work through dedicated phone lines and high-speed network connections. It's more like a corporate than an individual trading platform. And these systems integrate the trading platform with a plethora of high-performance information "push" feeds to create a complete trading platform. We're *not* talking about something offered through traditional brokerages but through special online trading service companies. These high-performance systems are the subject of Chapter 16, "A High-Performance Trading Jet."

Brokering the Internet

Internet brokers are brokers that provide trading and information services through the Internet. You connect to their Web site, and the rest is history.

You can access information, often by linking to connected sites. You can get quotes, sometimes real-time quotes. You can trade using the different types of orders presented in Chapter 12, "May We Take Your Order?" You can trade on margin. And you can keep track of your portfolio and investment performance. All of these form the core of an Internet broker, and all of these services are performed directly on the Web site. We'll talk shortly about some of the specific things to look for.

Vanilla, Chocolate, or Strawberry

There are three main types of firms providing standard Internet brokerage services. Some have emerged as exclusive Internet brokers while others have evolved from some form of full-service or discount broker.

Full Service Meets E-Service

A few full-service firms have ventured into the cybertrading world. Speed of adaptation has varied greatly among firms. A few, like Donaldson, Lufkin, and Jenrette (through DLJ Direct) and Morgan Stanley Dean Witter (Discover Brokerage) have taken big steps to embrace the Internet age. Others such as Merrill Lynch, eager to protect their thousands of registered representatives, have only stuck their toes in (Merrill now offers it only to certain well-heeled customers who have large portfolios and meet specified trading criteria.) Others still have yet to announce their online trading plans.

Commissions are heavily discounted and more closely resemble true Internet brokerages, normally $15-$30 per trade. You do get the backing of a much larger, more stable firm, and of course you're still connected to the more complete financial and portfolio planning services the full-service broker offers if that's your preferred ice cream flavor.

At a Discount

Discount brokers have been a quicker on the uptake. Charles Schwab, Quick & Reilly, Fidelity, Waterhouse, and others have online trading platforms. They are good but mostly not state of the art. However, you do get access to the old style of trading, too—by phone to an agent or through touchtone trading. This can be a significant advantage when network performance is poor, when you travel, or when other problems arise. Most discounters offer Internet-based trades from $15 to $30. At the lower end of that scale you'll often find a $5-7 add on for fixed price (limit/stop) orders.

"E" from the Ground Up

"E-brokers" include the dozens of firms springing up all around us that are 100 percent Internet based. There are no gleaming retail offices in fancy new commercial developments. Only a high-performance Web site and a central staff to set you up and resolve problems. Performance on these sites is very good, and they're getting increasingly easy for the less experienced user to use. They're also growing rapidly. Popular examples include E*Trade, Datek, Ameritrade, and Web St Securities. They offer all of the standard services, and a few offer or link to some of the high-performance services we've been talking about. Performance is generally on the rise; now Datek guarantees 60-second trades on major stocks or no commission. When you do pay commission, e-brokers are usually the cheapest: mostly $7-15 per trade.

Kicking the Tires

Now we'll get to work and describe some of the specific things to look for in an Internet brokerage. Things like:

➤ Features and services

➤ Performance and dependability

➤ Manual backup

➤ Ease of use

➤ Cost and cost factors

➤ Minimum account requirements

Features and Services

The menu of services at any online brokerage is impressive. Most offer quotes, news, and trading in a variety of well-delivered packages. Look for:

➤ **What you can trade:** Stocks only? Or can you trade equity options, futures, and indices? A few of the big-name e-brokers still have yet to offer option trading, which can be a significant disadvantage for some short-term traders.

➤ **Quote services:** All provide delayed quotes. Are real-time quotes available? Unlimited, paid for, or paid for after a certain number? These can make a difference for the active trader.

Alarm Bells

The rapid growth of e-brokers is both a blessing and a curse. Rapid growth means that more and better services become available at reasonable prices, but customer growth has exceeded capacity growth in a few cases. Major snafus and headaches can result! It's a good idea to check the ratings, hit the chat rooms, or even try a few trades yourself. And be warned: What works today can be down tomorrow!

Trading Terms

An **intraday chart** shows trading during the course of a day. You can see all up and down price movements, usually in five minute intervals or less. A parallel volume chart shown in the same window is very handy. This is an important day-trading tool.

Also look at what's provided *in* the quote. Are there any plans to include Level II access? (Most don't today.) At what cost?

➤ **Charting and technical analysis:** Do sites provide charting tools (can be by links, too). How many different types of charts? Can you set the parameters? Important intraday charts? Is the charting tool efficient (fast)? Is the intraday chart current (up to the 15-20 minute delay)?

➤ **News services:** A site should make available at least the major wire stories (Reuters, AP, Business Wire, CBS Marketwatch). Check to see that news stories are fresh and up to the minute.

Performance and Dependability

Performance and dependability don't mean too much for the average long-term or retirement investor. Can't buy it right now? Later today, tomorrow, or even next week is probably OK. But for the day and swing trader, it can mean everything.

➤ **Execution speed:** It's gotta be fast. On normal or calm days, most online brokerages execute listed and NASDAQ stocks in a matter of seconds. Five to ten seconds for an active stock. As mentioned earlier, Datek even *guarantees* executions in less than 60 seconds or no commission is paid. Try a few trades, on different stocks, in different markets, at different times of the day, during different kinds of trading days (quiet ones, big selloffs, big up moves) and see. Check the time the order is placed and the time the order is filled. See how fast *and how consistent* the broker is. Some may actually share performance data. You really should be able to execute the majority of your trades in that 5-10 second window for that active stock.

➤ **Rapid confirmation:** Quick, easy-to-understand confirmations are very important. It's difficult to know what to do next if you can't confirm your last move.

➤ **Dependability, reliability:** Much has been made of the recent "blow-ups" at E*Trade, Schwab, and a few others. Investors were literally offline for several hours at a time due to computer glitches, new technology situations, and the like. Things can stop altogether or slow to a crawl without warning, especially on fast-market days when you

Daily Specials

It's rare that someone gives you a better deal than you ask for, but it can happen in the market through price improvement. Price improvement simply means that your broker attempts to get the best price, even better than your set limits. This means attempting to trade in the venue where the best price is available, which can mean an ECN or a regional exchange for listed stocks. "Paid for order flow" usually denies this opportunity, as the firm who bought the order tries to make its profit on the price improvement. It doesn't get passed to you. If you want price improvement, avoid firms who sell orders to others.

can make the most money! Test this, ask around, read up, talk to the broker. Ask how many outages they've experienced in the last month. If they blame NASDAQ or SuperDot, check it out. (It may be true—NASDAQ has had a few problems with confirmations, but this is the exception rather than the rule.)

➤ **Order routing:** This one can separate the men from the boys, especially for very active day traders. Does the firm execute its own orders? Or go through another intermediary? Does it "sell" the orders through that intermediary? Can you get "price improvement"? Does your broker offer the opportunity to route an order to an ECN, such as Island? If you trade heavily, good order routing can be worth a lot at a "teenie" or an eighth per trade.

➤ **Rapid account updates:** A good online brokerage will keep your positions updated at least to the 15-20 minute delay. A better one will track your yearly, year-to-date, and sometimes monthly or (we'd like) even daily performance.

Alarm Bells

Selling orders to other intermediaries can but doesn't always degrade price and speed of execution. Check with your online broker, then see how fast and accurately executions occur. Your broker should also monitor executions and attempt to route orders to dealers and market makers that provide fast, high–quality executions. Most brokers disclose their execution policies. Most that sell their order flow will tell you that the $3 or so they receive for each trade helps to reduce your commissions. Decide for yourself if it's worth it!

Router Rooter

Order routing and handling is becoming more of a calling card for e-brokers. Some new firms are hanging up their shingle just on that premise.

Witness CyberCorp of Austin, Texas. Their new "CyBereXchange" system, just unveiled, electronically routes orders to whichever trading venue offers the best price. These are often ECNs. Not only do they eliminate "paid for order flow" intermediaries, but they also frequently avoid the market makers themselves. Hence, CyBereXchange purports to have the best prices and executions available.

But they aren't alone. Datek executes trades on the Island ECN (in which it is a part owner. E*Trade just bought 25 percent of the Archipelago ECN. Others advertise their policy of not accepting order payments. It's becoming a common theme, although nobody's really sure what it will mean to the day trader at the end of the day. The lines are becoming more blurred between full-service brokers, Internet brokers, information service providers, and ECNs.

Datek Online—cheap trades, free charts, ECN access.

Manual Backup

Redundancy is important, especially in the high-tech, high-performance world. If something happens to your broker's online facility, the Internet, your phone company, or your computer, you're out of business! And don't forget, you can't (and we hope you don't want to) always sit in front of your computer! From the beaches of Kona, at least until wireless Internet access arrives, you'll want to use a backup system to trade.

➤ **Agent backup:** It's mandatory to have someone you can call to execute a trade "by hand." It may be more expensive (although good online brokers will reduce the price of a trade with an agent to the Internet commission if they recognize their own fault). It may be slower. It is also necessary from time to time for problem resolution to handle "stuck" orders or transactions or anything else that might not have worked right.

➤ **Touchtone backup:** Most "older" online traders got started with touchtone trading with the likes of "Schwab Telebroker." We still like it, especially as a backup and remote trading capability. It's fast, and provides a good alternative for those really busy days, too. It's also a handy way to trade from the road (or from the gym) when you don't have time to plug in your computer and dial-up. You can easily check the status of your executions, get quotes, or check balances this way. And if trading from work is frowned upon at your company, you can use a touchtone system and no one will be the wiser.

Ease of Use

This is primarily a matter of preference. Check the information and trading screens to make sure they are:

➤ Easy to read

➤ Easy to navigate

You want something that is easy and fast from one page to another. We hate waiting for screens to load, and toggling back and forth unnecessarily to get from quote screen to trading screen to confirmation screen. Once "in," you should have to do very few new screen loads. And another thing (while we're at it), we also hate being dumped out onto other people's sites with no easy way back home.

Cost

This one's big, especially for some of us! Save five bucks of commission on 50 round-trip trades a month...let's see...that's 500 bucks! A big enough chunk to make a difference to your bottom line success as a day trader.

But of course you get what you pay for, and sometimes a little less. You should continually examine and reevaluate the comparison between cost and service provided. And usually cost will need to be evaluated as a total package. Like any retailer, brokers will have loss leaders and other store items to make up profits.

➤ **Commissions:** The big one. There's a large range advertised, from $7 to $30. Look at share limits (many have a per-share charge over 1,000 shares, for instance) and surcharges for limit and stop orders. Look at the cost for real-time quotes. Look at the cost for manual or manually assisted trades and at options commissions. On the other side, look for "volume discounts"—brokers who give you a break if you reach certain trade volumes. Favorable commission rates for serious day traders should be $15 or less.

Behind the Screen

Commission rates seem to get lower as the months go by. How are these online brokers making money? A recent article in the *New York Times* Sunday magazine drew up an estimated breakdown of an $8 transaction fee. Here are their guesses of where the money goes: $1.48 is spent on advertising, the second biggest expense (behind employee compensation); $1.62 goes to professional services like the cost of processing trade confirmations, lawyers, technology consultants, and executive travel. Expenses like communications, exchange commissions and clearance, and occupancy and equipment further chipped away at the profit. And what was left? An estimated .58 out of the $8 transaction fee is profit.

➤ **Margin rates:** This is the interest rate the broker charges for margin buying (and short selling). It can vary a lot: from 6 to 10 percent, at the time of this writing. Different rates can be charged for different sized accounts. Many firms will subsidize a low commission rate with a high margin rate. If you're not a credit trader, this can work to your advantage.

➤ **Real-time quotes:** These can be free, and you should be able to earn a reasonable number of free real-time quotes by making trades.

➤ **Clarity:** All charges, fees, and prices should be clearly listed and explained, even if we don't need to use the service.

Minimum Requirements

Each online broker will have minimum requirements for opening an account. These requirements, along with cost, performance, and feature, are an important part of a broker's "mix."

Most require fairly minimal amounts of money to open an Internet trading account. Figures like $2,500 or $5,000 are common. But there are a few, such as Brown & Co who are trying to connect with a more sophisticated investor, and want a minimum of $15K plus demonstrated investment experience. We find none of these firms to have extremely high hurdles, however, not compared to the direct access trading firms we'll talk about in Chapter 16, "A High-Performance Trading Jet."

Checking Out the Service Department

Before buying the car, we should take a cursory walk through the service department, shouldn't we? Just to satisfy our curiosity, if nothing else. A good online brokerage, like any other business, provides good service behind their product. A few key areas:

Customer-Service Desk

Isn't it frustrating to buy a high-tech product these days and find the service and support behind it a bit lacking? Has anybody out there experienced this? You bet—we all have.

An online broker should have a good, *toll-free* service desk that can answer any question or resolve any problem. They should be able to deal with the experienced and inexperienced investor alike. We insist on minimal telephone hold times, and we like (but have learned not to expect) helpful and courteous representatives.

Customer-service quality is hard to judge objectively, but the broker rating services and chat room will give you an idea. Just make sure it's available. We *are* dealing with a high-technology product.

Training, Education

Good online brokerages should provide information, training, and education. There should at least be references or links to get what you need. Our kudos go to E*Trade, which has one of the best "learning centers" we've seen anywhere.

Security

Everyone is concerned about e-commerce security, although more and more methods are being devised to ensure safety. Make sure that *you* are the only person who can access your account! Most of the bigger name firms have adopted standard security platforms that make this a relative non-issue.

What Does *Consumer Reports* Say?

Online broker services are getting so pervasive that they will become a regular feature in *Consumer Reports*. Even now there are good tools that collect relevant comparative data and take a few test drives themselves.

On the Magazine Stand

OnlineInvestor magazine provides good consistent coverage of the online investing world with frequent articles about Internet brokers. In addition, there's a well-organized reference section listing a bounty of other Web-based resources.

On the Web

A few dedicated "broker-watch" sites and a few other investing sites provide broker-analysis pages. Among those we've looked at:

➤ *Gomez Advisors* provides advice on all kinds of things—shopping, where to spend your summer vacation—but in our context they offer a complete broker-rating and comparison service. Brokers are scored using several well-crafted sets of criteria, including some which are more useful than others to the day trader. (We suggest the scoring for the "Hyper-Active Traders.") Detailed information is shown for each broker, its services, and insightful customer commentary about the firm. "Community" chat rooms include one specifically for day traders. (www.gomez.com)

➤ *Smart Money Broker Rankings* provides "just the facts, ma'am" in table format, allowing easy comparison. Ranking capability allows you to choose the features you consider most important, then re-rank the brokers right there online. A nice feature, but little of the "scuttle" and no test drives to provide a good behind-the-scenes comparison. (www.smartmoney.com/si/brokers)

➤ *Internet Investing* gives a real straightforward peek at all the major online players. Short, crisp, one-paragraph descriptions hit the highlights and go a long ways towards helping you differentiate one broker from another. (www.internetinvesting.com)

➤ *Online Investment Services* is a site created by an individual investor named Don Johnson, which compares broker services with an eye on the experienced investor. This report is full of "scoop" and anecdotal experiences shared by others (and by you if you want). The discussion of trends is nice—who's getting better, who's getting worse. Brokers that don't meet stringent criteria (such as $15 commissions) are excluded from some of the reports, however. (www.sonic.net/donaldj/best.html)

Gomez Advisors Internet Broker Scorecard.

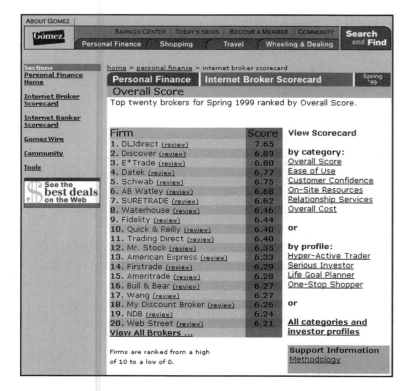

Taking It to Level II

Now, at last, we're ready to talk about the most powerful instrument in the day trader's panel. This tool separates the men from the boys and makes the amateur look like a seasoned pro. It's the ultimate in-the-know tool. It isn't available to everyone, and everyone who has it must study it and learn how to use it from experience. We're talking about the NASDAQ Level II screen.

But didn't we talk about information tools earlier? Hasn't the discussion shifted to *trading* tools? Well, yes. But Level II is so immediate and powerful that we think of it more as a trading tool. And most high-performance trading platforms that offer Level II integrate it with advanced trading tools anyway.

A Color Radar Screen

The NASDAQ Level II screen lays bare the forces behind the market. It is a specialized quote board that shows all bid and ask prices of all market makers, not just the "inside" or best bid and ask shown on a typical online brokerage quote screen. (These typical quotes are called Level I quotes).

You can see who's bidding what for how much, and who's offering what for how much, both *at* and *away* from the current market price. It's like being able to look around an otherwise blind corner while driving down the road. Some refer to this visibility as transparency.

It's unfortunate that this book is all black and white—the NASDAQ Level II screen presented in most trading packages is absolutely dripping with ebullient color, vividly depicting the size and speed of quote movement and market activity.

Remember the Market Maker

Remember that NASDAQ is a market created and run by market makers—large securities firms and investment banks that buy and sell NASDAQ securities for their clients and their firm's profit. These market makers post bids and offers, what they will buy for and what they will sell for. They make a living (for their firm and for themselves) trying to collect the spread between shares they buy on bid and sell on the offer, as many times as possible. They are dealers like the dealers at an antique show. They make money by trading with the public and with each other.

Market makers post their bids and offers in NASDAQ. NASDAQ Level II gives us visibility to those bids and offers. Remember that every market maker must make a market on "both sides"—that is on the bid and on the offer—at all times. So Level II will show the whole picture if we scroll down far enough on the screen.

Behind the Screen

Bids and offers don't *necessarily* represent actual orders. They *can* represent orders, especially those of the firm's clients. *Or* the firm and its market maker may be trading for its own account. You don't know for sure, because market makers, especially with big orders to handle, may hide their intentions so as not to unduly influence price. This is understandable from any dealer's viewpoint: If you have a container load of Louis XIV chairs, you might only show a few at a time so as not to drive the price back to eighteenth-century levels! We'll see later that it isn't always easy for the market makers to cover their tracks.

Displayed on the screen before your eyes you can see the bids and offers quite clearly (and we will shortly)! Each market maker has a four-letter code, for example GSCO for Goldman Sachs, BEST for Bear Stearns, MLCO for Merrill Lynch. Level II shows the code and the market maker's bid or ask price. It is sorted from best price to worst, and absolutely updated in head-spinning real time.

Supply and Demand

Ever see a picture of supply and demand? Sure, you can *explain* supply and demand to your friends, co-workers, and even your kids, but have you ever *seen* it? Maybe in the gas lines of the mid '70s and early '80s, but otherwise you'd be hard pressed to *see* supply and demand. Price, yes, but we all learned in ECON 101 that price is a *result* of supply and demand.

You already know what we're going to tell you: With NASDAQ Level II, you *can* see supply and demand! By looking at...

➤ The number of bids and offers at a price

➤ The size of those bids and offers

➤ Who's bidding and offering

➤ How consistently they bid and offer

➤ And how they *move* (important!)

...you'll get pretty good at predicting the direction of the stock. A large number of bids at or just off the inside market, with new market makers coming in to replace old stock sold to them, indicates *demand*. Especially if the bid price increases. Similarly, a large number of offers at or just above the inside price, persistent replacement of these offers, and declining offer prices signal a down move. These dynamics change with the beat of a jackhammer in an active stock, and watching it will keep you busy. That's the reason good Level II tools use color.

Picking Up the Echo

So, are you ready? Excited about the Level II voyage into the thin air of the market and all the intriguing possibilities it can bring? Let's put on the flight suit and take 'er up!

Ground School

Aw, heck, you knew we'd have to spend time looking at boring diagrams before heading to the wild blue yonder. OK, let's make it quick—here's a first look at our screen:

Wow—look at all those numbers. Well, we warned you—what we can't show so well in this book are the colors. Please use your imagination. The "gray areas" showing the bids and offers are actually brightly colored—yellow, blue, red, green, purple. This is so you can more easily track the *number* of bidders and offer makers at a given price level. This is key.

Level II screen for Dell Computer.

DELL	40 3/4 ↓	- 5/8	1000
High 42 1/2	Low 40 1/8		Vol 15455000
Bid ↓ 40 3/4	Ask 40 7/8		Close 41 3/8

Name	Bid	Size	Name	Ask	Size
MLCO	40 3/4	10	ISLD	40 7/8	10
ABSB	40 3/4	5	BEST	40 15/16	10
ISLD	40 3/4	8	MASH	41	20
MONT	40 11/16	10	TSCO	41	8
SNDV	40 11/16	10	PWJC	41	10
WEED	40 5/8	10	SNDV	41	10
TVAN	40 5/8	9	MONT	41 1/16	10
RSSF	40 5/8	10	CANT	41 1/16	5
SBSH	40 9/16	40	GSCO	41 1/16	10
JPMS	40 9/16	10	FBCO	41 1/16	10

Now let's take it apart:

Level II map: Level I quote (A), inside bid and offer (B/D), bids and offers away from the market (C/E).

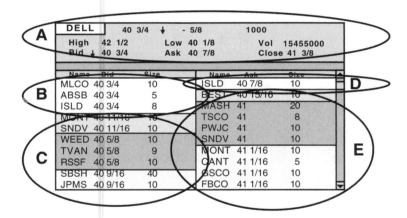

Back to Level I

The A area is essentially the Level I quote, the one you would see on any "detailed" quote at an Internet portal or brokerage screen. The last trade for Dell was at $40^3/_4$, down $^5/_8$ from the close of the previous day. It has traded as high as $42^1/_2$ and as low as $40^3/_4$. Volume is healthy at over 15 million shares. Yesterday it closed at $41^3/_8$. So far, so good, and we sincerely hope you've been trading long enough that you didn't need us to explain that part of the screen.

Another number to know is the "1000" in the upper right corner. This is the maximum order size available through SOES. (Sometimes you'll see this as "SM10," for SOES maximum 10 100-share lots.) Most active stocks have a SOES maximum of 1,000. More thinly traded stocks will have 100, 200 or 500 as the SOES maximum lot.

More noteworthy are two sets of figures. The "Bid" and "Ask" show the current inside, or best, bids and offers on the stock, in this case $40^3/_4 \times 40^7/_8$. That is, if you placed a market order to sell, you would get $40^3/_4$, and if you placed a market order to buy, you'd pay $40^7/_8$.

Also check out the "down" arrow next to the Bid. We have a downtick—the current bid price is lower than the previous one. What does that mean? No short sales, right, class?

Where else do you see these numbers? At the *top* of the two columns in the body of the screen where the market maker codes are. That's where we're going next.

Locking In on the Crowd

Now let's move on to the B, C, D, and E parts of the screen. This is where the action is, where the second level of Level II comes in.

There are two columns here. Doesn't everything in business seem to have two columns? Thankfully, we're not going to do debits and credits. The left column is the list of market-maker bids, the right column is the list of market-maker offers. Each bid or offer is represented by a four-letter market-maker code. Alongside the code is the bid or offer price. So "MLCO $40^3/_4$" is a bid of $40^3/_4$ from Merrill Lynch & Co. The small number to the right is the size—10 is 1,000 shares, 8 is 800, 5 is 500, and so on.

What Do I Hear Bid?

Now shift your attention to B and C. This is the bid side of the market. The bid column is sorted in *descending* order of price, first the best or highest bid price available, then falling away sequentially to the less attractive bids. The top bid is the inside bid (in this case $40^3/_4$). These bids are shown in B. Bids at prices lower than the inside bid are "away" from the market and are shown in groups below the inside bid. These are shown in C.

Daily Specials

You may find it hard to keep track of who is selling and who is buying. The market maker's offer, or ask price, is an offer to sell you shares, thus it becomes your buy price. The market maker's bid is what he/she is willing to pay you for shares, so it becomes your sell price.

Daily Specials

What's an Island order doing in a NASDAQ market maker bid/offer list? Wasn't it supposed to execute in Island to "bypass" market makers? An Island order that can't be executed inside the ECN is routed to NASDAQ and gets on the list, if the person placing the order allows it to (more next chapter). Each ECN has a four-letter code too.

Each shaded (or colored) area groups the market makers making a bid at a particular price. Of course the list goes on well beyond the bottom of the page for an actively traded stock with lots of market makers.

In area B, we have three market makers bidding at the inside price of $40^3/_4$—MLCO, ABSB (Alex Brown) and ISLD. ISLD isn't really a market maker—it is the Island ECN!

Moving "away" from the market (C), we have next in line two market makers bidding just slightly off the market at $40^{11}/_{16}$. "MONT" is Montgomery Securities, "SNDV" is Soundview Financial. Then three more at $40^5/_8$, and at least two more at $40^9/_{16}$. (We don't know yet what lies below the bottom of the screen.)

What happens now? Suppose the top three inside bids get filled by stock, or "taken out" in trader lingo. When MLCO, ABSB, and the ISLD order get their stock, these bids go away. The screen rolls up to the next price level of $40^{11}/_{16}$ with MONT and SNDV.

What happens to the inside bid? The NASDAQ Level I bid quote? You got it—it drops to $40^{11}/_{16}$, unless MLCO or ABSB decide to refresh their bid at $40^3/_4$. Or if another market maker posts a bid at that price.

Behind the Screen

A market maker usually has 20 seconds to refresh a bid or offer after a previous bid or offer is "taken out." Remember, they're supposed to post a bid *somewhere* to make a two-sided market. If they refresh at the previous price of $40^3/_4$, in our example, you might assume that they really want more stock. Either they have a firm order that they are trying to fill from a customer, or they simply believe that the stock is going up (after all these years, still a major reason to buy!). Watching what MLCO and ABSB do after being taken out gives clues to the underlying strength or weakness of the market.

An Offer We Can't Refuse

On the D and E side of the ledger we see the list of offers. Now we have only one inside offer of $40^7/_8$, another order through the Island ECN. This is shown in D.

Then, away from the market in E, there is only one offer, just a "teenie" off the market at $40^{15}/_{16}$. It is from "BEST," or Bear Stearns & Co. Then we get to a bigger list at 41, headed up by "MASH"—Mayer Schweitzer Inc—who just happens to be both a market maker and a dealer handling most Charles Schwab retail orders. Then another group at $41^1/_{16}$ headed up by Montgomery Securities (MONT).

So What Happens Now?

You now see and comprehend the inside market and close-in market for Dell. But this is a snapshot in time. At Dell's pace of trading, this market will last in exactly this form for about one nanosecond. Still, it's useful to look at what this screen is telling us.

As bids and offers on the inside are "taken out," one of four things will happen:

➤ Other bids and offers away from the market will "scroll up" to become the inside bid and offer, or

➤ The market maker will replace the bid or offer at the same price

➤ New bids and offers will come in, or

➤ (Usually) a combination of all three

Market makers watch these screens. In fact, that's what the Level II screen was designed for. Market makers look for opportunities in the market, and use them to meet their own and their customers' objectives. If a market maker has stock he/she really wants to get rid of, then as soon as the ISLD offer of $407^3/_8$ is taken out, that market maker might jump right to the head of the line and put in a new offer at $40^7/_8$.

And Now, Live from Level II

Let's interpret this Dell market just for fun. To simplify, we'll assume that no other bids and offers show up while we take out the bids and offers on this screen. A refresh:

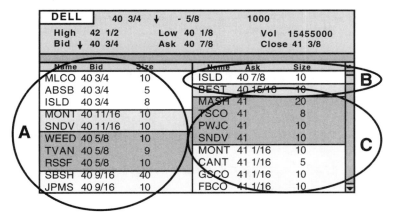

A simple example: strength, then resistance.

It appears that Dell will briefly head upward, then stall when it hits the 41 level. Why? Because with the information on the Level II screen, we can draw the following conclusions:

➤ There is a fairly orderly demand for the stock. Multiple bids show up at all price levels, including the inside market.

➤ There isn't much supply at or one sixteenth above the market on the offer, or ask, side. Single hits on ISLD and BEST will take out both $40^7/_8$ and $40^{15}/_{16}$, leaving a supply of stock at 41.

➤ If no new supply or demand come in, the stock will trade at $40^3/_4 \times 41$ after the first two makers in each column are taken out. As market makers are now getting

163

minimum 41 for their shares, it's likely more bids will show up at 40³/₄ or even higher, as market makers and traders see the opportunity to capture spread up to ¹/₄ of a point. At the same time, 40³/₄ is a mild support point—the three bids at that level can withstand some selling pressure. A market that is "thick" on the bid and "thin" on the offer has an upward bias.

➤ Finally, the stock will hit resistance at 41, then again at 41¹/₁₆. There are a lot of offers at these levels and all will have to be taken out for the stock to "break through."

We realize we glossed over this. In Chapter 20, "A Piece of the Action," we'll learn more about how to "read the tea leaves" in Level II through a more developed example. Here our objective was only to get you acquainted.

Bells and Whistles

So far we've walked you through the standard features of the Level II screen—the Level I quote summary and the bid and offer columns. Enterprising software platform developers recognize the need to give the day trader a little relief from the constant eye and math strain of watching all the action go by. They also see the need to differentiate their product. Necessity—and increased market share—are today's twin mothers of invention! A couple of ideas they've given us are worth mentioning.

The Corner Color Bar

Remember that in the last section we saw "soft" price points and harder "resistance" points in the price of Dell stock. The price points at which there were more bids or offers were *points de resistance*; the points where there were only one or two bids or offers were quick to be taken out and moved through. Fairly easy to see, but easier in a quick glance with a color bar.

See the following figure (sorry again for the lack of color!). The color bar illustrates the market bid-and-offer sequence graphically. At each price level, the color corresponding to that level is scaled exactly to match the number of bids or offers occurring at that level. So if yellow is the color used to show the inside bid, the

Daily Specials

The astute observer (and market maker) will see the uptick and the fact that other market makers are now offering and selling stock at 41. The best bid is 40³/₄. What will that sharp market maker do? Jump in and post a bid at 40¹³/₁₆, hoping to get stock (they will become the inside bid, thus next in line), then turn around and sell for 41 or higher for a ¹³/₁₆-plus profit. Market makers do a lot of this. Day traders can, too—more in Chapter 21.

Alarm Bells

You can see by now that the more market makers there are at a given price level, the more strength there is at that price and the less quickly the stock is to *break through* that price. Conversely, a lack of bids or offers at a price signal rapid movement through that price level.

yellow bar will be 2-wide if there are two inside bids, 3-wide if there are 3, 4-wide…you get the idea. Just next to the yellow bar is, let's suppose, a red bar, scaled to the number of bids at the first away price. And so on. The color bar gives a good, *quick*, easy-on-the-eyes read of the market.

DELL	40 3/4	↓	- 5/8		1000
High	42 1/2	Low	40 1/8	Vol	15455000
Bid ↓	40 3/4	Ask	40 7/8	Close	41 3/8

Name	Bid	Size		Name	Ask	Size
MLCO	40 3/4	10		ISLD	40 7/8	10
ABSB	40 3/4	5		BEST	40 15/16	10
ISLD	40 3/4	8		MASH	41	20
MONT	40 11/16	10		TSCO	41	8
SNDV	40 11/16	10		PWJC	41	10
WEED	40 5/8	10		SNDV	41	10
TVAN	40 5/8	9		MONT	41 1/16	10
RSSF	40 5/8	10		CANT	41 1/16	5
SBSH	40 9/16	40		GSCO	41 1/16	10
JPMS	40 9/16	10		FBCO	41 1/16	10

The Level II color bar— a good visual indicator.

Market Maker Watch

Many of the Level II platforms provide tools to help you keep track of market-maker activity—the actions of a *specific* market maker. One tool we've seen places an up, down, or sideways arrow next to each market maker's bid or offer. The arrow indicates whether that market maker's bid or offer is higher, lower, or the same as the last. That helps the day trader decipher whether the market maker is aggressively buying or selling, or just going through the motions. Aggressive behavior can indicate large orders behind the scenes or fresh news about the company that has yet to "go wide."

Other tracking tools can be set to monitor the activity of a particular market maker in a separate window on the Level II screen.

A Time for All Sales

One Level II accessory that most day traders can't do without is the "Time and Sales screen." While Level II shows bids and offers, Time and Sales shows actual transactions. Time and Sales is normally provided as a configurable window in a high-performance trading platform.

Daily Specials

Even without a color bar, as you gain experience you will be able to look at the bids and offers and create a quick number pattern to read it. For example, "3 2 3 2" would describe the bid pattern—3 bids at the inside, 2 at the next away, 3 at the next, and 2 at the bottom. A fairly flat sequence, foretelling small, smooth price movement. On the offer side we have a "1 1 4 4" pattern, indicating rapid price movement followed by resistance. You still have to look at the detail to know what prices are being shown at these levels, but it's a good quick–read tool.

Time and Sales screen.

DELL			
Time	**Price**	**Volume**	
10:39	40 7/8	1000	
10:39	40 3/4	1000	
10:39	40 3/4	500	
10:39	40 3/4	800	
10:40	40 15/16	3000	
10:40	40 7/8	10000	
10:40	40 3/4	1000	
10:40	40 11/16	500	
10:40	40 11/16	1000	
10:40	40 7/8	4500	
10:40	40 5/8	1000	
10:41	40 5/8	500	
10:41	40 13/16	6000	
10:42	40 3/4	1000	
10:42	40 7/8	1000	
10:42	40 7/8	1000	
10:42	40 15/16	2000	
10:42	41	1000	
10:42	41	4000	

Trading Terms

An **ax** is a market maker acting as a driving force at a particular moment—or even hours, days, weeks—holding his/her bid or offer position or even improving it after every execution. The ax probably has a large order from the firm they are representing and are aggressively trying to acquire or dispose of stock to meet the order.

Sort of an advanced ticker set up for an individual stock, time and sales allows you to read momentum. You can see actual volumes. Market makers may post a bid for 1,000 shares but really trade much larger blocks, or they may make trades without posting an inside bid or offer at all. You can see ECN executions. Time and Sales allows you to see what's going on right now, while Level II lets you look ahead. If the "prints" (executions on time and sale) are trending downward and market makers are "stacked" several offers deep and growing, and bids are retreating, you're probably looking at downward momentum. Many "less is more" day traders use these two tools alone.

At Your Local Avionics Store

OK, we've convinced you of the power of the Level II and Time and Sales radarscopes. So where do you go to get one, and how much are you going to have to fork over?

These advanced tools usually come packaged with an advanced information or trading platform. Lately we've seen them delivered as a "bolt on" feature to the high-performance data feeds. Also they're usually integrated into the advanced trading platforms that we talk about in the next chapter.

What's It Gonna Cost Me?

Unfortunately, Level II ain't cheap. We're talking high-performance software and data linkages, and NASDAQ has to get its cut, too. Hence, we've seen Level II offered for figures in the range of $150 a month, with some discount for a prepaid year subscription. Speaking in round figures, plan on $1,000 to $2,000 to bring this baby home. Figure a little more for training and self-paced video.

Upshot: Level II is for the more committed day trader or the well-heeled dabbler.

Training Wheels

Most advanced trading-platform providers are willing, even eager, to send self-paced training packages and demos to help you get started with Level II. The free video or CD-ROM is one of their chief forms of advertising! Not a bad way to get started.

These free demos usually lead to paid-for self-paced training and even classes and seminars, sometimes with one-on-one instruction on a real trading system. We mentioned some simulators in Chapter 11. A few of the platform providers make available a live demo on their Web site. There is also one "independent" site we found that gives a good walkthrough: www.phactor.com.

The investment—and the rewards—of Level II may not make you a top gun, but will definitely earn you a squadron medallion.

The Least You Need to Know

➤ The NASDAQ Level II screen was created for market makers and professional traders and gives visibility to bid and ask quotes of all market makers in a stock.

➤ Each market maker has an identifiable four letter code, i.e. BEST for Bear Stearns, MLCO for Merrill Lynch.

➤ The information on the Level II screen changes second by second as orders are taken up and new bids and offers are posted.

➤ Bids and offers are sorted in descending order, from the highest price available.

➤ With time and experience on a Level II screen, the astute day trader will learn to visualize what is likely to happen to the stock's price.

Chapter 16

A High-Performance Trading Jet

In This Chapter

➤ High-performance trading platforms

➤ Bells and whistles you should look for

➤ Understanding the market-maker ticker

➤ How to choose a trading platform

➤ A word about trading rooms

When getting properly outfitted for a modern-day Gold Rush, forget the picks and shovels. Nowadays for the serious miner it takes a bit more—power-sluice boxes, dredges, even satellite imagery to find the best spots. Sure, they still sell picks and shovels, but there's a lot of new high-tech gear on the market, and a lot of folks selling it.

The same goes for day trading. In an effort to mine this new gold vein, rapidly developing power-trading tools help the day trader reach new heights of trading proficiency. Based on what the professionals themselves use, these tools put the day trader on a level playing field with the pros. They offer premium performance, integrating the best information and trading platforms into a single package that also includes up-to-the-minute account-management tools.

But as you might expect, all this performance comes with a price. A lot of those "free seminars," free training videos, and even some of the popular day-trading books, are really trying to sell a platform package. This chapter will help you decide whether this type of advanced "mining" tool is for you.

Behind the Screen

Several times during our country's history the entire nation has been swept up in the idea that there was gold in them thar hills. Men from all walks of life dropped what they were doing and headed for California, Alaska, or the Black Hills of South Dakota. After a few years of largely fruitless activity, they all drifted away, leaving the gold fields empty. But some clever miners never abandoned the effort, just reshaped it with newer, better tools. We live in the California gold country, the Sierra Foothills, and believe us, the place is still crawling with dedicated miners, but instead of crude hand tools, they're using the latest technology. Why are we telling you this? Because long after today's crowds have gone home from day trading's gold fields, there will still be a hardy band of dedicated traders. And the tools will just get better and better.

An Advanced Weapons System

So, you might ask, what's so special about these advanced trading platforms? What if you like your Internet-broker based pick and shovel? It's cheap, you can see and understand what you are doing, and you find enough gold to keep you going!

No problem. If you're happy (or think you would be) with your Internet broker, that's OK. In fact, it's fine to start in the shallow water to pick up what you can in profits and (especially) experience. "Dabble" away. You may never need to move to the more dangerous current in the middle of the river. But if you do, we think you might want to seriously consider some of these tools.

Engines and Controls

Advanced day-trading platforms combine the best information and trading engines. We've already talked about the high-performance information feeds and what makes them high performance: real time, "push" based, quotes and news, multiple wire feeds, charting and analysis tools. We won't reopen that discussion here, except to say that most of the advanced trading platforms provide the same kinds of information as Signal Online, PCQuote, and the others discussed in Chapters 10 and 11. In some cases, they "OEM" these feeds and pass them right on to you.

What does the advanced platform add? It adds an integrated high-performance trading engine and the capacity to act as "broker," executing trades for a commission like any other broker, except in near-real time and without middlemen.

The trading engine is a high-performance transaction program, often Java-based. These engines are integrated into the complete platform with unique, user-customizable controls. Engines include Cybertrader, Attain, Javatrader, and Tradecast, among others.

These engines are designed to connect directly to the exchanges and clearinghouses. No broker intervention or opportunity for middlemen to redistribute and profit from orders. You're essentially operating in a wholesale capacity.

Launch Your Own Invasion

Believe it or not, the advanced trading platform really owes some of its design to military battlefield technology. They are designed to take in incredible amounts of information, process it, and deliver it to you, the field general. But they're also designed with the user-configurable intelligence to make a lot of decisions for you. Finally, they're set up with rapid-fire "kill-keys" that allow you to launch missiles into the marketplace with minimal keystroke overhead on your part. We're talking about an environment where mouse clicks are often too slow!

And who is the "enemy"? Well, we don't want to take this analogy too far, do we? No live ammo for *our* day traders, no sir! We want you to carry on as good citizens in high standing. But to carry on with the imagery, the professional day trader (especially the "scalper" variety) does battle with market makers, launching "missiles" (often in the form of SOES orders) to hit targets before the market makers can adjust quotes—reposition *their* armies—to make trading more profitable *for them*. It's a wargame of sorts, and the advanced trading platform gives you, the individual do-it-yourselfer, a measure of weapons parity.

What's in the Cockpit?

It's pretty amazing what these systems can do, and how impressive they look to the casual bystander! Completely configurable information and trading windows. Tickers of all sorts. Lots of color. Anyone using one of these will quickly recognize the need to invest in a large monitor—at least 19" and 21" is even better.

The Instrument Cluster

We've already talked about most of the instruments in the day trader's information panel. News feeds, quote tickers, and the like are old news. Yes, the NASDAQ Level II screen is an integral part. What starts to make this fun is that you can now have more than one—as many as four—Level II screens going at once. (Beware: at a greater cost!)

Alarm Bells

Sign up for a basic Level II screen and you'll get one screen. And that will only let you track one stock at one time. Probably all you need when you are first starting out, but if you plan to actively day trade several stocks at once, you might need to upgrade to a fancier system showing as many as four different Level II screens all at once.

For Your (Many) Eyes Only

Remember those three-eyed day traders we described in Chapter 4? Watching quotes, news, trades all at once? The advanced trading platform will help you automate what you'd have to watch "by hand." This is done through a plethora of automated tickers and filters. But are you really back to using your two natural eyes?

Probably not. Because these advanced trading platforms allow you to watch all this stuff on more than one, usually several stocks at a time!

Tickering Around

Tickers—and the "intelligence" they provide, are key to your being able to interpret and act upon the deluge of market and news data you receive. Tickers can be set up on one or several stocks at once. There are many different kinds of tickers, and you can set them up as you please through screen-driven menus. A sampler:

➤ Price tickers, the most basic, show up-and-down movements on a stock. Usually up movements are shown in green, down movements in red.

➤ News tickers show news stories about companies you follow.

➤ ECN tickers monitor activity through individual ECNs, providing sort of a Time and Sales screen for that ECN. You can use that to watch what large traders are doing, or to see if there are successive bids inside the market to aggressively pick up or sell stock.

➤ Market-maker tickers are more advanced. They will "lock on" to a particular market maker and watch his quoting and trading activity.

Tick This

Why would you need all of this info? Let's examine just one ticker closely to see how much more you'd know with this function. Here's how you'd use the Market Maker ticker:

A market maker ticker will track, for a given market maker or set of market makers, when they:

1. Make the high bid. (Translation: They need more stock for a client order or they think it's going up.)

2. Make the low ask. (Translation: They want to sell more stock for a client or they think it's going down.)

3. Refresh a bid after a transaction. (Translation: They are maintaining their position and want more of whatever that position was.)

4. Go from bid to ask. (Translation: They probably just acquired shares. Probably didn't need them but were next in line in the market. Got hit by a SOES order and now want to dump the shares back into the market.)

5. Go from ask to bid. (Opposite of #4.)

6. Drops the bid. (Translation: Don't want any more stock, they think it's headed lower, they have enough inventory, or they just want to focus on something else.)

7. Raises the ask. (Translation: Don't want to sell any more stock, maybe it's going higher?)

8. Joins (or leaves) the bid at a price. (Translation: Competing for stock at that price but doesn't want to pay more than the current market.)

9. Joins (or leaves) the offer (ask). (Translation: Competing to sell stock at that price but won't accept a lower "inside the market" price.

Daily Specials

The market-maker ticker tracks a market maker's behavior in vivid detail. From this you can determine intentions—whether they're really buying or selling stock for a large client or just trading to profit from the spread. When you get better at deciphering these intentions, you'll get better at predicting future price movements. That, of course, is what day trading is all about....

We've given you a sneak preview of the "market-maker game," which will be covered in Chapter 21, "The Day Trader's Playbook." The market-maker ticker gives you a lot of intelligence to help you figure out and play the game.

On Alert

Complementing the tickers nicely is a series of alerts or "FYIs" that flash across or sound on the screen when preset criteria are met. A price target is met? A volume target? Bingo! Alerts include:

➤ **Print** alerts that tell you when a stock trades at a particular price

➤ **Quote** alerts that tell you when a bid or ask quote reaches a certain price

➤ **Volume** alerts that tell you when the volume reaches a certain level (possibly indicating momentum or a momentum change)

➤ **Spread** alerts that tell you when the gap widens between the inside bid and inside ask (foretelling an opportunity to jump inside the inside market with a limit order and capture some of the spread for yourself)

You've Locked In—Now What?

We've surveyed the information tools that help you figure out what's going on. When the alarm goes off or the time feels right, it's time to do something. That's where the advanced platform really excels—giving you a high-performance trading "joystick" to maneuver your aircraft and hit your targets with high-performance trades! Let's fly onward and upward!

A Trader's Joystick

The "joystick" is the set of tools that manage the trading part of the platform. Buy and sell, rapid fire, real time.

Here's what they offer and what to look for:

Immediate Execution

These systems are set up to route orders directly to the exchange "floor" by direct-connecting to SuperDot, SOES, or an ECN. No middlemen, no delays. Some platform providers describe the more traditional Internet broker platform as "e-mail" trading—your order is basically an e-mail message to the broker, who sends another e-mail message to the trading venue and vice versa. E-mail communications are good enough for e-mail messages, but for the high-performance trader the seconds delay can be huge.

Behind the Screen

Top performance depends on top connections. Communication speed allows you to take full advantage of the power of this software.

These systems already dispense with the Web's full-screen protocol, bringing up screens that can take several seconds to paint or refresh. These are straight-ahead real-time connections. But you're still subject to the vagaries of your ISP and phone-line situation.

Many platform providers recommend a high-speed connection. The standby 56K modem is OK, but performance can be improved through ISDN, DSL, or some of the other new technologies. And performance can be improved further by dedicated corporate network style connections. Pretty soon, bandwidth enhancements through cable and even satellite wireless will again change the connectivity landscape. We hesitate to provide too much detail here. You'll get service recommendations and costs when you talk to the platform providers.

Confirmation

How do you know if your order was filled or not? An e-mail based broker confirmation may not tell you until after it's time to "close out" (reverse) the trade. Internet broker confirmations can be excruciatingly slow on busy days. A high-performance platform tells you *immediately* when your order executes and at what price and sometimes from which market maker.

Flipping to the ECN Channel

Most trading platforms offer the standard SOES (and SuperDot) order routings, but also offer one or many ECNs. Buttons or keystrokes point your order to Island, Selectnet, Archipelago and other ECNs. While SOES hits existing bids and offers, the ECN provides a way to set your own price in the marketplace or trade around restrictive SOES rules (such as the five-minute rule). You either get a fill through the network or display your order in the market at your price.

Divergence

Divergence allows you to place an order and have the system search an ECN or group of ECNs for the best price before executing it on SOES.

Preferencing

Trading tools allow you to preference a market maker, that is, to choose to trade only with that market maker. As an example, if you think that market maker might be soft on price (in other words, has a big client order) you can "fish around" with fixed-price limit orders off the market to see if they will take them, thus getting a little bargain on the stock. These orders are placed via SelectNet to the specific market maker chosen.

Alarm Bells

Online trading has already spawned an apocryphal tale or two—stories that might have happened, but no one can pinpoint where.... So have you heard the one about the dentist who placed a trade for 100 shares of Dell and never got a confirmation? He placed it over and over, and ended up owning (and owing his broker for) 10 times what he originally wanted. We don't know whether or not he profited from this trade, but regardless, *be warned!*

Time in Force

No, this isn't your required time of enlistment in the Day Trader's Air Force! Time in force refers to the time you want your order to be open. Remember when we talked about Fill or Kill, Day, and Good Till Cancelled? This goes one better by allowing you to set the number of minutes to keep an order out there. Handy if you're trying to do several things at once (which most of us are, most of the time).

Changing Your Mind

When moving this fast, we all make mistakes, and things can change very quickly. Absolutely critical to all high-performance trading platforms (and well worth the money) is the ability to cancel, very fast, one order or all orders in a stock. Like confirmations, many mid-performance Internet brokers don't do a good job here. Look at cancellation performance—and cost. Some platform providers charge per-cancel fees.

Let's Take a Closer Look

It takes a thousand words to create a picture, and for a lot of the material presented in this and the last chapter, we think it takes a lot more. So without further ado, here's the picture:

A high-performance platform Level II screen with trading access. From Trendtrader LLC.

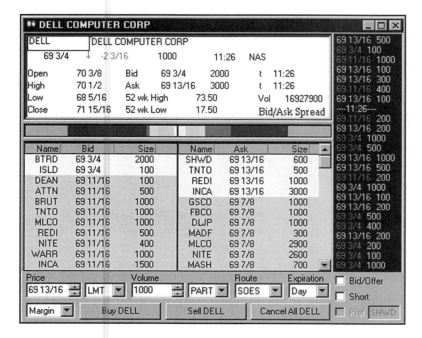

What do we have here? An information and trading window open for Dell computer. This is a fairly simple one. Keep in mind—this is probably only one portion of your 21" trading-platform screen! There are news and market ticker feeds and perhaps additional windows open for other stocks. For now, we'll look at just this window.

You're already familiar with the top ⁴/₅ of the screen. A NASDAQ Level I quote and a Level II screen with a color bar. At the right we have a Time and Sales screen. The part we're interested in now is the bottom. This is the trading "block." This one's set up for NASDAQ. Let's walk through it together:

➤ **Price 69¹³/₁₆** is the limit price we have chosen. Note the up/down arrows to avoid clunking in big fractions on the keyboard!

➤ **LMT** is a limit order; this would say **MKT** if you had a market order in place. Different platforms have different codes for other kinds of orders, but most day traders using these systems use either limit or market.

➤ **Volume** for this trade is 1,000 shares.

176

➤ A **partial** fill is OK; in other words, don't wait for a market maker or ECN to offer an exact 1,000 share lot before executing, picking up partial lots is OK.

➤ **SOES** is the chosen path. SOES automatically fills at the inside price. By choosing a limit on SOES, you're protecting against price slippage should supply at the inside price disappear to other orders ahead of you. You won't pay 69⁷/₈. Alternatives could be "ISLD" or whatever ECN you designate.

➤ This is a **day order**. Some platforms call it "Time In Force" and allow you to set it to the minute here.

➤ **Bid/offer**. You can set the order to buy automatically on the bid or sell on the offer instead of manually entering these prices yourself.

➤ **Short**—check here for a short sale.

➤ **Pref(erence)** isn't lit here because we have a SOES order. A SelectNet order (SNET) might show a preference if we want to deal with a specific market maker.

➤ **Margin** is the normal case; the system will check to see if you have the appropriate buying power.

➤ **Buy, sell, cancel all:** This is where you indicate, in a single click, what you want to do. The other stuff we just covered is the detail. This is the "fire" button on your joystick!

Hotkeys

For a more combat-ready system, many advanced-platform providers have keystroke configurations that allow you to define keystrokes (macros) to perform your trades. These macros can execute simple transactions or be programmed to do more complex expert system sequences. For the really serious combatant, they can be still faster than the mouse-driven screen. Smartkeys, Hotkeys, Killkeys—they have lots of names in the ads. These are tools for the advanced trader that we won't cover in detail here.

Picking Out Your Jet

This one's hard. There are so many tools out there. Internet sites run advertising banners for some new service almost every time you log on. These are little companies, not your household names in the industry. We ran across probably 15 or 20 of them in all while researching this book. What do you choose, and how and from whom do you choose it?

Alarm Bells

Professional day traders often describe a tradeoff between performance and the number of markets accessed by a trading platform. In other words, very diverse platforms don't do as good a job on the basics—NASDAQ stocks. Less can be more. We're not sure this is true in every case, but it's good to keep in mind.

Speed, Climb, Payload, Cost

The first thing to look at is whether the platform trades in the markets you want to trade in. Some trade NASDAQ stocks only, while others cover NYSE, equity options, index options, futures—the whole nine yards. If you want to trade options behind your day-trading activities, you might want this feature in your platform. Or maybe your Internet broker is OK. Many platforms promise to include other markets "in the near future." Be clear on what that means.

You should also look at which ECNs are available. Some platforms offer several, others are limited to one or two. That might be OK, depending on your style and strategy. Or it might not.

A Checklist

We've talked about information and trading tools as being the two key components of a complete high-performance trading system. A few other services round out and "accessorize" the product. First, a high-level checklist, then a feature-set checklist for each category:

➤ Information and decision support

➤ Trading and execution support

➤ Account management

➤ P&L performance tracking

We owe GRO Corporation some recognition here for their explanation of their "GROtrader" platform. This is the best explanation and demo Web site we've seen. (www.grotrader.com)

GROtrader, from the GRO Corporation.

A High-End Integrated Trading Environment For Active, On-Line Stock Traders

Information and Decision Support

You should look for:

➤ News

➤ Real-time market tickers

➤ Individual stock tickers

➤ Special tickers, such as market maker or ECN tickers

➤ Configurable "smart" tickers

➤ Alerts and alarms

➤ Real-time charts and charting capability

➤ Position management (tailored tickers and alerts that help you watch movements and market-maker activity in stocks in which you hold positions)

Trading and Execution Support

You should look for:

➤ Trading "block" design. Easy to read? Easy to use?

➤ Direct-access trading (no intermediaries)

➤ Connect methods

➤ Execution speed

➤ Available ECNs

➤ Divergence and preferencing capability

➤ Change and cancel capability (and cost)

➤ Time-in-force capability

➤ "Hotkey," "smartkey" setups

➤ Programmable intelligence, "expert system" capability

➤ "Execution manager" to show executions with price and market maker

Account Management

Account managers show summaries of activity and positions—orders entered and executed, with price, time, and closeout if the order is already closed. Included:

➤ Positions open

➤ Positions closed and profit/loss on positions over a period of time

➤ Margin position, interest charged, and so on

➤ Problem resolution, network bypass. As with the Net brokers, you should always have a live person to call.

P&L Performance Tracking

It is *oh* so important to know where you are and how you are doing. Not only for the taxman in April, but to guide your immediate trading strategy and to *learn*.

If you don't know what happened, you can't learn from it, and you'll make the same mistakes again. A successful day trader knows up-to-the-minute how well he's doing, and will act accordingly. Profit-and-loss summaries will help you with this, and we think they're a "must" in your platform.

179

What About Training?

Day trading is a new art and a new science, and these day trading firms don't make much money unless they can attract new clients (and keep them!). So training and education become a big part of their value proposition. Most offer free demos of their software and self paced training. Many also offer classes and seminars, some in a city near you!

OK, Who Makes These Jets?

The list changes daily, and we won't go into too much detail, but here is a handful of current companies with Web addresses. These companies sell software and provide online executions for commission. We have no preferences.

➤ On Site Trader (www.onsitetrading.com)

➤ GROTrader (www.grotrader.com)

➤ Navillus Securities (www.navillus.com)

➤ Castle Online (www.castleonline.com)

➤ TradePTN (www.tradeptn.com)

➤ MarketWise Trading (www.getmarketwise.com)

➤ UltimateTrader (www.abwatley.com)

➤ Watcher (www.broadwayconsulting.com)

➤ EdgeTrade (www.edgetrade.com)

➤ Pacific Day Trading (www.day-trade.com)

➤ TrendTrader (www.trendtrader.com)

➤ Milestone Daylight Trading (www.daylighttrading.com)

Heard of any of these companies? We doubt it, unless you're an experienced day trader. You won't find full-page ads for any of these companies in the *Wall Street Journal;* look to the sides of the page for smaller ads that will alert you to new folks getting into the market.

Are Internet Brokers Seizing the Opportunity?

Yes, but slowly. This changes daily, too. Datek Online has gone the farthest, offering the 60-second guarantee we mentioned earlier and claiming to eliminate intermediaries (no paid-for order flow). You can also route orders to the Island ECN (which they just happen to own in part). But at the time of this writing they still do *not* offer Level II, although they claim it's coming....

We suspect the Internet brokers are trying to see which way the regulatory and public relations winds blow before sinking any more money into these options. With the right climate, the day-trading revolution could go mainstream and spread rapidly.

Is It in Your Defense Budget?

Noticeably absent until now (we noticed it anyway)—a discussion of *cost.* Yes, people are trying to make money selling these mining tools. They're powerful software packages with connect capability, intelligence, and decision support that are used by professionals. Sound expensive? Yes, but maybe not in the grand scheme of things.

How Do They Charge?

There are usually three components to pricing. All handle this a little differently, but there seems to be a pattern. Fees are based on the following criteria:

➤ **Data service:** All those data and quote feeds, and especially NASDAQ Level II, cost money. Most firms offer feeds ranging from $150 to $300 per month, with some break if they are paid up a year in advance (remember the big customer retention issue). This is the "razor."

➤ **Trade commissions:** These are the "blades." "Per ticket" costs run from $15 to $25 or so. (Not $7—remember these are high-performance trades with no additional profit from paid-for flow). When you reach a break point, suppose 50 "round-trip" trades a month or so, the "razor" becomes free. Let's see: 50 × $20 × 2 (round trip) = $2,000, or something like that in day-trader's arithmetic. Yes, you're paying for the razor.

➤ **Little fees:** Like buying a house, there are lots of little nuisance fees that crop up. Some are by force, such as ECN per-share fees (ECNs don't get commissions, they make their money on a per-share basis, usually a penny or two at a time). SOES can charge 50 cents, SelectNet a buck.

Exchanges charge fees for higher level quotes, such as NASDAQ Level II, which may or may not be bundled into the data service fee. Finally, these "brokers" themselves may charge for changes, cancellations, and so on. Not a lot, but it adds up.

Adding it up: Not including the cash you'll need to trade with, it will cost anywhere from $300 to $2,000 a month or more to be an active trader on a high-performance platform. Is it worth it? Only you can decide. But be aware of the up-front cost.

Minimum Requirements

Most firms have a minimum amount of money required to start an account—usually $10,000 to $50,000. They may also require a certain level of proficiency or training.

Trading in the Parlor

A slightly older and different high-performance platform is available if you live in the right place and qualify. There are actual day-trading *rooms* offered by specialty day trading companies. These were the only game in town before some of the high-performance communications and PC-based software packages were available.

These rooms are operated by small independent trading firms, just like the at-home trading platforms. A few offer both, such as Cornerstone Securities. These rooms consist of rows of workstations, each loaded with high-performance feeds and trading tools. "Member" traders show up before the market opens, sit down, and start trading. Most firms have fairly strict "member" qualification.

What does it cost to get in? Each trading room has its own minimum investment level; some require that traders have $20,000 to trade with, others might require up to $100,000. Day-trading rooms make most of their money through commissions on the trades that they handle, $15 is the average commission.

Trading rooms can be devilishly hard to find. They do *not* want the typical retail customer to come through their doors. We've checked the phone books in the major financial centers around the country—New York, Chicago, LA—and haven't seen a single one advertised.

Behind the Screen

You've got money in your pocket and you're ready to go. Can you just sign up with a trading room and start firing away? No. "I've turned down many traders before, even folks with check in hand," Tom Burton of On-line Securities in Rancho Cordova, California, told us. Why? "I turned them away for several reasons, either because they were computer illiterate, or because I thought their trading style was too unsophisticated to succeed as a day trader. I asked one fellow what kinds of buy signals he'd like to see on a stock before he got into it. His answer was this—that he'd buy a stock if he saw a little green arrow pointed up next to the stock symbol as it scrolled across the bottom of CNBC's screen. Sorry, not good enough."

Trading-Room Advantages

Advanced communication technology and high-performance PCs and software have just recently provided the high-performance trade-at-home alternative. So why would you choose a trading room? The compelling value proposition today is training and teamwork.

A trading room can offer lots of direct, hands-on training. You can have pros look over your shoulder and guide you towards getting it right. You home-based traders are mostly on your own in this regard, whereas at some day-trading rooms you'll spend a few months trading "side-saddle" with a professional trader before they will let you loose.

Teamwork is the biggie. A room full of people has more collective eyes than any individual, even a three-eyed individual trader. Somebody sees something, and if they're part of the team, shouts it out so the others can take advantage. Ten heads and twenty eyes are better than one and two, respectively. Day-trading rooms can also give you comradeship, encouragement, and a good joke or two to cut the ever-mounting trading tension.

Another advantage is account and technical support. You have someone right there to answer technical questions and questions about your trading account. This can be a lot easier and quicker than doing it by phone.

Behind the Screen

Let's say you do start trading in a trading room, and let's suppose you turn out to be extremely good at it. The money is rolling in, and you're on top of the world. You might also end up being sought after by other trading rooms. Day-trading rooms are always quietly on the lookout for "alpha traders": super-successful, high-energy traders whose success keeps everyone pumped up and coming back for more. If you're an alpha trader, expect to be offered a better commission rate, or perhaps a free trip or two to entice you to come and trade with another firm.

Where to Look

Trading rooms are kind of hard to find. They aren't listed in local phone books nor in mainstream investment publications. Many do advertise on CNBC. But there's still a touch of an "underground" feel to the trading room industry. They aren't available everywhere.

Here are some firms you can check with to see if they operate in your part of the country:

➤ LaSalle St. Trading (www.lasalletrading.com)

➤ Navillus Securities (www.navillus.com)

➤ Harbor Securities (www.daytrading.net)

➤ Cornerstone Securities (www.cornerstonesecurities.com or www.protrader.com)

➤ Momentum Securities (www.soes.com)

➤ Online Investments, Inc. (www.onli.com)

Cornerstone Securities Web site.

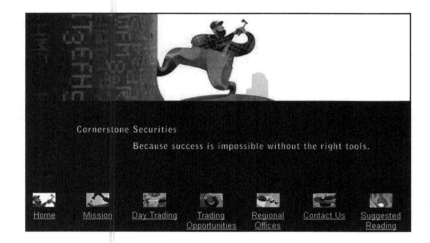

Licensed for Action

In Chapter 5, we touched on a touchy topic—the fact that there is some talk that day traders who trade from trading rooms might someday need to have a securities license to do so. The Philadelphia Stock Exchange has already proposed such a rule, which we understand has recently been shot down. But stay tuned…. A Series 7 exam is no stroll in the park—it's a tough test that covers the characteristics of different investments, the securities laws, the proper way to figure margin requirements, and other intricacies of finance.

Meyer S. Frucher, chairman of the Philadelphia Stock Exchange, summed up the way he and many others in the industry would like to see this requirement put in place: "Sometimes people need to be protected from themselves. If the firms enticing people to come in and trade aren't going to do it, the exchanges are."

The Least You Need to Know

➤ Advanced day-trading platforms combine the best of information and trading engines, giving the trader all of the analysis and info tools, plus the ability to execute trades.

➤ These trading engines are designed to connect directly to the exchanges and clearinghouses without broker intervention, allowing the day trader to operate in a wholesale capacity.

➤ "Tickers" allow you to further track the information you want on a particular stock, from price movements and breaking news to locking on and tracking a particular market maker's moves in that stock.

➤ Expect to pay anywhere from $300 to $2,000 a month to be connected to these platforms.

➤ Day-trading rooms are located around the country where you can become a member and take advantage of the equipment, training, and expertise that they can provide.

Part 5
Reading the Tea Leaves

You want to choose a stock that moves in the direction you need it to—but how can you ever begin to predict what it will do? Well, you'll learn a trick or two in this section. From gauging the indices to charting and stochastics, you'll be visualizing and predicting the price moves with ease. And, with time and practice, your predictions might even be accurate!

Immerse yourself in the patterns that stocks on the move can produce, and learn how to shadow the market maker's own moves to your benefit. The more you learn here, the stronger your skills as a trader, and the greater your chances for success.

By examining the behavior patterns of the big market makers, you will learn how to tease out their intent. This is like a big card game, and you get to try to figure out what cards they are holding. Watch that screen carefully and all will be revealed....

Chapter 17

Getting an Attitude

In This Chapter

➤ Examining the major market indicators

➤ Using technical analysis

➤ Why data doesn't replace judgment

➤ Applying trading science to market chaos

➤ The importance of S&P futures

Whew! If choking down seven chapters on information and trading platforms and the tools they contain seemed like an awful lot to absorb, we sympathize. It's all necessary, because they form the backbone of day trading. But hey, haven't we skipped a step? We've discussed all these tools and sources of vital information—but we still haven't said much about how you actually use them! We sympathize here, too, and now we're going to shift into high gear—to get value out of it all.

Of course, this topic *could* be a whole 'nuther book (and, publisher permitting, maybe it *will*)! Volumes have been written on "reading the tea leaves"—on market forecasting. What we intend to do here is give an overview of market forecasting and some of the key predictive indicators the pros use.

Over the next two parts, we'll discuss predictive market indicators, beginning in this chapter with the direction of the overall market and its influence on individual stocks. In Chapter 18, "Getting Really Technical," we'll explore how indicators can foretell *individual* stock price movements, and take a look at indicators together with the trading behaviors and motivations of the people doing the actual trading. Chapter 19, "Games People Play," explains a few behaviors and motivations of market makers, brokers, dealers, and professional traders and how they influence markets. In Chapter 20, "A Piece of the Action," we'll watch indicators and trading behaviors unfold through the real time lens of the Level II screen. Finally, in Chapters 21, "The Day Trader's Playbook," and 22, "Getting Personal," we'll talk about how indicators become part of your own personal trading system.

The Day-Trading Picnic

You're planning a picnic. For most of us, picnics are better in good weather: sunny, warm, not too windy. At the start of the day you're faced with the decision whether to go or not go. That decision is based on a number of factors, weather being just one. How is everybody feeling? Do you have the right food and equipment? Is your car running? How crowded will the park be?

So, let's look at the indicators: Sun's out, but it's a little windy. Wind is out of the southeast. There are a few clouds overhead. Feels humid. Temperature is 71 degrees. Everyone's feeling OK, and your car ran the last time you checked. Plenty of sandwich stuff, and nothing else comes to mind that has to be done today. Should you go on the picnic? Your indicators are positive. Sunny, everyone's happy, you have what you need. But there are a few distant rainy-day indicators—wind from the southeast, humid, clouds….

The point is, you don't know for sure based on these indicators alone, do you? You still have to make a judgment from your best read of all the indicators together, then add your own "gut feel" as you look out the window.

Data Doesn't Replace Judgment

In a similar way, day trading is a picnic! (And here we've been telling you what hard work it is, how much concentration it requires, and how risky it can be!) You can choose your indicators, some of which point in the same direction, some of which raise doubts. *In the end, you must have your own system for weighing them all and making a decision.*

Trading Terms

Predictive indicators use historical patterns and statistical analysis to try to predict an outcome or most likely outcome. They can be used to predict trends, strength of trends, and/ or trend reversal.

The main thing to keep in mind about predictive indicators: They are nearly all based on history—the record of a market or stock's previous performance. A lot about the future can be read in the past, as any good historian can tell you. But it can't possibly give you the whole picture. If it could, all historians (and stock technicians for that matter) would be fabulously wealthy!

You choose the indicators, decide how much weight to give each one, and finally, apply some judgment to the bits and pieces of data you retrieve. A perfect combination of art and science!

I Thought My Computer Could Do This

With all this technology and sophisticated analysis tools, it seems like all you'd have to do is to switch on your computer, set up the right programs, and head for the golf course. The computer uses mathematical indicators to make all your decisions and make all your money. (Then you would *never* be mad at your computer, right?)

Unfortunately, it can't be that simple. No mathematical model can predict things 100 percent of the time. In fact, they're pretty good if they're right more than 50 percent of the time, and exceptional if more than 70 percent. (Don't you wish you were graded so "easy" in school?) Just when things start to fall into a pattern, the pattern changes.

Part of the change is driven by the pattern watchers themselves! They see the patterns, then change their behavior. What happens when behavior changes? The pattern changes. Add to that the chaos of other events, all of which change the pattern in their own secret little way, and you can see why no analysis program, no matter how fancy and expensive, can completely replace you and allow you to play golf all day!

> **Daily Specials**
>
> An overlooked skill among successful traders is a knowledge of history—history like wars and pioneers and migrations. In fact, famed market strategist (and newly minted partner) Abby Joseph Cohen of Goldman, Sachs, believes that a knowledge of history is critical. If you don't understand the things that have happened in the past, how can you anticipate what might happen in the future?

IS It a Random Walk?

We talked a little in Chapter 8 about action in the marketplace and the *predictability* of this action. A market is an aggregate of thousands, millions, even *billions and billions* of specific trading events. A few of them might tie together; that is, one trade may cause another trade: You buy something, and sell something else to pay for it. But for the most part, stock transactions do not *cause* each other. In that sense they are random events; the results of millions of independent human decisions. But this doesn't mean there aren't patterns to these events, some of which might even be predictable for a period of time.

Applying Science to Chaos

Pure science attempts to find cause-and-effect relationships that can be utterly predicted into the future. Believe it or not, weather forecasting is based on cause-and-effect science. Temperature, humidity and air pressure—all measurable causes having their own causes—have specific, known effects on the weather.

So why do the weather people blow it all the time? Because there are *so many* causes that change rapidly and work differently in different combinations; no mathematical model yet devised can figure it all out. They're getting better, but a glance out the window still works best.

Scientists look for things that happen in patterns, too, that *correlate*, to try to predict the future. In using these patterns, the scientist says, "There is certainly a pattern here. I can't find the exact cause underlying the effect, but it happens with such regularity that there must be one. Every time I see that pattern, the same underlying cause is likely to be present."

How do the scientists find these patterns? Tea leaves and crystal balls may work for some things, but we doubt they go far in practical weather or stock price forecasting.

Scientists (OK, let's start calling them "statisticians" or "gurus"—a spade should be a spade) look at vast amounts of previous history—previous behavior—and use powerful models to discern a pattern. In theory, the more data crunched and the stronger the pattern, the more predictive it is. The process of finding patterns by "crunching" history is called "back testing."

Daily Specials

Remember, indicators are just that, indicators. They are based on patterns that may or may not repeat, and they combine with each other and other random behavior in ways that in the end may not be predictable. Indeed they can help, but you must have your own *system* for weighing them in and using them to help make trading decisions. Science plus art equals a better chance towards trading success!

What's This Have to Do with the Markets?

Market "scientists" apply pattern analysis to market history and trading data. They also look for underlying causes when they can find them, but these are usually elusive. Like the weather, there's too much interplay to use cause as a predictor, even when it can be established.

You can't measure the temperature, humidity, and air pressure of each individual stock trader! You can't measure their *motives*, but you *can* collectively measure the resulting behavior. These aggregate behaviors are usually measured at three levels: the market as a whole, by sector or industry, and for individual stocks. We'll start with market and sector measures.

Why Have an Attitude?

What do we use all this stuff for? Seems like a lot of trouble and expense to go through just to tell ourselves that, yes, the market is down, or goody, my stock is up. Why else do we need these indicators?

We've already talked about how indicators can be part of your trading methodology. That's the short answer. But more specifically, market and individual stock "attitude" indicators can help you with…

➤ **Focus:** What to watch more closely—industry sectors, stock groups.

➤ **Stock selection:** Which individual stocks to look at (stock selection).

➤ **Market and trade timing:** When to buy, when to sell, when to avoid—what's changing and when.

Be with the S&P

The most frequently used indicator of market direction is the S&P 500 index and the futures that trade on that index. The S&P is considered the most representative basket of stocks in the marketplace. Simply put, if the S&P is rising, the market as a whole—and your stocks—are most likely rising.

Let's Be Futuristic

All this stuff about how indicators dwell on the past, and look, the first one down the chute is a "future"!

If the S&P futures are rising, what do you think that means? Always the same hands—the market is going to rise, right? Like everything else in life and prediction, you can't be sure, for anything can happen between now and the future. But it's a darned good indicator that the most likely direction is up, that there is upward pressure on the market.

The cool thing about the S&P500 futures is that they trade 'round the clock, 'round the world. While you're fast asleep in Illinois, Europeans, Asians, and certain insomniacs in the West are slugging it out in the pits. Result: Even before the market opens, the futures will have likely moved a few points from the previous close. By the time your alarm clock goes off, there is already a good sense of "which way the puck is going."

What Do the Arbs Say?

S&P 500 futures movements are dictated by the collective motivations and buying behavior of traders all over the world—both long-term and short-term investors. When the S&P 500 is up, simply put, the collective mind thinks the market is going up. That's a good sign in itself.

But to fully assess how much a futures move indicates a move in the underlying stocks, we must look at the difference between the value of the futures contract and that of the underlying stocks as represented by the S&P cash index. Small differences can emerge as the result of trading strategies and risk arbitrage that are way beyond the scope of this book. But if the futures contract is trading at a

Trading Terms

S&P **futures** are financial index futures for the S&P 500 or 100 stock indices. They are the collective investment community's prediction of where the market will go for a time period up to several years forward. Because of their high visibility and active play by so many traders and money managers, they are considered one of the best overall market indicators.

Trading Terms

S&P futures are financial index futures for the S&P 500 or 100 stock indices. S&P **cash indices**, on the other hand, represent an aggregate price of the top 500 or 100 stocks today. The cash indices tell us where stocks have already been—a lagging indictor. The difference between the two, when adjusted for fair value (interest and dividends forward for the futures), reveals more about the short–term direction of the market.

premium (or discount) to the aggregate of current stock prices, professional arbitrageurs (and their "computer buy programs") are likely to show up at the party to drive underlying stock prices up (or down) to eliminate the gap.

Daily Specials

S&P 500 index future activity can be an excellent before-the-bell indicator of directional pressure and stock price movement. Once the market is open, the "PREM" index reveals even more about possible short-term market swings.

Daily Specials

How much data do we want to look at? Data examined only in small increments can lose meaning, because it's more likely to be influenced by random noise or short-term events perhaps irrelevant to the underlying trend. Technicians want to include as much data as possible because it helps to increase the reliability of the answer.

But not *too* much, because we want new data, the freshest, most recent events and trends, to influence the answer too. This new information might really be trying to tell us something!

There is an indicator called "PREM" shown on CNBC cable financial news broadcasts and perhaps elsewhere. PREM shows the premium—or discount—of the futures contract vis-á-vis the stock "market basket." A positive PREM can signal a time to buy, as arbitrage-related buy or sell programs may be about ready to kick in.

Declining Your Advances

Every day when you hear the market report you hear what the averages did, usually a major average or two. Then you hear "…advancers led decliners by a near 2 to 1…" and it goes on from there. What is this and how do we use it?

Does the Market Have Bad Breadth?

Advance/decline is a measure of market breadth. That is, are most stocks participating in the direction shown by the index? Or not? If the Dow 30 Industrials are up 150 points but decliners lead advancers 2 to 1, that says something about the overall market. There is some downward pressure although not indicated by the indexes. Happens a lot these days.

Is there a cure for bad breadth? No, and we still don't know *why else* the market is declining your advances, but it's a further sign of where the market is going.

Making It Cumulative

A daily advance/decline figure (1677 advances, 831 declines) is a number, and an OK one, to smell the breadth of today's market. But does it tell us anything about longer term market direction, or momentum?

A daily advance/decline tells us about today but not the overall trend. So stock watchers have developed a cumulative advance/decline line that keeps a running cumulative score of advances and declines over a period of time. That period of time is set to the investor's preference. So, if for the last three days:

	Day 1	Day 2	Day 3
Advances	1300	1400	900
Declines	600	500	1000

The cumulative three-day advance/decline is 3600/2100, a fairly strong bullish signal, even though Day 3 (today) is slightly bearish. Pressure is still upward, although looking at Day 3, especially if Day 2 looks like a "top" in our charts, we might be seeing a downturn. Many cumulative advance/decline watchers use much longer periods, and often the *comparison* of long term, short term, and one day A/Ds tell us the most.

A Tick in Your Arms

S&P futures and advance/decline can be part of the day trader's pre-opening bell homework, to be continued throughout the trading day. The next two indicators, TICK and ARMS, are extremely short-term, minute-by-minute indicators that tell us what the market is doing, really, at that exact moment in time.

Making Us All Tick

TICK as an indicator shows the net total of all stocks trading on an uptick minus the stocks trading on a downtick. Remember, upticks and downticks represent the difference from the previous trade levels (or bid level on NASDAQ). A TICK of −677 means that 677 more stocks declined from their last trade than advanced. A down market, for sure. TICK indexes of 100 + or - are usually said to be neutral; 100 to 400 +/- are moderately bullish or bearish; and greater than 500 +/- are strongly bullish or bearish.

TICK is reported regularly on CNBC and more advanced information feeds, and is also available on some financial Internet portals. CNBC also shows the direction of TICK, whether it's moving up or downward.

Trading Terms

TICK is a *very* short-term indicator showing the net total of all stocks trading on an uptick minus the stocks trading on a downtick.

Daily Specials

A good short-term indicator of whether the markets are weakening or strengthening is to look at the direction of the TICK index. Is it getting more positive? Less positive? More negative? Less negative? Watching the direction can help you figure out which way the current is moving right now.

ARMS Strength

TICK is useful but has built-in two problems: It is very, very short term—like *right now*; and it isn't weighted by volume. The short-term "pulse" measure is OK for some day-trading strategies, but when you're trading, these short-term stock price movements are often more important than those of the market. About volume: TICK is purely the number of upticks and downticks, without regard to the activity or volume of the stock. A stock may trade only 200 shares in a day but its tick will carry the same weight in TICK as the most active stock.

So there's a more complete, volume-sensitive indicator that many use to get a sense whether the big money is going in or coming out. This is the ARMS, formerly known as "TRIN." *ARMS* looks at uptick and downtick stocks and incorporates an up-volume and down-volume scaling factor. Never mind the math: an ARMS of less than 1.0 is considered bullish and an ARMS of greater than 1.0 is considered bearish. Again, this is a short-term daily market indicator.

Behind the Screen

What does ARMS stand for? Some high-tech acronym, maybe the American Registry of Market Strategists? Wrong. It's a guy's name. Richard W. Arms Jr. first developed this index, which shows the relationship between stocks that are advancing in price and the volume associated with these stocks. The index is calculated by dividing the advance/decline ratio by the upside/downside ratio. You know, the kind of idle calculations you do to kill time at a red light, right?

Strength Is All Relative

Relative strength has nothing to do with your six-foot-five first cousin who plays for the New Orleans Saints! It's one of the key indicators of momentum, whether for a market sector or an individual stock.

Trading Terms

Relative strength is the strength of a stock or a sector *relative* to other stocks, other sectors, or the market as a whole.

Relative to What?

At its roots, relative strength is just what the name implies: it is the strength of a stock or a sector relative to other stocks, other sectors, or the market as a whole. Combined with volume and change in volume, relative strength can be very powerful indeed. A change indicated by relative strength is especially significant and likely to last if it is sustained and reasonably gradual.

At the "macro" level, which is the focus of this chapter, relative strength applies to a stock versus an industry group, or an industry group versus the market. If the semiconductor or Internet industry is behaving very well with respect to the rest of the market, that's where you ought to pay some day-trading attention. Likewise, if Hewlett-Packard is up sharply while Dell, Compaq, IBM, and Gateway are all down, that also tells you something.

Are We Relatively Strong Today?

You can look at relative strength over differing time horizons and find very different results. Long-term relative strength—over say, the last year—points you in a direction that you probably already knew by reading the daily paper. We all know as the millennium turns that Internet stocks are the big play.

The shorter term view can be more revealing. What has been strong during the last week? Two days? The last hour?

Do I Have to Go to the Gym?

Relative strength, like all other forms of strength, is a bit elusive. So, as with most other things elusive, sometimes you have to be creative!

Investor's Business Daily offers stock relative strength versus the market as a whole, but only over a 12-month period. That's useful, but not extremely telling, for the day trader. Short-term individual-stock relative strength is often more a matter of eyeballing—you can, for instance, put all PC manufacturers up on a quote ticker and watch them together. You can do the same for industry sector indices. Or, if you don't have ticker windows that align these for you, you can simply watch by rotating through quotes and charts "by hand."

Sometimes you can also pick up industry sector trends by looking at the most active and "changes up/down" lists. Gold-mining stocks as a sector have frequently underperformed lately, and their stocks dot the "15 Largest Decreases" list. Semiconductor stocks are frequently seen on either side of the "changes" list depending on the day.

Getting Sentimental

"Sentimental" indicators, as the name implies, attempt to guage market strength by applying measures to optimism and pessimism. Difficult to do in the best circumstances, these indicators are interesting—and make nice cocktail party talk—but they have only modest relevance to the day trader. But we'll discuss them because most likely you've heard a lot about them.

Behind the Screen

Chief Strategist for Goldman, Sachs, Abby Joseph Cohen, predicts, "You'll frequently see strategists quoted, boldly forecasting where they think the market will go and when they think it will get there." Do the professional market strategists look at the kinds of things we've examined—short selling, relative strength, and ARMS strength? Most market strategists are looking in a different direction, towards the economy, unemployment, interest rates, the strength of various industries, and the nation as a whole. You, the day trader, must tend to individual tea leaves, not the just whole pot of tea!

A Sentimental Journey

Sentimentalists—if you wish to use that term—look at things like odd-lot trading, short-selling activity, insider trading, and the number of positive and negative articles in the media.

Higher odd-lot sales are supposed to signify a market top—that all the "dumb, small" money is now getting in, so it's time for the "smart" money to leave. There is probably some basis in history for this, but we don't think it's a good nail to hang your day-trading hat on.

Short selling is another indicator. Always difficult to interpret (increasing short interest says people are betting against the market, but also foretells a rally in that people *someday* have to buy to cover), short interest has less meaning today as many large players short stocks while buying futures in arbitrage deals. You can't really read much into this. If one of your stocks is in the "Top 10 Shorts" list, it might be something to watch.

Insider trading could be a very good indicator except that it so greatly lags the event. Disclosures often come months later, long after any effect on trading action has dissipated.

Media articles are kind of fun. Some can become self-fulfilling prophecies but can also provide great kindling for the contrarian. The contrarian believes that by the time the "hype" arrives about a market move, the underlying reasons are already past. A boom in "Dow 10000" articles may or may not have made it that much harder to reach. There are so many other factors to consider that it's hard to tell.

That's our read on sentimental indicators in general. Interesting, often entertaining— but usually not the most robust indicator for day and other kinds of traders.

The Least You Need to Know

➤ Data never replaces judgment. Your computer can't make your trading decisions for you.

➤ Market indicators measure collective behavior, which may or may not repeat itself.

➤ Market and stock performance indicators can tell us what to watch, which stock to trade, and can help with in and out timing.

➤ The S&P 500 index and futures are probably the most useful aggregate market indicators.

➤ Relative strength helps day traders focus on stock groups and individual stocks.

Chapter 18

Getting Really Technical

In This Chapter

➤ Crunching the data and selecting trading stocks

➤ Using charts to visualize stock moves

➤ Analyzing trendlines and patterns on a chart

➤ About oscillators: RSI, stochastics, and momentum

➤ Identifying support and resistance levels

So where are we? We know a little something about gauging market strength and moves. How does that help with predicting the movement of individual stocks?

Believe it or not, there *is* a connection. You've heard the expressions: "All boats float in a rising tide," or, "Even turkeys fly in a high enough wind." But you can't day trade just on "connections." If the day trader's goal is to trade on movement in *individual* stocks (which it *usually* is), we must take a deeper look at "micro" indicators to read individual tea leaves.

Danger: Sharp curves ahead! We're probing the murky depths of statistical analysis. Technical stock analysis fills many a cubicle with high-powered mathematicians and "quant" (quantitative analysis) specialists, few of whom speak a language we recognize. Much of their material comes from 2-pound, 500 page, $69.95 textbooks and million-dollar supercomputers.

We aren't "quants," and we have only one little chapter to deal with the topic. Result: You'll get an overview of some of the more useful technical indicators and how to use them, but we won't turn you into a "quant." We suspect your spouse would take a dim view of that.

Nestle's Data Crunch

Let's put this into perspective. In the last chapter, we regretfully informed you that you couldn't just let your computer do all your work for you. How no predictive system is totally right, or even right a high enough percentage of the time to get on the school honor roll! So why do a day trader and his trusty computer need to "crunch the numbers" to make all those nice multicolored charts?

Not Just for Decoration

Why bother? Individual stock analysis and charting can contribute in many ways to the day trader's arsenal. In this case, a picture is worth a thousand datapoints! Buckets of data show up as an easy-to-comprehend picture, the better for your three tired day-trading eyes.

Timing Isn't Everything

Do charts and technical indicators provide magic timing signals to help day traders time trades? Most day traders, including yours truly, stop short of using technical indicators alone for timing. Too much else is involved. Things change too fast, and by the time you draw the chart and get the signal, things have changed again.

For pure day trading, real-time quote and trading activity (such as viewed on NASDAQ Level II) must be brought into the timing picture. For swing traders looking for short-term but not necessarily *hourly* moves, technical indicators can play a greater role in timing trades.

Pick Me a Few Good Ones

We think these indicators are best used for stock *selection*. Every trading day we need to figure out which stocks to watch closely, which stocks to set up tickers, alerts, and Level II windows. Stocks that appear poised for a move, up or down, are the ones we want, right? Indicators can help us find the nuggets in the sand.

Alarm Bells

The best use of charts and technical analysis is to identify day-trading opportunities. As a stand-alone tool, they usually don't tell us how or when to trade.

Keeping It Simple

Again, we aren't trying to turn you into pocket-protected statistical gurus. Don't fret about Bollinger bands (although they're really quite useful and simple), Parabolic SARs, and Ultimate Oscillators. We'll keep it simple—and introduce what's important about charts and give a sampler of a few of the many types. If you want to impress others with your math and statistics skills, there are other books to buy that fit nicely next to this on your bookshelf, in your bathroom, or wherever!

The Art of the Chart

There are as many types of charts as there are day traders, or so it seems. The main point of the chart is to help the user *visualize* trends, patterns, and signals in the data that would otherwise go unnoticed. Good charts are clear, easy to read, and constructed for maximum visibility of the point they convey. Now for a few more thoughts about charts....

What Are We Looking For?

Normally the chartist focuses on price and price fluctuation from one chart interval to the next. As we'll see, much is made of statistically analyzing and correlating price movements. But most charts also show volume. Price movement and volume work together. High volume often signals a change or confirms a price trend.

For individual stocks, charts can help us find

➤ Strength

➤ Trading ranges

➤ Breakouts

➤ Patterns

➤ Trends

➤ Trend changes, crossovers, buy/sell signals

➤ Gaps

➤ Combinations of all of the above

In the following sections, we'll explore how charts follow each of these price and volume phenomena, and how they add extra indicators to clarify the picture.

The Long and Short of It

Charts can be constructed to view whatever time horizon you choose. The art of charting is built on the choice of time horizons. There's always a tradeoff—the more data in your chart, the more significant the trends for the long term. But you may lose the short and especially the *very* short-term view.

Long-term investors look at monthly charts, 50-day, 200-day, yearly, and even 5-year charts to gauge a stock's long term direction. For the day trader, this is geologic time. The 50-day or 2-month chart is a day trader's long-term chart. A lot of analysis is done on one- or two-week trends. Day traders will frequently look at intraday charts to try to decipher trading ranges *within the day* and "breakouts" from these ranges. It all depends on your objective.

Another decision you must make is the size of the time intervals within the time horizon. Short-term charts can be set to look at intervals of 1, 3, 5, 10, minutes, hourly, or pretty much as you desire. Many busy day traders keep their eyes glued to 1 minute charts.

Compare and Contrast

A good charting package will allow you to chart the "raw" data alongside several sets of indicators. These indicators can either be in the same chart as the raw data or presented in a series of charts in tandem to the price chart. The point is, you can see how the data and its indicators compare, and you can compare indicators with each other. Sometimes it's important to see how they work together.

Most charting packages let you see and compare the price and volume performance of an individual stock with the market as a whole or an index of that market. Some of the better ones allow you to compare an individual stock with *another* individual stock or an industry index.

Smoothing Out the Bumps

Charting and technical analysis packages are stuffed full of ways to smooth or average data. The objective: Filter out the "noise" in the data and get to the underlying trend. You can make the resulting "smoothed" trendlines more or less sensitive to recent events by varying the time period or how much the most recent events are weighted in the calculation. More heavily weighted recent history makes the chart more "jumpy," while even weightings and longer periods create smooth, flat trendlines. You can play with these parameters for days on end.

Trading Terms

A **trendline** is a straight line, or two parallel straight lines bracketing highs and lows, indicating the direction in which a stock has been moving, and is predicted to move.

The "art in the chart" in this case is deciding just how "jumpy" you want the resulting trendline to be. Too smooth and you might miss important recent changes. Too sensitive and you can't detect the underlying trend because of the noise. Different settings will work better for different stocks at different times. Your job is to experiment, "back test," and watch for changes in the underlying pattern you started with.

Fast Lane, Slow Lane

Charts can have individual trendlines or systems of multiple trendlines. These multiple trendlines can be highly smoothed to reflect "old" and "new" data more or less equally, or they can be set to be sensitive to more recent data. Many technicians watch with great interest for these "fast" and "slow" trendlines to converge, diverge, and to cross each other. "Fast" lines crossing "slow" lines to the upside can give a "buy" signal. "Fast" lines crossing "slow" lines to the downside can give a sell signal. Fast lines that try but fail to cross a slow line can indicate a reversal or failure to confirm a trend.

Remember, "fast" trendlines reflect shorter time periods and heavier weighting of more recent data. They move more on either side of the long-term average. "Slow" lines bring in a longer time horizon or less weighting to recent events, or they can be "second order derivatives"—moving averages of moving averages. (We won't go there.) Anyway, they're more stable and indicative of longer term base trends.

Which do you use? "Fast" if you think the recent past is the best predictor of the future. "Slow" if you want to look at the longer term underlying trend. Or the interaction of both to signal significant shifts in direction.

On with the Show

Normally we'd let these chapters play themselves out, but here we thought it would be good to have a little navigation. We'll take a closer look at:

➤ **Relative Strength Index and Momentum:** The mathematical index "RSI" and momentum indicators are simple, measures to help gauge a stock's strength against its own recent performance (RSI not to be confused with group relative strength, introduced in the last chapter).

➤ **Trading ranges:** We'll draw "support" and "resistance" lines and tell you about "breakouts," stocks that are either off to the races or the glue factory.

➤ **Pattern analysis:** The public aggregate trading chaos often unknowingly falls into recognizable patterns. Some are as clear as the Big Dipper, others may leave you wondering how they saw the "bull" in all those stars. We'll learn to recognize a few key patterns.

➤ **Trend analysis:** How to discern the underlying trend or trends, and watch for "crossovers" and other signals that indicate change.

➤ **Gap analysis:** Gaps are a form of breakout occurring at the opening of trading in a stock. We'll explore how to read these gaps as a day trader.

We'll leave this section and move on with the reminder that no mathematical model or resulting chart is automatically right, and while they may help you with your work, they aren't a substitute for it. Enough said.

Strength Is All Relative, II

One of the most basic indicators of the underlying strength of a stock is the Relative Strength Index, or RSI. RSI is straightforward, based on the strength of stock versus its own recent performance. It compares the number and magnitude of recent "up" closes and "down" closes. A related measure called momentum tests the strength and consistency of a price move. Both are simple and useful to screen stocks for a closer look.

RSI in Your Eye

The Relative Strength Index is expressed as a single-figure indicator. When RSI is above 80 it's a sign of an "overbought" condition, that is a "sell signal." When it's below 20 it signifies an "oversold" stock, and we have a "buy signal." We captured the following screenshot from CBS Marketwatch to illustrate a custom chart with RSI. This is a 90-day chart with daily price ranges represented as individual bars. There is a long-term (for day traders) 50-day moving average. Multiple connected charts show volume and the RSI. RSI was calculated as a 14-day moving average: We didn't want to overemphasize what AOL did *today*, so we averaged against the last 14 days.

CBS Marketwatch chart showing price, volume, moving average, and RSI. Note RSI "sell signals" just prior to price dips.
Courtesy CBS Marketwatch/Data Broadcasting Co.

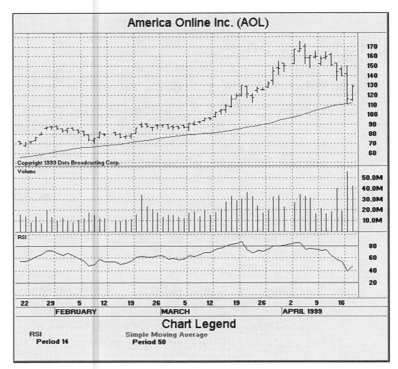

Mighty 'Mo

Another simple indicator is momentum. Momentum is the accumulated net change of a stock's closing or ending price over a defined series of time periods. A growing momentum tells the day trader to buy; a contraction may signal that the move is over.

Momentum is usually shown as a tandem chart to the price chart. The cumulative upside move is shown on the momentum chart. "N=6" means that momentum is measured over the last six periods.

How does the momentum chart help when you can plainly read the price move itself? Good question. Does a look out the window beat the weatherman? Maybe, but remember—it's easy on this chart. When up and down moves are more complex and "nervous," the momentum indicator can help separate the move from the noise.

We've made up (we hope) a phony company stock to feature in the following charts. Please don't rush out to place orders for trademe.com based on these examples. These are just illustrations to help you better understand charts.

Trading Terms

Momentum is the accumulated net change of a stock's closing or ending price over a defined series of time periods.

Momentum indicator.

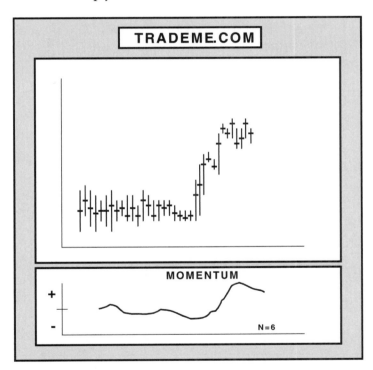

At Home on the Trading Range

Stocks, particularly in the absence of fundamental news—earnings, splits, acquisitions, and the like—will often trade in visible ranges. When it gets up to the top of the range (resistance), sellers come in and knock it down. When it gets to the bottom of the range (support), bargain-hunters come in and snap it up. The pattern repeats and the

Trading Terms

The **support level** is a price at which a stock will receive considerable buying pressure. This develops when investors consistently buy a stock when down to a certain price. The **resistance level** is the price at which a stock will encounter selling pressure. It forms where investors consistently sell stock when it approaches a certain price level.

stock tracks "sideways" until something happens to change the pattern. See the following chart.

Often you can draw the support and resistance lines by hand. Most technicians look at the daily high (not close) prices to define resistance and the daily lows to define support. There are more complex algorithms for determining support and resistance. (Remember those Bollinger bands and Parabolic SARs? They draw resistance and support levels by taking into account previous volatility and trading patterns). We'll save the details for another book.

Note that the trading range *narrows*. This is common. Why? More and more traders see the range and jump in with more buys and sells as the stock moves to support and resistance. These additional orders blunt the move and narrow the range.

Trading range and breakout.

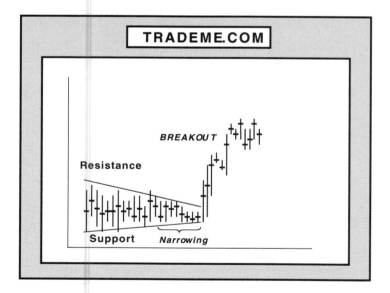

Everybody Over the Wall!

Finally, we get a breakout. Something happens to rejuvenate interest in the stock, often just a sustained move a period or two in duration above (or below) the range. All bets are off, and the stock can run away in the direction of the breakout move.

Stochastics, Anyone?

We know "stochastics" sounds scary. Before you put the book down or skip to the next chapter, we promise to keep it simple. No long, dry, technical explanations, and no quizzes or exercises at the end of the chapter!

Stochastics simply measure the position of a stock's closing price relative to its price range over a specified number of periods and relative to its overall trend. If a stock starts closing near the low of its daily range but is on a strong uptrend, it's a sign of a potential "overbought" condition and short term weakness. Like RSI, the stochastic indicator will register high (over 80) and give a sell signal. Conversely if the stock starts closing strong every day during an overall downtrend stochastic will suggest read "buy," especially if under 20.

Stochastics can predict tops, bottoms, and reversals. Usually technicians look at the interaction of "fast" and "slow" stochastic indicators. Often stochastics will be looked at in combination with other indicators. Specific details and interpretation are beyond this book.

See the following figure for an example of the stochastic indicator. When above 80, a "buy" is signaled, especially if other indicators also signal "buy" concurrently.

Trading Terms

Stochastics measure the position of a stock's closing price relative to its price range over a specified number of periods and relative to its overall trend. Stochastics are a type of **oscillator**, which tell us if a change is significant and sustainable, or weak and likely to reverse.

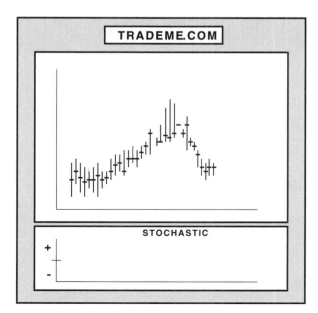

Stochastic indicator.

Higher Highs, Lower Lows

From stochastics we now arrive at a more common-sense indicator. If a stock is making higher "high" each trading interval, it is a sign of an upside breakout. It isn't closing at the high yet, but the mere fact that new ground is plowed at each interval is significant. Of course, this works on the downside, too.

Say, What a Cute Pattern

Pattern analysis is one of the classic forms of technical analysis. The technician looks at a chart to identify a pattern, much as the psychology patient sees a butterfly in a Rorschach diagram. Certain patterns seem to recur, especially for certain stocks.

This isn't pure chance—remember, we're analyzing collective human behavior. Traders, market makers, brokers, and owners of a given stock are likely to behave in like patterns over a time period—at least until they realize that they're getting predictable! Technicians have a few "stock" patterns that they routinely look for.

Head and Shoulders Above the Rest

"Head and shoulders" patterns cleanly reflect underlying activity. See the following chart.

Head and shoulders, or "triple top" pattern.

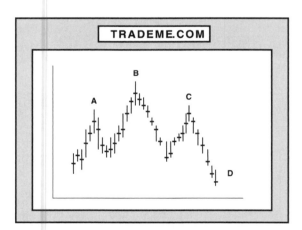

There is an initial upside "smart money"–driven surge (A), which falls back on profit taking. Those that missed the initial move "buy the dip" and cause the biggest surge (B). The stock tires again. Finally, those who missed both moves, the least nimble or "informed" money of all, buy into form C. Finally, all the buying interest is gone, and the stock breaks down at D. This pattern is fairly common, and is sometimes called a "triple top" (or bottom, if reversed). "Double tops" and "double bottoms," are milder versions of the same thing.

Love Triangles

Interesting patterns emerge as buying or selling pressure dries up on a stock. A stock may have solid upside resistance or downside support at a particular price level. A stock showing clear upside resistance may at the same time show ever higher downside support levels as selling evaporates. If this is the case, an upside breakout is often in the cards. See the following chart.

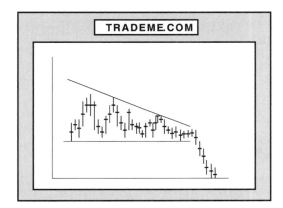

Triangle down pattern.

Similarly, a solid support level with a steadily decreasing resistance level may indicate a breakdown in buying pressure. Result: A price breakdown when support is broken. See the following chart.

When resistance and support converge with both on diagonals (instead of one a straight line) it is called a *pennant* formation. A breakout is usually in store, but it's harder to tell which direction. The first few periods of movement after the pennant convergence will usually tell.

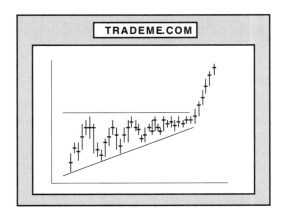

Triangle up pattern.

Little Round Tops (and Bottoms)

A gently rounded bottoming pattern (like a small bowl) can signify upside movement ahead. Sellers tried to take the stock down but were unable to deliver any kind of breakout. There were always enough buyers. Eventually the selling pressure gives out and the stock begins to creep higher. Momentum starts to build, and it's off to the races. Similarly, a round "top" signifies failed buying and the "creep lower" can turn into a rout.

Cups and Handles

Moving from technical analysis to doing the dishes? Is this our way of politely reminding you that if you wash out as a day trader you can always get a job doing dishes at Denny's? Nope. A cup-and-handle formation is a variation of a rounded bottom. See the following chart.

Cup-and-handle pattern.

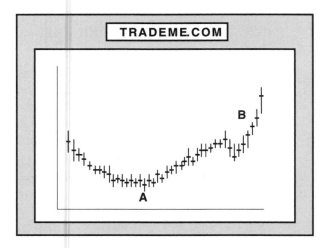

A represents a typical rounded bottom. The up move gets tested by selling, which quickly dissipates and confirms the up move (B). Off to the races.

The Trend Is Your Friend

Trend analysis is probably the most developed and sophisticated form of technical analysis. Higher mathematics take over as we try to quantify trends and changes in trends. It gets even fancier when we compare the differences between trends and trend changes calculated from different time intervals. For example, if the short-term trend change is bearish and "crosses over" a longer term more confirmed bullish trend, what does that mean?

We're getting a bit beyond our scope here. First and second derivatives of moving averages are easy only for computers and their pocket-protected math-geek friends to comprehend. We won't go there.

Moving with the Averages

One of the most popular visual tools is the moving average. Individual price behavior can be so erratic as to be confusing on a chart. Moving averages simply reduce—but not eliminate—the noise. Moving averages take the most recent data value and average it in with a defined set of previous period data values. The result is a "smoothed" representation of history.

You control how much smoothing is done. As we said earlier, greater smoothing means greater discounting of the most recent data, which can cause you to miss real indicators. On the other hand, making the smoothed trendline too sensitive to recent values reintroduces "noise" and may give false directional indicators that aren't really there. Experience will tell you the best formula.

Moving averages can be smoothed in different ways:

➤ **Simple moving averages (SMAs)** are as simple as adding up the last 6 data points and dividing by 6. No more or less weight is given to recent or earlier figures, and any action 7 or more periods ago is left out altogether.

➤ **Weighted moving averages (WMAs)** can weight the most recent data values a little more heavily (or less if you choose). A 6-period average might give the most recent value a 25% weight, then weight previous values a steadily declining amount until the oldest carries, say, only a 10% weight. How you set up these weights (and the number of periods) determines the sensitivity to recent events.

➤ **Exponential moving averages (EMAs)** never drop off the old data. The average is calculated by multiplying the most recent figure by a determined constant percentage called "alpha," let's say 20%. Then the previous single EMA figure is multiplied by 80% or (1-20%). This pattern is continued indefinitely. The influence of a single period will decay exponentially but never be left out altogether. Larger "alpha" values make the average more sensitive to recent data.

Regardless how you do it (and it's fun to play with the choices), remember that the point is to get a better, more representative view of the trend.

Let's look at a couple of moving averages in the following chart.

The 9-day simple moving average is calculated by taking a straight average of the last 9 periods. This "black line" tracks individual stock price movement fairly closely. Contrast this with the 18-day average which moves with the data but more slowly. This one probably better represents the underlying trend, while the 9-day average gives a clearer view of the pattern.

Trading Terms

Moving averages take the most recent data value and average it in with a defined set of previous period data values.

Simple moving averages—9-day and 18-day. The 18-day average is less sensitive to single interval prices.

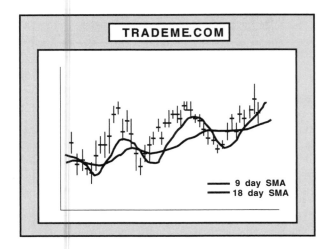

Crossovers

One popular signaling technique is to look where the moving averages cross over each other. When the short-term moving average crosses over the longer term average, it can signal a significant move in that direction. The illustrated pattern is pretty simple, but you can see that when the black line crosses the gray line to the upside, it's a pretty good time to buy. The converse is true for downside movement.

One More for the Road

Much is made today of the Moving Average Convergence Divergence indicator. MACD mathematically measures differences between short- and longer-term moving averages (which you define) and plots a signal line. Crossovers, line divergences, and line position work together to create strong signals. Sometimes MACD and stochastics or other indicators will be used together to identify and confirm a move. These types of complex indicators are getting beyond our scope. The following chart illustrates the use of MACD and stochastics together to identify a move.

Summing it up: Charting and technical analysis can give you a good look-see at short-term and long-term trends, and how both play together to indicate strength or weakness in a stock.

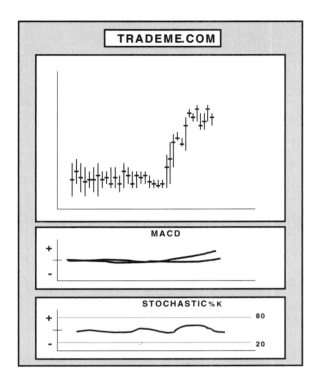

Compound chart with MACD and stochastic indicators.

A La Carte Menu

You'll hear about a couple of other patterns from time to time that would probably be best described as pattern analysis: thermals and gaps.

In a High Enough Wind

Sometimes you'll look at a chart and say to yourself, "That stock is trying its hardest to move up (or down) to a certain price level, but just can't seem to make it." Chartists call these thermals. A stock might be "buoyed" at a level short term by active buying. But if the real "smart money" pressure is downward, that's where it goes as soon as the buying volume dissipates.

Price ambles along or may rise a bit with sustained high volume. It looks like it could go somewhere but doesn't. Then volume (buying pressure) starts to taper—when that happens, look out below! Sellers were always there to meet the buyers when the stock was stuck at the higher plateau; the buyers went away, volume drops, and selling takes over. Volume picks up briefly as selling momentum builds, then everything stabilizes at the lower level. The same thing can happen in reverse.

Thermal support and breakdown.

Fall into the Gap

Gaps are a favorite day-trader's play, and we'll dig in further when we examine trading strategies. Basically a gap occurs when the opening price of a stock is much different, or "gapped" from the previous close. Often it's driven by news events or rumors.

Trading Terms

A **gap** occurs when the opening price of a stock is much different, or "gapped" from the previous close.

Specialists or market makers meet the excess demand or supply often trading from their own accounts. They have to stick their necks out some to do so, either buying excess shares or selling short to meet the public's "buy" orders. As a result, they will look for any and all opportunities to reverse the positions favorably. If a stock "gaps up" on the open, the specialist or market maker sells short to meet the demand. On weakness, they will quickly bring the price back down, often lower than the open, to cover their positions advantageously. Sharp-eyed day traders on the watch for this sort of behavior will see the stock either reverse below the previous close or continue higher (if buying pressure continues)—and trade into those patterns.

Just in Case You Want More

Now that we've pushed the limits of what can be squeezed into a single chapter, you're probably more than ready to move on. But first we thought we'd take the opportunity to share a few technical-analysis resources.

Free Charting

Two free Internet-based charting platforms are worth mentioning:

➤ CBS Marketwatch provides a complete charting platform sourced from Data Broadcasting market data and charting tools. Lots of flexibility and control, easy to read. But it doesn't provide intraday charts nor charts comparing individual stocks. (cbs.marketwatch.com)

➤ Bigcharts.com overcomes some of the short-comings of CBS Marketwatch but the result is a bit harder to read. Both of these services have decent "help" tools to educate the new user on terminology but not as much on interpretation. (www.bigcharts.com)

➤ Most Internet brokers have something but we haven't seen much beyond normal price/volume charts, a few with simple moving averages. E*trade has a very good "Learning Center" guide to technical analysis.

Daily Specials

A final reminder of our position on charting and technical analysis: Use it to find day–trading opportunities; you're on thin ice if you use it alone for trade timing.

And Not Free

Most of the high-performance trading platforms have sophisticated charting tools. There are also a few software packages specializing in technical analysis and advanced backtesting, such as Omega Research. (www.omegaresearch.com)

In the Bookstore

There are dozens of books on technical analysis, most of which are well beyond the average trader's needs. (But good for impressing friends, parents, co-workers, and the like!) They are not very fun reads! Most of them aren't tuned for the day trader either.

One is worth a mention: *The Compleat Day Trader,* by Jake Bernstein, although focused on day trading in commodities, gives a useful and well-illustrated guide to various techniques of the technician. Maybe not the first book you should read (after ours), but one for the day trader's self-improvement list if you think charts and indicators will help.

The Least You Need to Know

➤ Charting can be used in a variety of ways to visualize both actual movement, underlying trends, and structural changes in those trends.

➤ Relative Strength Index, Momentum, and Stochastic "oscillators" track stock activity against recent behavior and give buy and sell signals when a trend reversal appears likely.

➤ Trading range and pattern analysis reveal recognizable, patterned behavior on the part of traders, market makers, brokers, and money managers.

➤ Several free Internet charting platforms can help you create and use technical charts. "High performance" charting software tools are also available—for a charge.

➤ Technical and charting tools normally aren't used alone for day trading. They can identify trading opportunities and then be used together with other tools to determine trade timing.

Games People Play

In This Chapter

➤ The inner motives of market makers and how they can work for—or against—you

➤ Market makers as day traders

➤ How to identify a market maker's motives

➤ How to tell if a market maker is bluffing

➤ Learning to buy at the bid and sell at the ask

You've no doubt heard this one before: "Markets are driven by greed and fear." Greed pushes them higher and fear pushes them lower. We're talking *collective* greed and fear—greed and fear on the part of the general public, the pros, the traders, market makers, the institutions. Greed and fear are emotions. Greed and fear often show up on the market "scene," and yes, they do drive markets. This conclusion is something of a no-brainer.

But let's take this one step further. Our contribution: "Markets are driven by motive and behavior." The motives and behaviors of the general public, pros, traders, market makers, and institutions. But we'd like to single out one segment of this population for closer examination: the market makers (and specialists, for you NYSE fans). Why? Because their motives and resulting behaviors both indicate and dictate the direction of the market. Better, at least in the very short term, than all the graphs and charts we just spent 20 pages talking about.

In this chapter we'll explore the inner actions and behaviors of the market makers and specialists, what they mean, and how to best read them from your new frame of reference as a day trader.

Market Makers Are People, Too

The day of 100-percent automated markets hasn't arrived yet. Even with the best electronic order routing and automated SOES-style execution, the human factor is still alive and well (and the thousands of folks employed in the industry are grateful for that). In both the NYSE and NASDAQ markets living, breathing, and (we hope) thinking humans remain at key steps along the path.

The Human Factor

Why are people still involved in automated order execution? There are probably three reasons: 1) We haven't invented a computer that can do it all, 2) We wouldn't trust it if we *had*, and 3) Profit opportunities for the folks currently involved (and their firms) would disappear otherwise.

The focus for this chapter, anyway, is the NASDAQ market maker and NYSE specialist. For the most part we'll consider them one and the same for this discussion. Any key differences that emerge will be pointed out.

Brokering and Dealing

As each of the major markets were discussed in earlier chapters, we made it a point to detail the roles and responsibilities of market makers and specialists. You do remember all of the details, don't you? They're qualified and chosen by their respective exchanges to act as transaction principals. In the NYSE case, they match orders. In the NASDAQ case, they show bid and offer quotes and buy and sell stock directly from brokers, other market makers, or the general public through ECNs.

Trading Terms

A **broker** is an agent who buys and sells something on behalf of others, usually for a large clientele. A broker's objective is to find players (or their brokers) on the other side of the deal and transact on the client's behalf at the best possible price. For this work they receive a commission, but don't normally take title to the goods and services being rendered, in this case, stock.

In this capacity they provide order and liquidity to the market. Controlled, predictable executions without fanfare or emotion. Given what it *could* be, with 100,000 institutions and 70 million individuals trading with *each other,* we should be quite thankful for market makers and the services they provide. Day traders, give these guys a hand!

But it also must be recognized that, just like the rest of us, market makers and specialists are motivated by profit. Market makers make profit in two ways: as a broker and as a dealer.

As a Broker

The dictionary defines a broker as an "agent who buys or sells something on behalf of others." An entirely suitable definition. Both specialists and market makers execute the orders of others. They make their money on commission.

The NYSE specialist job description is close to the definition of a broker. One specialist from one firm handles all orders in the stock for every market participant. You could get away with saying that the specialist is a very specialized broker.

For the NASDAQ market maker, it's a little different. Market makers represent their firm in the market. For the firm's clients, clearly the market maker acts as a broker, representing them in the marketplace. These clients could be large institutions, individuals, or other brokers who "wholesale" their orders to the market maker. But while they play an active role in trading their clients' orders, market makers also actively trade for their own—their firms'—accounts. In this capacity, they are dealers.

Deal Me In

Dealers buy and sell something from their own inventory. They buy it from one party at one price, hoping to sell it later to someone else at another (hopefully higher) price.

For market makers and specialists, this occurs when they trade "from their own account," buying and selling shares from their own—or their firms'—inventory.

How do they get paid? By pocketing the difference between what they paid for shares and what they sell them for. This can be the bid-ask "spread"—or it can be more, depending on how long the inventory has been kept and how the market has moved.

NYSE specialists can and often do act as dealers when the supply of orders from the general public dries up. In fact, they are often *compelled* to do this by rules and the prevailing obligation to create an orderly market. In some cases they may *want* to trade from their own accounts to make profit for their firm. But there are rules about this, too, that prioritizes the public interest ahead of their profits.

Not so, or not at least as *much* so, for the market maker. The market maker is buying and selling fast and furiously from other market makers, brokers, and the general public (yes, *you*) with the hopes of turning that stock and making a profit. This profit is for the firm that employs the market maker, not the market maker person him/herself (but it does turn into rather spectacular five- and six-figure year-end bonus checks…).

Understanding these roles, motives, and resulting behaviors will help you "read the tea leaves" and improve your day-trading success.

Trading Terms

A **dealer** buys and sells something, in this case securities, from their own inventory. They hope to profit from the difference between purchase and selling prices, and may hold the commodity for as long as needed until the right selling conditions arise. The main difference between the broker and dealer is that the broker wants to collect commissions while the dealer wants to profit from price differences in the commodity itself.

Behind the Screen

There's big money in acting as dealer for NASDAQ member firms. Does NASDAQ have the same rules as the NYSE? Not quite—in theory competition between market makers helps govern where the "monopoly" of the specialist might fall short. But it didn't work perfectly. The January 1997 rule changes eliminated some dealer practices that fattened profits. Spread-fixing was reduced by monitoring market-maker communications (to stop collusion) and by forcing market makers to post customer orders *inside* the spread (Limit Order Protection Rule).

And They Are Also Day Traders

You thought day trading was a new thing? Think again.

In their role as broker and *especially as dealer*, specialists and market makers are really super-charged day traders. Their sincere hope and wish is to buy shares from the public, institutions, other brokers, other dealers—*everyone*—"on the bid," and then resell the shares "at the ask" to other people, institutions, brokers, and dealers as quickly as possible.

Fine Used Cars

They want to pay low blue book and sell at high blue book, over and over again. Like any dealer, the more times they do it, the more money they make. Profit is driven by the number of transactions, number of shares, the spread, and the amount of inventory held. Frequency, spread, inventory. High trade frequency and high spread bring in more profit, lower inventory reduces risk (of a downturn) and ties up less capital.

There are limitations to the amount of spread, as we just discussed. Competitive forces and rules keep it to a minimum, usually a "teenie" for very actively traded stocks. So the market-maker dealer makes money in volume by flipping transactions over and over again and minimizing exposure to inventory held overnight. You should, by now, recognize this as day trading!

Must We Always Compete?

So as a dealer/day trader, market makers compete with each other. With all the new technology and know-how, you are right there in the mix, too! As a day trader, you're competing with market makers to be a dealer in the stocks you are day trading. You want to buy as close to the bid and sell as close to the ask as possible. Or, for a higher ask. Market makers are competing with each other *and you.*

This is also true, albeit to a lesser extent, with NYSE specialists.

You're One of the Crowd, Now

That market makers and specialists as dealers are day traders *just like you* is very important to remember. And you're a day trader just like them. It's a frame of mind you need to remember and acquire as a day trader.

Alarm Bells

Don't ever forget that a market maker is also a day trader, just like you. The more you understand this, the better you will be able to understand the moves they make.

The Market–Maker Card Game

We've talked about what a market maker *is*, now let's talk a about what he/she *does*.

Let's start by taking a closer look at the NASDAQ market maker. Day in and day out, the NASDAQ market maker makes a market by quoting prices. Remember, the rules stipulate that, in normal circumstances, they must make a two-sided market, posting at least one bid and one offer at *some* price level. The rules also say they must honor any quote they post. Beyond that, they're pretty much free to do as they please, whatever meets their own and their clients' objectives.

It's like a card game. The market maker is dealt a hand of client orders and gets a stack of chips—investment capital—from his firm. Goal: To trade with other market makers, brokers, and the general public (including day traders) at the card table to win! In this case, winning usually involves not taking the whole pot but taking a few chips out at a time.

They win if they play their cards right. Let's take a look at how the market maker plays those cards, and *why.* Let's look at the behaviors—and the motivations behind them.

Drawing for an Ace

The market maker is required to post a bid (to buy stock) or an offer (to sell stock) to other market makers, brokers, and the public. Remember that other market makers and brokers can trade with market makers through ECNs, particularly SelectNet. Meanwhile the public trades with market makers electronically through SOES, and now also through ECNs if their trading platform supports it.

If the market maker posts a bid, does it mean that he/she will get stock? If the market maker posts an offer, does it mean he/she will sell stock?

Answer: It depends! Whether or not the market maker "gets filled" depends on two things—the bid or offer price and the size of supply and demand.

Daily Specials

Let's say it again, this time with emphasis: A market maker who really wants to buy stock will quote the highest bids. A market maker who really wants to sell stock will quote the lowest offers.

➤ **Price of the bid or offer:** If the bid or offer is *competitive,* it is more likely to get filled. A good bid is more likely to get "hit" by a seller; a good offer will get "hit" by a buyer. What is a "good" bid or offer? The "best" bid or offer is one at the inside market—that is, the *highest* bid or *lowest* offer available.

➤ **"Size" and supply/demand at the price:** If the market maker makes a competitive bid at the inside price, but they are Number 10 on the list, they won't sell stock if there only 9 buyers. Remember: Bids and offers at the inside market, including those from ECNs, are "taken out" *in the order posted* unless a market maker is "preferenced" in the trader's order.

Bottom line: *A market maker who really wants to buy stock will quote the highest bids; a market maker who really wants to sell stock will quote the lowest offers.*

Is This Guy Bluffing?

A market maker who wants to buy stock will quote the highest bid. But is the converse true? Does a market maker who quotes a high bid *always* want to buy stock? The answer is: *Usually, but not always.*

Market makers can use quotes to do whatever they want. Normally, it is to buy and sell stock at the quoted prices. In this case, their bids (or offers) reflect their true position. But sometimes market makers want to hide something they have—or show something they don't have—with their bids and offers. Why? To achieve a particular price or trading objective. Let's examine what some of these "ulterior motives" might be.

Straight, Flush, or Pair of Deuces

Here we resume the discussion of the market maker's role as broker or dealer. What they try to accomplish in the market depends on what role they are playing at a given moment. That role changes continuously through the day.

Let's look at some of the roles, or "hands" that a market maker may hold, and how they're motivated to play them out. Later on, we'll show you how to recognize these hands.

Hand #1: Capturing the Spread

This is the routine, everyday, "steady-state" role of the market maker. Simply, he/she tries to buy shares at "wholesale" (bid) and sell them at "retail" (at the ask or offer), pocketing the difference. A market maker can do quite well, grabbing a teenie, an eighth, or a quarter off of hundreds of thousands of shares per day. The more times this trade is made, the fatter the total profit at the end of the trading day. You'll recognize this as a dealer role.

This opportunity doesn't come free, however. To get stock to sell, the market maker must bid competitively with other market makers (and now, the public) to buy the stock in the first place. This drives the price upward. The market maker can't just sit at a lower price and hope to get filled—it won't happen. So the market maker risks paying too much for the stock if they are *too* aggressive in the market. And they risk holding too much stock in a downturn—the risk of holding inventory we described earlier.

Behind The Scenes

Who are the market maker's competitors? By now, you've probably figured out that you, the day trader, are part of that elite club. Up until the advent of professional information and trading access for everyone, market makers only had to worry about each other—and sometimes chose to illegally cooperate with each other instead! Now, powerful technology and virtually unlimited access put you right in the middle of the game, right on the virtual trading floor competing for spreads with the pros. A great opportunity for you and other traders to play that also, by the way, has reshaped the whole marketplace. Compete with the pros? You've gotta know what you're doing, but the good news is that you no longer have to sit on the sidelines!

Still, market makers will play hand after hand, drifting in, playing the bid to pick up stock when the opportunity presents itself, only to sell it moments later when *that* card becomes the one to play. As long as there is stock to buy and plenty of "market orders" from the public to fill at the "ask," the game goes on.

Hand #2: Playing the Market

If "capturing the spread" is a fairly placid, passive way of picking up small profits over and over with minimum risk, then "playing the market" is the opposite. Here the market maker, again in a role as dealer, is trying to capitalize on an anticipated market move. Just like most of the trading public, only they're better at it!

Market makers are professionals, connected with all the best information sources, public and private. They know what's going on. We're not saying they know *more* than the public, but it's safe to say they know it *sooner* (although that gap is closing with the high-performance data feeds we've discussed). Since they are, after all, market makers in a company's stock, it can be assumed that they already know a lot about the company in the first place. What does this mean?

It means that market makers often have a pretty good idea of where a stock might be going.

And what does *that* mean? It means that they will bid in the market, often aggressively, to pick up shares they think will go up. They will also offer aggressively to get rid of shares they think will go down. In some cases, they will even short shares they don't own into the market, expecting to buy back later at a lower price.

Hand #3: Wild Cards

A market maker, acting as a broker now, has just drawn a big card. An institutional client wants to buy 100,000 shares of WXYZ. What happens?

Deep down inside, the market maker is just excited as all get-out. Why? He/she will not only get a big commission from the client, but can also, if the cards are played right, profit from the spread on 100K shares. Easy—what's the catch?

If the market maker simply shows the order to the market, the world sees the demand increase. Offers are pulled to wait for a better price. Result: The price at which the market maker can acquire the stock he/she so desperately needs to fill this huge order—goes up! Does the market maker want that?

Nope. So the market maker puts on his/her best possible poker face in the market bidding war. Can't show wild cards to the rest of the table. Must get the shares wherever and however possible, either in the open market or through ECNs, and try to disguise intentions all the way.

Hand #4: Bluff Hand

Here the market maker has a mediocre hand; not a winner, not a loser. But they want to make something happen. So they draw a few cards and put up a small bluff.

Daily Specials

"Lifting the offer" is a euphemism for hitting the offer price; in other words, buying stock at the ask. Often the result is a "lifting" in the offer price as offers at the current inside market are taken out. If there are three offers at $52^1/_2$ and they are all taken out or "lifted," it would leave the next highest offer at the inside—say $52^9/_{16}$.

The bluff comes in the form of a bid or offer that exaggerates their true position. If they want the price of a stock to go up—suppose they hold a lot of inventory—they might suddenly put a big bid out there, with size, for everyone to see. It can be priced anywhere but has the most effect if priced at the inside market, or even *above* it to define a new inside market. Whether it's true or not, the rest of the world will play their hands as though this market maker just got the biggest client order in the world.

Result: Offers will be "lifted" and up goes the price. Which is what the market maker wanted in the first place. The risk, of course, is that other market makers and traders call the bluff and continue to sell stock. The price doesn't go up, and the initiating market maker may get stuck with expensive stock if his/her bids are filled.

Finding the Poker Face

Why are we dragging you through all of this? Are we trying to prepare you for a glorious, lucrative career as a market maker?

Well, sort of. What we're really doing is showing you how to read a market maker's actions, how to "read the tea leaves" of market-maker activity. You'll be better prepared to day trade *with* the market makers. As you get more experience, you'll be able to play some of these market-maker games yourself using limit orders and direct trading access.

One or Many

What we're about to show is how to assess the behavior of a single market maker or market makers as a collective whole.

Sometimes you'll want to watch a single market maker, especially if he's a "heavy"—a Merrill Lynch, Goldman Sachs, Bear Stearns, etc. You can assume they know a lot. They also get lots of big client orders. As a day trader, you're happy to play follow the leader.

Other times you'll watch the collective bunch—if everybody's doing much the same thing, capturing spreads for instance, it's a signal that no big price moves are in the offing. If on the other hand, market makers are falling all over each other to get on the inside offer, they're trying to sell stock as fast as possible. Translation: Down move coming!

Daily Specials

These behaviors aren't the same across the board. Different market makers do different things, and different stocks will behave differently. Within a market-making firm, different people manage the price quotes. Behavior may depend on the behavior of the other market makers in the stock, or how many day traders are involved. You'll have to watch, pick up the behavior pattern, and be aware that it can change at any time. Keep in mind the reason we watch this behavior so closely: *To predict near-term price movements.*

The Spread Catcher

The "capture the spread" player is fairly easy to find: Their "close in" (at or near the inside market) quotes jump back and forth between the bid and the offer.

Suppose Merrill Lynch is trying to capture spreads in WXYZ. They show a bid of "MLCO 52$^1/_2$ 10," at the inside. (Bid to buy 1,000 shares at 52$^1/_2$) It gets taken out. What do they do? They don't refresh the bid—instead they jump right over to the offer. Now you see on the inside offer: "MLCO 52$^9/_{16}$ 10." They will take the first buyer coming to the market and pocket the teenie. Likely: As soon as their offer is lifted, they will jump back to the inside bid. Et cetera.

If they are aggressively pursuing this strategy, you'll see jumps back and forth at the inside. The goal is to reap as many "teenie" profits as they can! But they may also disguise this a little—or mix with another strategy such as trying to raise the price—by jumping to the offer one or two *levels* away from the inside. How should you interpret this? Business as usual, no big immediate price moves.

Behind the Screen

"Level" is the term for a trading increment in the stock as lined up in the Level II bid or offer queue. Most active stocks trade in one-sixteenth increments, so the levels are defined as "teenies." If the inside offer is $52^9/_{16}$, then the offer one level away is $52^5/_8$, two levels away is $52^{11}/_{16}$, and so forth. For less active stocks, levels may skip the minimum trading increment (maybe the next level is $52^7/_8$). Stock prices change as trading moves through the levels.

What does it mean if there are lots of "spread catchers" in the market? Probably things are quiet for now, no immediate breakout moves are likely.

The Market Player

Remember these aggressive market makers who are betting on the move in the price of the stock? How do they behave? With determination, that's how.

Suppose a market maker is convinced a stock is about to run, or go up with momentum. Guess what? They want to buy as much stock as possible without driving their own price up. So how does this poker-faced player drop his/her hints?

➤ By staying on the bid. His/her inside bid is taken out, and guess what? The bid pops right back up again, it is refreshed.

➤ By increasing the bid. If there's a pack of bidders at $52^1/_2$, he/she may want to post a new bid of $52^9/_{16}$, a new inside offer, to "win the race" to the next lot of stock to come in on a market order. This market maker wins the competition. Why? Because he/she thinks the stock is headed north, and wants to profit from the move.

When you see this going on with more than one market maker at a time, it confirms the suspicion: Something is up, and the stock is about to be. Watching these close-in indications for soon-to-be momentum is one of the most powerful strategies of the day trader!

A Man with an Ax

This is the "wild card" guy we talked about before. Has a big order, has to do something with it. What?

Like the market player, he/she will stay persistently at the bid (if trying to buy, at the offer if it's a sell) to try to get stock. Sometimes the rest of the market will fall away, and this 600-pound gorilla is still there buying stock. Like we said before, this market maker doesn't want to make his/her intentions too obvious (driving the stock up or down), but just the same, wants to get or sell stock.

For a "buy," you may see this market maker also picking up big chunks on ECNs—something you can track with your ECN/market maker alerts if you have an advanced platform. And this market maker will usually fall away several levels on the offer so as not to *sell* stock he/she just picked up. He/she wants to save it for the client.

Sometimes this player will back off bids one level, just to bluff the market a little. And if the stock "comes back" to that level, why, they've made a little more profit on that order, especially if they've agreed with the client up-front on price.

Trading Terms

The trading community has a name for everything, and "600-pound market-maker gorilla with a big order" takes too long to get out at the frenzied pace of daily trading. So traders refer to the market maker with a big order as the **ax**. Short and sweet, easy to say, and if you don't like it, you can call them a "hammer." "Following the ax" is a mainstream trading strategy.

The Bluffer

Bluffers are hard to spot, because they're doing just that—bluffing! They're trying to get a stock to move, or *look like* it's going to move. Why? To shake out "weak hands" and make the price move in their favor. Sometimes you'll see aggressive bids or offers posted, only to back away or change as the market reaches them. Maybe they're really the ax—sooner or later they will have to come forth lest they lose their commission (and the client's business)! If you see a lot of quote manipulation without many "prints" (trades) from a particular market maker, look out. Like players at a poker table, sooner or later you'll figure out who the bluffers are!

Let's Return to New York

Haven't been to New York in awhile? No, we haven't either. We've dwelt on the activity of the NASDAQ market makers, at the expense of the NYSE specialists, for the last six pages or so.

What's the Difference?

Market makers post quotes for the world (the Level II world, anyway) to see. That's what makes the NASDAQ world go round—aggressive quotes at the inside, weak quotes away, the interplay, the action, the dynamics. What happens, as in the case of NYSE, where you only have one market maker?

With the NYSE, the queue isn't made up of bids and offers, it is made up of actual orders. Limit orders, to be precise (market orders are just filled at the inside price, not posted on the book). So how can a specialist "play games" with the trading public?

Answer: They can place a kind of "limit order" of their own, to buy or sell stock from their own account (or sometimes, sell short).

Get Out Your Magnifying Glass

Suppose a floor broker comes to a specialist with a big ax order. The specialist and the floor broker want to make the trade without driving the price up. Do they just post it at the current bid? No—because other traders and brokers would see it and "hold out" their orders for a better price. The specialist needs stock to fill the order. So he/she places new size at the current offer, indicating selling pressure. Why? To encourage the buying public to keep hitting the current bid with market orders. This allows the specialist to accumulate stock without driving the price up, and the big "ax" order is filled.

This is fairly hard to detect. Like market maker bluffing, a concentrating trader may see size come up, then go down without corresponding "prints" on the Time and Sales screen. Without the Level II screen, it's hard to see demand and supply away from the price, and it's hard to identify where the specialist himself is acting as a dealer.

If a specialist is trying to manipulate price one way or another (for instance, to shake out day traders), they might post bids or offers inside the current prices just to feint upward or downward movement or hide size at the former inside bid or offer. Again, you don't know for sure where they came from, but often these specialist "orders" are in neat increments of 500 or 1,000 shares (size 5 or 10).

Hitting Your Limits

Now that you have some idea of the game, you're anxious to play your own cards! Understandable.

Often the limit order card is the one you want to play. You want to buy at the bid or sell at the ask price, just like the market maker does. You want to become a market maker yourself, collecting spreads as you go. You don't want to pay the spread like the public at large does.

We'll talk about strategy a little more in Chapter 21, "The Day Trader's Playbook." But here's the question you're probably asking: How can I possibly buy at the bid and sell at the ask? Aren't the market makers firm on the prices they quote? This *is* America after all—as a retail customer we don't haggle every time we buy something, do we? That's only for big-volume, mostly wholesale deals, right?

The answer—not really. You can try to buy at the bid, buy wholesale, yourself. Why? Because market makers, with their many motives, may sell to you at a more favorable price despite what they indicate to the public. If they need to sell stock to fill a large order, they need stock. If your order is there, even if the price isn't quite there (for them) it will get taken. Supply and demand.

This can be a good thing…but look out. If instead of having a big order, the market maker really believes a downturn is imminent, you'll get your stock. Then you may get your head handed to you. The market maker is relieved to have gotten rid of it, and what follows may not be pretty.

Bottom line—stay close to the behaviors and motives, and you'll become a better trader. Charts and graphs can give you a bigger picture, but a close look usually tells more.

The Least You Need to Know

➤ NASDAQ market makers and NYSE specialists can act as both brokers and dealers.

➤ Market makers and specialists make much of their money by capturing the spread on normal market orders.

➤ Market makers compete with each other openly to acquire and sell shares. In many ways, they too are day traders.

➤ Market makers and specialists use different tactics to achieve different objectives at different times. You can read market-maker behavior by watching NASDAQ Level II closely.

➤ You can, by using limit orders, buy "wholesale" and sell "retail," just like a market maker.

A Piece of the Action

A picture's worth a thousand words. A chart is worth a thousand datapoints. We've preached it, but especially in the last chapter, we didn't practice it.

We've presented the Level II screen, and showed some of the dynamics of the market—the motives, behaviors, and external factors that influence a stock's activity. In this chapter, we'll try to bring it all together. We'll show the dynamics of all the different market influencers and how they would play out on Level II.

Unfortunately, we're a bit constrained by the lack of color and depth of information that you would see on an integrated trading platform. So what you see here would look much clearer on an advanced platform—once you know what you're looking for. This presentation is a bit simplistic, but aimed to give you the idea so you can get started.

We'll show a sequence of events: a steady-state balanced market, a simple spread-capture transaction, a market downdraft, a news-driven stock updraft, with the appropriate commentary along the way. Here goes!

Steady as She Goes

You'd probably guess that a balanced market has an equal number of buyers and sellers evenly distributed at all prices, at and away from the inside market. You're right.

Balanced market.

DELL	40 3/4 ↓	- 5/8		1000	
High 42 1/2		Low 40 1/8		Vol 15455000	
Bid ↓ 40 3/4		Ask 40 13/16		Close 41 3/8	

Name	Bid	Size	Name	Ask	Size
MLCO	40 3/4	10	ISLD	40 13/16	10
ABSB	40 3/4	5	BEST	40 13/16	10
ISLD	40 3/4	8	MASH	40 13/16	20
MONT	40 11/16	10	TSCO	40 7/8	8
SNDV	40 11/16	10	PWJC	40 7/8	10
WEED	40 11/16	10	SNDV	40 7/8	10
TVAN	40 5/8	9	MONT	40 15/16	10
RSSF	40 5/8	10	CANT	40 15/16	5
SBSH	40 5/8	40	GSCO	40 15/16	10
JPMS	40 9/16	10	FBCO	41	10

Trading Terms

A **balanced market** is one in which there is an equal number of buyers and sellers evenly distributed at all prices, both at and away from the inside market.

Here we are, back at the Dell example used in Chapter 15. The stock is off a bit for the day. Currently there are three market makers lined up at the inside bid and each of the next two levels away. Same for the offer side. The size on the ask is a little larger, but not enough to draw any conclusions. This screen doesn't foretell much market movement.

Remember that on an active stock like Dell, this screen will roll very quickly, at "jackhammer" pace. So what may be true this instant isn't likely to be true for long!

Chasing the Spread

Now let's suppose somebody "takes out" the MLCO (Merrill Lynch) offer. Let's see what MLCO does:

MLCO jumps to the offer—trading for spread.

DELL	40 3/4 ↓	- 5/8		1000	
High 42 1/2		Low 40 1/8		Vol 15455000	
Bid ↓ 40 3/4		Ask 40 13/16		Close 41 3/8	

Name	Bid	Size	Name	Ask	Size
ABSB	40 3/4	5	ISLD	40 13/16	10
ISLD	40 3/4	8	BEST	40 13/16	10
MONT	40 11/16	10	MASH	40 13/16	20
SNDV	40 11/16	10	MLCO	40 13/16	10
WEED	40 11/16	10	TSCO	40 7/8	8
TVAN	40 5/8	9	PWJC	40 7/8	10
RSSF	40 5/8	10	SNDV	40 7/8	10
SBSH	40 5/8	40	MONT	40 15/16	10
JPMS	40 9/16	10	CANT	40 15/16	5
SALB	40 9/16	10	GSCO	40 15/16	10

Did they refresh the bid? No—MLCO doesn't appear at 40³/₄. Do they want more stock? Probably not, at least not at these prices. They may want more at 40⁹/₁₆ or below, but we don't know that (many bigger screens show more lines than our example). What happened?

You'll notice they showed up on the offer at 40¹³/₁₆! A brand-new offer, next in line behind the ones that were already there. As soon as ISLD, BEST, and MASH are taken out, the next market order in will take them out, and they will have made their teenie.

Will they make this teenie for sure? No. There are three offers ahead of them. If the stock turns south before those offers are lifted, or if other lower offers come in, they will be stuck with the shares at least until they lower their own offer. (They don't want to do that, otherwise they would take a loss!)

There's a good chance that, if/when they *are* taken out, they'll show up on the inside bid again. They could have gone for a sale at ⁷/₈ or ¹⁵/₁₆, but it would have taken longer to get this fill and there's more risk of a change in direction.

Daily Specials

Suppose the inside offer was at ⁷/₈, not ¹³/₁₆. Then what? MLCO could post their offer at ¹³/₁₆ and be first in line, guaranteed fill for the next market order in. This action serves to narrow the spread and make prices more competitive for the public, generally a good thing. It also points out a strategy that you, yes you, can do as a day trader. You can put yourself in line ahead of the pack with limit orders to get faster executions at guaranteed prices.

Uh-Oh. Time to Sell?

You may see the first signs looking at a "macro" indicator. (Remember Chapter 17?) The S&P may have turned lower, or maybe the NASDAQ 100 or CBOE Technology index or whatever. Or the TICK or ARMS go way negative, or breadth gets bad. You get a notion that the market may be ready to go south.

Behind the Screen

With all this talk about day traders addicted to watching the financial news on television and trading on whatever stock is being talked about, does that mean that there is a lull during commercial breaks? Do all day traders head for the bathroom or the kitchen while the mutual fund commercials are on? "No, we don't see a drop in trading during TV commercials," Tom Burton of Cornerstone Securities told us. "The only time there is a noticable lull is when Alan Greenspan is talking, when the Federal Open Market Committee is meeting (about interest rates) or when Joe Kernan gives one of his active stock reports on CNBC."

Or maybe you've been watching a chart. Over the past few days when Dell starts the day up but shrivels as the day wears on and gets to a certain price level, it drops. Something tells you it's time to take a closer look at trading activity.

Maybe the Motley Fool just released its lunchtime Fool Plate Special condemning the computer industry to yet another Compaq attack.

Or maybe Dell is already your stock of the day, month, year, whatever. So you watch Level II like a hawk all day long, come Dell or high water.

Whatever the trigger, now you take a look at Level II and see some cracks starting to form:

Selling pressure builds. Market makers on bid leave or don't refresh. Bid levels get smaller, inside offer gets bigger as more market makers try harder to sell.

DELL	40 3/4 ↓	- 5/8		1000
High	42 1/2	Low 40 1/8		Vol 15455000
Bid ↓	40 3/4	Ask 40 13/16		Close 41 3/8

Name	Bid	Size	Name	Ask	Size
ISLD	40 3/4	8	ISLD	40 13/16	10
MONT	40 11/16	8	BEST	40 13/16	10
TVAN	40 5/8	10	MASH	40 13/16	20
JPMS	40 9/16	10	MLCO	40 13/16	10
SALB	40 9/16	10	FBCO	40 13/16	10
MASH	40 9/16	9	MHMY	40 13/16	10
UBSS	40 1/2	10	JPMS	40 13/16	15
ISLD	40 1/2	5	TSCO	40 7/8	8
LEHM	40 1/2 40	10	PWJC	40 7/8	10
MSCO	1/2	10	SNDV	40 7/8	10

Daily Specials

This is where the power of Level II really comes to light. The public, through their Level I screens, sees the same quote as before: $40^3/_4 \times 40^{13}/_{16}$. Do they know anything's amiss with the market? Nope. They don't have the same look-ahead capability you and all the other pros do! Acting quickly and before the crowd is the name of the game, and Level II and good trading access are your tickets!

What's going on?

➤ ABSB (Alex Brown) is either filled or leaves the bid (check Time and Sales or your market maker ticker to be sure).

➤ The ISLD ECN order is still there, but since that's an individual trader you can be pretty sure it won't be renewed.

➤ SNDV and WEED leave the bid one level away.

➤ RSSF, TVAN leave two levels away.

➤ A whole bunch of players—FBCO, MHMY, JPMS come into the inside offer.

More offers, fewer bids. In fact, bids look pretty thin all the way down to $40^1/_2$, where some support might be found. There are lots of sellers in line to get out on the offer. Upshot: Downward pressure is starting to build.

Strategy: Time to close any open position, might be time to short on an uptick.

Is There a Man with an Ax?

It's too early to tell if there's an ax, or a strong market supporter with a large client order on either side. While preparing to enter or exit positions, you might keep an eye on MONT (Montgomery Securities) for example—a fairly large player. If that bid at $40^{11}/_{16}$ hangs around or gets stronger, we may have an ax here.

Getting Clocked

Three-eyed day traders (and most others) are always looking for ways to recognize these patterns without digging their tired eyes into the details of these screens. There are (at least) four short cuts that will help you get the verdict without detailed cross-examination:

➤ Up/down arrows. Many advanced platforms show the direction of market maker quote adjustments as a small up or down arrow next to the price. That arrow represents the direction of change, usually from where the quote was 5 minutes ago. A screen full of down arrows is trying to tell you something.

➤ Color bars (which we can't illustrate) can help. They show each level sized according to the number of players. Suppose yellow is used for the inside level bid and offer. If there's a big yellow bar on the right and a small one on the left, selling pressure exceeds buying pressure, at least on the inside market.

➤ Number system. The bid side could be represented as "1 1 1 3 4" while the offer side is "7 3" and we don't know what's beyond. But the big numbers are on the offer, while the bid indicates many levels to go before support is found.

➤ Appearance of clockwise or counter-clockwise flow.

Bids and offers change in real time as you watch and quite quickly. If the flow *appears* clockwise in your "live" view—that is, if the left gets smaller and the right gets larger—that shows a bearish trend. Offers are expanding while bids are contracting, supply is exceeding demand.

Note: This flow is a perception and is only real when a market maker actually jumps from the bid to the offer or vice versa. The following picture illustrates:

Alarm Bells

Clockwise "flow" in the Level II screen indicates a possible downtrend.

Motion appears clockwise—indicating down move likely.

DELL	40 3/4 ↓	- 5/8	1000
High 42 1/2	Low 40 1/8		Vol 15455000
Bid ↓ 40 3/4	Ask 40 13/16		Close 41 3/8

Name	Bid	Size	Name	Ask	Size
ISLD	40 3/4	8	ISLD	40 13/16	10
MONT	40 11/16	8	BEST	40 13/16	10
TVAN	40 5/8	10	MASH	40 13/16	20
JPMS	40 9/16	10	MLCO	40 13/16	10
SALB	40 9/16	10	FBCO	40 13/16	10
MASH	40 9/16	9	MHMY	40 13/16	10
UBSS	40 1/2	10	JPMS	40 13/16	15
ISLD	40 1/2	5	TSCO	40 7/8	8
LEHM	40 1/2 40	10	PWJC	40 7/8	10
MSCO	1/2	10	SNDV	40 7/8	10

Oh, Baby. It's Getting Worse

You keep watching, and it keeps weakening.

Selling pressure continues to build. Bids continue to drop, two big players (MLCO, JPMS) drop their offers.

DELL	40 3/4 ↓	- 5/8	1000
High 42 1/2	Low 40 1/8		Vol 15456000
Bid ↓ 40 11/16	Ask 40 3/4		Close 41 3/8

Name	Bid	Size	Name	Ask	Size
MONT	40 11/16	8	MLCO	40 3/4	10
TVAN	40 5/8	10	JPMS	40 3/4	15
JPMS	40 9/16	10	ISLD	40 13/16	20
SALB	40 1/2	10	BEST	40 13/16	10
MASH	40 1/2	9	MASH	40 13/16	10
UBSS	40 1/2	10	FBCO	40 13/16	10
ISLD	40 7/16	5	MHMY	40 13/16	10
LEHM	40 7/16	10	TSCO	40 7/8	8
MSCO	40 7/16	10	PWJC	40 7/8	10
ISLD	40 7/16	15	SNDV	40 7/8	10

What's going on?

➤ The ISLD order is filled and not replaced (no surprise).

➤ SALB (Salomon Brothers) drops their bid to 40$^1/_2$. Other market makers who were at 40$^1/_2$ drop to 40$^7/_{16}$. There seems to be some support there, but that's a long way down.

➤ At the same time, MLCO and JPMS (J.P. Morgan securities) get more anxious to sell and drop their offers to 40$^3/_4$.

Ugh! Declining demand, increasing supply available at lower prices. If MLCO or JPMS turn out to be an ax, we aren't going any higher for a while, and if their clients get desperate, look out below!

Strategy: *Time to get out!* Shorting is possible if there were to be an uptick (but not now!). Note that the down move hasn't really started—the Level I quote is the same—so there may still be time! You can see the power of Level II as an indicator of near term direction....

Whew. Glad That's Over

You're watching the action. The little downdraft subsides and bidders start to come back. Sellers let their offers get lifted and don't come back. Eventually the whole thing turns around:

DELL	40 7/8 ▲ -1/2		1000	
High	42 1/2	Low 40 1/8	Vol 15558000	
Bid ▲ 40 13/16		Ask 40 7/8	Close 41 3/8	

Name	Bid	Size	Name	Ask	Size
PIPR	40 13/16	25	TSCO	40 7/8	8
OPCO	40 13/16	10	PWJC	40 7/8	10
PRUS	40 13/16	15	SNDV	40 15/16	10
MSCO	40 13/16	10	NMRA	41	10
DAIN	40 3/4	12	MASH	41 1/16	20
NEED	40 3/4	10	ISLD	41 1/16	10
HRZG	40 3/4	20	INCA	41 1/8	10
MONT	40 3/4	30	MHMY	41 1/8	10
TVAN	40 3/4 40	5	PIPR	41 1/8	20
JPMS	11/16	10	MONT	41 1/8	20

Turnaround. New bids from big players show up while offers dissipate.

What's Going on Now?

➤ Strong inside bids and bids one level away. Big players on the bid—Piper Jaffray (PIPR), Oppenheimer & Co (OPCO), Prudential (PRUS), Morgan Stanley (MSCO). Can't read too much into the names, but they have the most money and the highest paid professionals, and often lots of big client orders.

➤ Offers are weakening at and near the inside market. Looks like the first resistance of any consequence is at $41^1/_8$.

Strategy: Buy *fast*. Try to get in before favorable offers are lifted and price jumps to $41^1/_8$. Watch the position closely for new bids (additional strength) or bluffing (bids falling away).

Alarm Bells

Just as a clockwise movement on the Level II screen indicates a downward move, a counterclockwise movement indicates an upswing in the price.

Clocking In

If clockwise movement suggested a downdraft, does counterclockwise movement foretell an upturn? Right again.

And here it is in picture form:

Motion appears counterclockwise— indicating up move likely.

DELL	40 7/8 ↑	-1/2		1000	
High	42 1/2	Low	40 1/8	Vol	15558000
Bid ↑	40 13/16	Ask	40 7/8	Close	41 3/8

Name	Bid	Size	Name	Ask	Size
PIPR	40 13/16	25	TSCO		8
OPCO	40 13/16	10	PWJC		10
PRUS	40 13/16	15	SNDV		10
MSCO	40 13/16	10	NMRA		10
DAIN	40 3/4	12	MASH		20
NEED	40 3/4	10	ISLD		10
HRZG	40 3/4	20	INCA		10
MONT	40 3/4	30	MHMY		10
TVAN	40 3/4 40	5	PIPR		20
JPMS	11/16	10	MONT		20

Behind the Screen

"What day is it? What time is it?" Peter remembers his first time in a day-trading room. After the market close he staggered away from the computer bleary-eyed and more than a little disoriented. After hours of total concentration and absorption, his mind zeroed in on the flashing numbers and charts of an advanced platform with no less than 15 active windows. It took a few minutes to re-enter the regular world. And this is from a guy who likes numbers!

On Our Way

Now you've had a simple tour of market dynamics as seen through Level II. As we said in the opener, this treatment is a bit oversimplified. But most treatments we've seen are overly complex and hard to follow for the inexperienced trader. Going straight to the trading platform without a stroll through the basics is like learning to ride a bicycle on a Harley. Training wheels are a good idea, especially when your money's at stake!

Once you get going, the more you look at these screens, and the more you watch, the more you'll know what to look for. Drawing quick conclusions becomes second nature.

You'll learn to combine bigger-picture market-strength and stock-strength indicators with this in-depth micro view of the markets and player behavior. Then you'll become more effective in executing good strategies and making required "snap" judgements.

Enough said...let's move on and share some of the strategies day traders use.

The Least You Need to Know

➤ The Level II screen helps you see the movement of bids and offers at and away from the inside market. You see things develop before they happen and before the average investor sees them.

➤ When downward pressure begins to build, it's time to close an open long position before demand dries up.

➤ If the flow on a Level II screen appears clockwise, (the bid levels on the left appear smaller and the offer levels on the right appear larger) a bearish trend is developing.

➤ Likewise, if the flow appears to move counterclockwise, (bid levels get larger while offer levels shrink) a bullish trend is developing.

➤ Smart day traders watch Level II very closely to detect changes in market balance and to observe who is driving them.

Part 6

Developing Your Own Day-Trading Style

Everybody's got style, and there are several day-trading styles to choose from. Which one will work for you? It depends on your own personality, of course, and your appetite for risk.

Will you be scalpin' teenies or chasing the big 'mo? Shadowing the ax? These are all different day-trading strategies, and not all will appeal to you—or work all the time. Read up and decide which style will fit you the best. Take a personal inventory of your characteristics, your lifestyle, and your goals—not to mention your finances—before deciding.

And then, if you decide that day trading is the thing for you, get started trading at the speed of thought!

Chapter 21

The Day Trader's Playbook

In This Chapter

➤ Basic day-trading strategies

➤ Capturing spreads, a.k.a. "scalpin' teenies"

➤ Spotting a momentum play

➤ Playing gap openings at the start of trading

➤ Following the leaders for fun and profit

➤ Practical trading tactics

Knowing how things work doesn't make any of us day traders. No more than knowing how an airplane works makes us a pilot, or how a piano works makes us a musician. Yes, it does take practice, but that isn't what this chapter is about (we'll save it for next). What we want to do here is turn notes and keys into music, turn metal and mechanical energy into flight.

Unless you're truly the Orville and Wilbur type, you probably would want to learn from the pioneers. You'd like to learn what they do and learn from their mistakes. Learn the tested strategies that work. And that's what this chapter is all about.

You'll learn the five principal strategies that real day traders use. We'll also toss in a laundry list of trading tactics that help to carry out the strategies. In the next chapter we'll get a little more personal and talk about style: *Personal* tactics and habits that will *make you a better day trader*.

It's Never Pure and Simple

Sounds simple, eh? Just learn five easy strategies and laugh all the way to the bank. Well, not quite. *Different strategies will work on different days at different times for different stocks in different markets for different day traders.*

Get all that? Go ahead—read it again.

OK? Now, to make matters worse, none of the strategies we're about to present are "pure." They overlap. The situation, stock, and market will often call for a combination of two or more.

Did we scare you? Sorry, that wasn't the point. Understanding these five strategies in "pure" form will bring you a long way. *Getting experience* with them will get you even further. You'll become comfortable with how they work together.

Without Further Ado

Let's get on with it. What are the five strategies?

1. **Scalpin' teenies:** Capturing spreads. Very short-term, fast trades designed to capture teenies, eighths, quarters, sometimes (but not usually) more. This strategy can take just a few seconds, or a few minutes.

2. **Momentum plays:** Figuring out the big movers, up or down, and playing them for what they're worth. A momentum play can take anywhere from a few minutes to a few hours.

3. **Playing gap openings:** Every action begets a reaction—especially at the opening. You can learn to play gaps without knowing anything about physics!

4. **"Shadowing the ax"—and other market makers:** Following the leaders and profiting from their moves. This can also take anywhere from a few minutes to a few hours.

5. **Playing events:** Earnings news, acquisitions and rumors, splits, IPOs. Trading on current events can take anywhere from a few minutes to a few days.

Discussion of these strategies centers around NASDAQ, but where we can we'll try to give the "listed" stock (NYSE) angle.

Scalpin' Teenies

Objective: Capture the spread between bid and offer as often as possible, make profit just like a market maker.

Strategy: Use limit orders to trade just like a market maker.

How and Why

When you're trying to capture a spread, you want to buy stock at the bid price and sell at the offer, or ask, price. Obviously if you bought at the offer like everyone else, there would be no spread to capture! But isn't the offer price *the* price available to you? Don't you have to buy at that price?

Answer: For the mainstream general public, that's true. Their "market" orders will get the offer price. The buyer accepts the price, pays retail sticker, and moves on. For a considerable segment of the public (and even institutional traders) this is OK. They have long-term objectives and care more about the position than the price. Paying another teenie or eighth is just fine.

Making It Work

So what do you do to be different from the general public? To trade more like a professional? Like a market maker?

➤ You place limit orders at the bid price

➤ If the spread is greater than one tick (for example, $52 \times 52^1/_4$) you place a limit order one tick *above* the inside bid (at $52^1/_{16}$)

What happens? Your order will be executed in the order received. If you place *at* the bid price, and there are four bids in front of you, the fifth sell-at-market order from the general public will sell you stock. Suppose you bid 52—you buy from a market seller who saw the 52 bid and accepted it.

You now have stock at 52. The inside ask is $52^1/_8$. What do you do? Just like a market maker, you turn around and put the stock up for sale, again using a limit order, at $52^1/_8$. Then you wait in the bushes for the next market order to come your way. You make an eighth, or $125 on a 1,000-share trade.

Enticing as scalping teenies for $125 profit all day long sounds, don't overlook the roundtrip price you are paying in commission. Subtract those fees for your real total. Also, don't forget that this isn't automatic—you may place an order to buy on the bid but it may never get filled. In some stocks your chances may be as low as 1 in 20 of getting a fill, depending on competition.

Cutting In

Why did we bring up placing the limit order *above* the inside bid? If the opportunity presents itself (through a large spread), you might as well jump in line in front of the others. It costs you a teenie, but it might be worth it to get the stock *now* and flip it right away. You have downside protection in the form of the bids that are lined up one tick below. You can flip faster than the others, leading to more round-trip trades each day and more total profit. Only works with a healthy spread.

Behind the Screen

The *number* is a round figure, usually an integer, without a fraction. So "52," "30," "75" are referred to as the number, while $52^{1}/_{16}$ is *away* from the number. What's the significance? Most people think in round numbers. They'll place a limit order at 52, not $52^{1}/_{16}$, unless they're trading very tight margins like you. If you place your bid at $52^{1}/_{16}$, you'll often be alone in your quest for the stock. At 52, there may be several other bidders. Stay in front of the number—to get the market to yourself where you can.

Repetition—doing it over and over again—is a cornerstone of the scalping strategy. The number of times you do it is more important than the price or size of the spread. And have we mentioned the choice of companies or industries? No. It doesn't matter. You're trading the stock, not the company.

Gotchas

If this were so dang simple, everyone would do it, and market makers would be out of business, right? You got it. So what are the pitfalls?

The big one is change. If you could guarantee that inside quotes would stay unchanged, you could scalp all day risk free. The only thing that would slow you down is the number of other day traders and the length of the inside bid and offer queues. You may not get filled.

Problem is, prices *do* change. And market makers have a lot of influence on price, as we've already seen. And—here's the rub—you're competing with market makers by doing this, eating what was their lunch. Do they like that? No. So what happens? Market makers try to derail day traders where they can. If they see you lining up and flipping trades over and over, they'll do what they can to move price. You buy at 52, the inside market drops to $51^{3}/_{4}$, and you lose!

How do you avoid this?

1. Avoid the most volatile stocks. They move too much, even without market-maker "games." You'll lose a point in the blink of an eye trying to pick up a teenie on Amazon.

2. Be careful on high-visibility stocks such as Microsoft, Intel, and so on. Investment firms put their most seasoned market makers on these stocks. They're getting quite good at figuring you out and messing up your well-crafted plans.

Best-Laid Plans

The keys to success are

➤ **Level II access:** This can be done without Level II transparency, but it becomes much closer to gambling. You can't see moment-by-moment support and resistance. You might catch a stock on a bid only to find out that buying pressure had evaporated at or immediately below. Down she goes. With Level II visibility you can see and feel this in advance.

➤ **High-performance ordering platforms:** You're trading a few seconds to a minute or two per round-trip trade. A normal Internet broker might work on a good day but won't be dependable if things are slow.

➤ **Stock selection:** Pick stable, predictable stocks. Rotate—don't camp on the same one all day. What works once or twice might get "sniffed out" and quickly turn sour.

➤ **Watch the action:** Watch market makers and other traders. If downward momentum is signaled by the Level II bid/offer queue, stay out. You don't want to be the only guy on the bid if there are 10 market makers lined up against you on the offer, and "support" in the form of bid strength is three ticks below!

➤ **Don't get greedy:** You may try to get an extra teenie or two by staying high with your "flip" offer, hoping inside offers dry up leaving yours to get hit. It may not happen. You might lose a half, a buck, while waiting for this ship to arrive. Worth a chance only if other momentum indicators are positive.

Down Broadway

We've said all along that day traders look for active, volatile stocks. Actually, the scalping strategy can be put into play on very "slow" stocks, and at that, on the NYSE.

There's a NYSE-unique rule that makes this possible. Remember on NASDAQ a limit order goes in the bid queue in the order it's received. Market makers who were there first will get the next market orders that come in, usually on SOES. You have to wait your turn, and the only way to "jump in front" is to improve your price. The 1997 limit order protection rule requires your "in front" order to be displayed.

It's a little different with NYSE. The specialist is the only "market maker." The order book consists of actual limit orders, not quotes. A market order coming in through SUPERDOT will get the matched to the best available limit order on the books. But sometimes there aren't any, or they are so far off the market that the specialist, in the interest of maintaining an orderly market (and making profit as a dealer), will put his own "bid" on the books. His goal: Trade and make money on his own account, buying at bid and selling at a higher offer.

A slow-moving utility stock can provide this scenario: There may not be any limit "bids" from the public at all! What does the specialist do? Quotes his own bid. What can you do?

Daily Specials

Remember, on the NYSE, a customer order gets priority over specialist orders entered for their own account. If there are no other customer orders at your limit price, you get the next fill from a public market order if you're at the inside market. You effectively have an advantage in competing with the specialist.

Here's where the special rule comes in. The rule states that any customer limit order will trade before a specialist bid or offer from his own account. So if the specialist creates a market by bidding 15, you can place a limit order to buy at 15, and automatically catch the next market "sell" coming in from the public. You get placed in line ahead of the specialist. You then turn around and put your own limit sell at the inside offer, and make your teenie, sometimes more.

Daily Specials

There's a brand-new book devoted almost completely to this strategy: *Day Trade Online* (Christopher Farrell, Wiley 1999). Check it out if you want to further refine your technique. But be aware—the more who use this technique, the less effective it becomes.

This doesn't work if other players are doing the same thing, or if there are lots of customer limit orders on the book. You only jump in line ahead of the specialist, not the other customer orders. So the trick is to find a very quiet stock and learn to tell when the specialist is the only game in town. That isn't an exact science, but if you see small "size" in round numbers of 5 or 10 on the bid or ask, chances are you're there, and you can find out by jumping in with your limit order to see what happens.

Of course, when the specialist wises up to who you are and what you're doing—eating his lunch by capturing spreads that are normally his—strange things start to happen. For this strategy to work, you need to pick low volume, slow moving stocks and rotate them during the trading day.

Meant for Momentum

Momentum trading and scalping are the two most popular strategies of the day trader. While scalping is almost a rote, repetitive, mechanical trading strategy, momentum play is an exciting, sensory experience requiring extreme skill and vision. Momentum traders are true three-eyed day traders! Your objective here—to jump on something that is going your way and jump clear when the time is right.

How and Why

Momentum traders seek the stocks that are "in play." Of course, this list changes daily! Momentum players watch news feeds, CNBC, S&P 500 futures, relative strength, industry groups, charts, trading ranges and breakouts, Level II bid and offer queues, and Time and Sale. Three eyes are seldom enough!

Once identified, the momentum player waits for the right time: the breakout. He/she buys or sells at a good price, but not necessarily the best. Momentum players know they can't time the market exactly.

The 'mo player lets the stock run, and hits the exit at the right time. What is the right time? As soon as the run starts to slow. How do we tell that? By looking carefully at the market activity in the stock through Level II. When the stock hits a "saturation" point, where orders start piling up on the offer, and bidding slows or "gets thin" at the current market and a few levels back, it's time to pull the trigger. The good momentum day trader sees this coming. The bad trader or the one without Level II visibility will miss the saturation point and be forced to sell on the way down again.

Trading Terms

Momentum traders are day traders who watch for stocks that are suddenly actively traded as a result of breaking news or other factors.

Alarm Bells

Remember that SEC rule about shorting stocks—you can only do it on an uptick in the stock's price, not on a downtick in the price.

Note that we've been talking about "buy" before "sell." Momentum play works almost equally well for *down* moves, too. The only limitation is the "uptick" rule, which prevents us from shorting any time we want. We must wait for an uptick.

Making It Work

Here's how:

➤ Watch the opening carefully. Futures, news, stocks that appear strong relative to the market or just don't seem to go down when the others are going down. We also suggest the morning equity options page. Stocks with call volume increases can be good upside breakout candidates.

➤ Pick the strong stocks to watch.

➤ Look at the charts. Identify trading ranges and breakout patterns.

➤ Watch Level II for signs of a push: bids lining up, levels coming up (towards inside market), offer evaporation.

➤ If a move starts, wait to confirm. A little patience can help here.

➤ Place a *market* order (usually SOES). Don't try to catch the extra teenie by buying on the bid. Remember, lots of others are waiting to buy if you've done your homework right. The teenie is meaningless—you're trying for a half, a buck, two bucks with this trade.

➤ If you're *really* convinced, you might want to "cut in" and bid a tick higher. You'll get filled before those other guys and show even more strength in the market, possibly drawing in still others.

➤ Continue to watch closely.

➤ Bail when the stock "saturates" and momentum starts to slow. *Don't wait too long! Don't try to catch the "top."* This is the most common mistake of the inexperienced trader.

➤ Bail if the trade "goes bad." If it doesn't work out your way, get out. Don't follow momentum downward, and don't "hope" for a reversal. Hope doesn't work. Good day traders lose on trades and they know it. The point is to be disciplined, accept losses, and make the winners bigger than the losers. It's not how *often* you win, it's how *much*.

Reverse most of the above for weak stocks.

Gotchas

You'll recognize that success depends on lots of dynamics. Some are in your control, some aren't. A few pitfalls:

➤ Getting in too soon (before move is confirmed)

➤ Getting out too late (after saturation and reversal)

➤ Loss of discipline, hoping for reversals

➤ Falling for market maker games (firms assign their most wily, experienced market makers to big-name momentum stocks)

Best-Laid Plans

A few other things to keep in mind:

➤ Level II access is important here, too. It helps to see when the move begins (market makers and ECN limit orders lining up on the bid) and when it ends (bids fall off, offers start to come in).

➤ High-performance order entry can be critical if trends and reversals are very fast. You must get out before the crowd.

➤ Stock selection is critical. It helps to know the prior price behavior of the stock.

➤ Keep your eye(s) on the ball. Watch for news and any trading signal that things are changing. Change comes fast.

➤ Again, don't get greedy. Greed and fear are the two worst enemies of the momentum trader. Act with confidence but don't hold out for the extra crumb.

Down Broadway

Momentum trading works for listed stocks, but because of the lack of transparency away from the inside market, it's a little harder. If you have access, watch the "size" build up on either side of the trade. When the bid or ask moves, look at the size at these levels. If an ask ticks up only to find huge size at that level, resistance is indicated. Same if the bid ticks up but there's no size at that level. And so forth.

Filling the Gaps

Scalping and momentum trading are the two basic strategy engines of the day trader. The next three are more specialized "situation" strategies.

What's a Gap?

"Gaps" occur when a stock opens at a materially different price from the previous close, either up or down. It can be driven by news, brokerage recommendations, or pure emotion. Often the trading at the end of the previous day can give clues. If the stock closed on a sharp upswing, professionals were probably at work, and there may be a short "squeeze" happening as well.

A stock closes the previous day at $59^1/_2$ and opens the next day at 61. What happened? Obviously a lot of demand piled up at the opening, from the public, from market makers, or both. Market makers and specialists providing the liquidity—the shares—had to get them somewhere, either from their own inventory or by "shorting" them into the market. If the buying persists, they're likely to lose; but if it subsides for any reason, look out! Pros do what they can to come out ahead, and they'll drive the price down if they can.

So they try to "test" the market. If successful, they break through the other way, down for a "gap up" opening. If not, strength is confirmed, and the stock will chase the opening price and beyond.

The Day Trader's Play

What does the day trader see? First, the gap-up open. Then, often, a short burst of continued buying as other "average investor" orders come in. Then, shortly after the open, usually less than an hour, it will weaken. Here's the point: If the stock crosses back below the open, it's probably headed lower. If it doesn't, the advance renews. This is a sign of strength. The day trader uses this inflection point to place a momentum trade, either up or down.

"Gaps down" represent buying opportunities if the reversal breaks through the previous close. If they don't, more prolonged weakness is signaled. You can see that gap trading is a form of "pattern" trading.

Down Broadway

Gap trading works both on the NASDAQ and NYSE. In fact, since the pattern is usually easily discerned on a chart, it doesn't really matter which exchange is involved. True, NASDAQ Level II can give a little more advanced notice of the inflection point or points, but this isn't a huge advantage in this case. Not as much as with scalping and pure momentum trading.

Shadowing the Ax

You don't want a guy with an ax following you around, do you? Didn't think so. But as a day trader, you're about to see that it's OK to turn the tables and follow *him* around. Let's take a look.

Remember the "ax"? The ax is a market maker, usually one of the big investment houses—Merrill Lynch, Morgan Stanley, Goldman Sachs, and the like—who often bring large institutional orders to the market. These can be buy or sell orders.

Large orders mean, of course, a lot of demand in the market. And they mean a lot of money for the investment house/market maker too. At the very least, the ax will give support or resistance in the market, and often be a strong enough force to drive it higher.

Is the Ax Sharp?

Usually the ax is "sharp"—a seasoned professional trader. Having said that, they have an order to take care of, and a lot of other things to do too. They will play persistently in the market until the order is filled. A day trader watching closely can see this.

The Day Trader's Play

The day trader first must identify the ax. The ax will show up persistently on the bid (if they have a large buy order) or on the offer (if they have a large sell). As the market contracts on the buy side, the ax remains pat. As soon as you see the ax emerge, your "trade" is to play the same market at the same price. You enter a limit order at, or maybe one tick above, the ax. The current bid stands firm as other traders panic and hit his (and your) bid, thinking the bid side is breaking down to lower levels. The bid stands firm, thanks to the strength of the ax.

Once others see that the bid is firm, the tide rushes in the other way. Prices run until resistance is hit and offers start to pile up.

The ax may play games to look less like the ax. He/she may drop the bid briefly as the market "comes in"—which may also serve the double purpose of producing greater profits on a previously negotiated client deal. The ax may put up a feint on the offer side, but it wouldn't be there for long. The ax doesn't want to sell when trying to accumulate 100,000 shares for someone else.

When they do start to sell, close your position and run. The ax's order has likely been filled. You may want to watch "Island" and other ECN trades for this market maker, too. The order might get filled through these "offline" channels. Watch Time and Sales and your custom tickers for "ax" market maker trading activity on your advanced platform.

Down Broadway

This one doesn't work on the Big Board. You can't see intentions—only orders. The game plays out in person on the NYSE, not on a computerized quote board. A floor broker will walk up to the specialist and indicate the large order. The specialist may sell from his own account or handle partial fills from the public. Occasionally they might nudge offer size to get sellers to come into the market, but these actions are subtle and hard for the day trader to follow.

Is This Event on Your Calendar?

Stock "events" can provide day-trading opportunities. Events can include earnings reports, splits, acquisitions and rumors, upgrades and downgrades, and the like. Usually they serve to foretell momentum, and the trader's strategy reverts to a standard momentum strategy.

Stocks often show strength before an earnings report and weakness after. (Buy on rumor, sell on fact!) This pattern has become so predictable that it can provide the basis for a relative strength–based momentum trade.

Splits are tricky. Rumors drive prices up, as usually does the actual announcement. Remember that splits themselves cause no change in the value of the stock or the company, they only divide the company up into smaller ownership pieces. Still, the investing public perceives splits as a forward indicator of success straight from the management team. So the news of a split frequently causes a rally—again a momentum rally. The rally subsides from the time the split is announced until after it

Alarm Bells

Although recently we've observed these patterns to be less repeatable (people are getting wise to the true meaning of splits, finally, and they're starting to anticipate these moves), splits can still provide a good day- or swing-trading opportunity.

happens. Often the stock weakens in the absence of other news. But then the split happens, shares then appear cheap, and a short run can occur the day the split is "distributed."

Financial news and rumors can trigger huge rallies or sell-offs. Brokerage recommendations (www.briefing.com) can have a huge impact. They usually start a pattern resembling a momentum trade, and often the momentum pattern will repeat through the day as more investors become wise to the information. Don't scalp teenies when four houses put out a strong buy recommendation! Look for a momentum trade instead....

Down Broadway

Earnings, splits, and news work the same way on Big Board stocks. Subject to the limitations of trading information, you can day-trade NYSE stocks based on these events, too!

Tactical and Practical

Here we supply a "laundry list" of tactics that good day traders (and day-trading instructors) will remind you of over and over. Use these tactics to make yourself better at the strategies we just discussed. Most, by now, should be self-explanatory.

➤ Buy strong stocks, avoid weak stocks (or the opposite for "short" plays).

➤ Don't "fight the tape"—if it's strong it will stay strong and get stronger.

➤ Watch S&P futures and other key leading indicators.

➤ Look for higher highs and higher lows to identify strength.

➤ Look for *relative* strength and weakness—stocks strong or weak when others aren't.

➤ Watch market-maker movement. Look for the ax.

➤ Know when to get out.

➤ Don't try to hit tops or bottoms.

➤ Press winners, cut losers. "Pressing" can mean "doubling down"—investing more. Never invest more in a loser. Dollar-cost averaging is OK for mutual funds but not here.

➤ Keep track of where stocks *have been*, how they've moved through the levels.

➤ Watch for feints and other market-maker games, such as showing low offer while buying stock on Island.

➤ Watch the time of day. Lots of amateur money and exaggerated moves on the opening. Pros and experienced investors tend to come in at the close.

➤ Know when to use limit orders and market orders. Paying the spread is OK when the rewards are bigger.

➤ Bid in front of (or sell beneath) "the number" when you can. That puts you in front of the other bidders or sellers.

➤ Watch the number of stocks you feel comfortable with. Some traders watch a hundred or more, others only one or two.

➤ Trade on news if you get it early, otherwise let it run.

We'll now move on to the more personal side of day trading—creating your style, defining your habits, in Chapter 22, "Getting Personal."

The Least You Need to Know

➤ There are five principle day-trading strategies—Scalping teenies, momentum plays, playing gap openings, shadowing the ax, and playing events.

➤ There is no one perfect play—different strategies work on different days, at different times, for different stocks, in different markets, and for different day traders.

➤ When scalping teenies, you act as a market maker, taking small profits of an eighth or a sixteenth at a time.

➤ Momentum traders seek stocks that are suddenly in play. There may be news or rumors or they may have broken through support or resistance.

➤ Good traders know good trading tactics and always have the discipline to use them.

Getting Personal

The ball's in *your* court now. We've spent 21 chapters describing the ins and outs of day trading: What it's all about, what's traded where, and the information sources, trading platforms, tools, techniques, and strategies. Now it's time to roll up your sleeves.

It's time to think about your own personal approach to day trading. It's time to build your day-trading strategy and style as well as your competence and confidence. This chapter is much more personal than it is technical. Getting through aviation ground school teaches you about flying, but it doesn't teach you to fly.

And you need to decide if this type of flying is right for you in the first place. Remember—it isn't for everyone.

No Two Day Traders Are Alike

Every day trader is different. Some of you are going to rise with the sun every morning, flick on your favorite financial television show while waiting for the coffee to perk and the market to open, raring to go for another day. You'll spend the entire length of the market day immersed in technical charts and buy signals, not moving from your chair until the market closes.

And then others of you might well decide to stay away from the action at the open of the market, preferring to watch from a distance to see which way things are headed before plunging in. You might return over and over to the same favorite stocks everyday, flipping Amazon.com and CMGI till the bell rings. Or you might rove all over the market, scouring the scene for stocks that are on the move. Different traders, different styles. Let's look closer at some of the differences.

Science

We mentioned earlier that day trading is both art and science. The science part is pretty straightforward—information, trading platforms, exchanges and exchange rules, charts, technical analysis. The science part is much the same for everyone.

Art

The "art" part is where every day trader becomes an individual. How do we interpret charts? Daily price movements? Market maker behavior? Momentum? We are all human, and we form our own interpretations and visions of the future from these phenomena.

But it goes even deeper than that. Different day traders have different goals. Some want to get rich, others want a steady income, others just want to earn a few bucks on the side.

A Question of Style

Day traders differ in their tolerance for risk. They have different appetites for information, numbers, and graphs. They have different appetites for speed and activity. They can become a "guru," intensely focused on one or two stocks, or they can scan the markets for what looks good this morning. They can scalp, play momentum, play gaps, or take short-term positions. They can play for seconds, minutes, hours, or even a few days. They can play for teenies, eighths, quarters, or full points. They can make 2 or 200 trades a day. And they can do it part time, full time, all day, or part of a day.

All of the above define a day trader's *style*. These are all matters of personal preference and personal vision about the day trader's self, the markets, and his/her *role* in the markets.

Compulsories

It doesn't matter if you can pull off a few double-axle triple-toe-loops in competition if you can't skate a basic figure-eight. There are a few behind-the-scenes "compulsories" that all day traders must incorporate into their personal style before trying the fancy stuff.

These common threads that tie all day traders together:

➤ **Detached emotions:** The day trader who gets emotionally attached to his trades and their results will get sucked into bad decisions again and again.

➤ **Passion:** You gotta *like* this stuff! The action, the thrill. It's like flying that high-performance jet—if you're nervous about throwing up and can't wait till it's over, this may not be for you. On the other hand, if you can't wait for Monday mornings—for the action to start again—that's a good sign!

➤ **Discipline:** The ability to create a game plan and stick to it is essential. When things get critical, follow your brain, then your heart.

➤ **Positive attitude:** Keeps you from being tentative and from dwelling on that last bad trade.

➤ **Willingness to learn:** The successful day trader learns from his mistakes and successes. The more "flight" hours logged, the more qualified he/she becomes. And there is always a well-kept flight log to keep track.

We'll dig further into the other style points and personal skills and tactics. Some would be classified as "compulsories"; others are truly unique to the day trader's style.

Alarm Bells

If you can't be cool and detached about the stocks you own—ready and willing to dump them at the first sign of trouble—forget about day trading. If you can't make a quick decision and act on it in a split second, forget about day trading.

Involved or Committed

Most of you with any experience in a corporate conference room have heard the "ham and eggs" parable. As you carefully volunteer your services towards the completion of a critical project, the project manager asks you if you are "ham or eggs." Immediately you know what he's asking—in the case of "eggs" the chicken is *involved*, but in the case of "ham," the pig is *committed*!

Does It Make a Difference?

The difference between involvement and commitment can be critical to any big challenge you face. Day trading is no exception. Commitment implies a prioritized, no-stone-unturned approach to getting it done, with a final, measurable result. Involvement implies that you'll attend a few meetings and jump in and contribute where you can.

From a day trading perspective, a "ham" day trader commits the time, gets the training, buys the tools, practices until perfect, prioritizes day trading as a profession, and closely monitors the result. This day trader isn't overwhelmed or discouraged by losses or bad trades—it's all part of the learning process.

The "egg" day trader dabbles—a few "part-time trades," maybe while at their desk during breaks, reads a few books, learns a few tools and techniques, but probably doesn't invest in a high-performance platform. Makes a few trades, may back away if unsuccessful. The "egg" approach is OK, but it probably won't make you a professional day trader.

Are you a "ham" or an "egg" day trader? The answer will tell more about your style and get-started approach.

Style Points

Once you decide your level of commitment (and you can rethink your decision after taking in what's coming), you need to think about your day-trading style.

"Style" refers to your approach to day trading and all investing in general. Style choices match your personal goals, interests, and traits to major day-trading and investing strategies. Style choices dictate *how* you will play the market.

You don't have to choose one and lock in on that choice, never to try another. Good day traders are flexible and can change their style to fit the situation. But they are aware of the tradeoffs.

Our "dimensions" of style include:

➤ Risk versus reward
➤ Time commitment
➤ Market "appetite"
➤ Trading "speed"

No Pain, No Gain

With any investing strategy, you're always taking risks. Day trading, being short term in nature and subject to the whims of volatility, is certainly no different. But like most other things in life, you can choose the amount of risk you want to take.

Everybody has a different tolerance for risk. Some like it hot—taking big risks to try for big returns. Others like to venture their capital, but keep some powder dry to hedge against the devil unknown or capitalize on the *next* best opportunity. You need to decide who you are. Go for it? Or go *with* it, but not all the way. Either is OK for day trading, so long as you understand the tradeoffs and base your decisions (at least in part) on rational intelligence!

You might choose to take smaller gains, with less capital risked—and always your *own* capital. Or you might decide to venture in a little deeper, with larger 2,000-share trades and margin leverage. It's up to you. The day trader's goal is to score the most runs possible, and you score runs by hitting lots of singles and doubles, or by hitting home runs and striking out.

If you have the capital and don't mind making a few outs, hitting a home run can be thrilling, and it can win the game in the bottom of the ninth after being down all the way. But you can also strike out. Most day traders strive to hit singles and doubles. But like a good baseball team, a few power hitters in the lineup can add punch. Unlike baseball, you can unleash the fence swinger any time you want—you're not committed to a batting order. Your approach to risk will determine, first, how many power hitters you place in your lineup, and second, when to bring them to the plate.

The more risk-averse trader might stick to less volatile stocks, and might stay closer to teenie-scalping as a core strategy. Trades are very quick and the fewer unknown "random variables" affect the result as compared to momentum trading. The rewards are small but consistent and can add up. True "singles" hitting.

Time Commitment

Are you gonna do this full time, part time, or during office breaks? The answer has a lot to do with style.

Serious day trading requires a healthy immersion in information of all kinds. It takes time to acquire all this information, digest it, and form a vision of where things are going. It takes time to watch closely enough to enter and maintain your positions. It takes time to track your trades, analyze the results, and learn from your experience. It's hard to keep up when you have to run off to a three-hour staff meeting.

This "style" point is somewhat related to your goals. If you're just learning, or trying to add a few bucks to your income, sharing day trading with some other job is probably OK. Those of us on the West Coast have a distinct advantage in that two hours of market activity are already behind us by the time we start work. You might be able to trade casually from your desk at work (subject to your company's approval) using the Internet, but it doesn't make sense to install a high-performance platform there. Watching a Level II screen on company time sounds like a good way to get fired.

Alarm Bells

This is as good a place as any to remind you that day trading should *not* be done with your household finances, nor your business capital, nor your retirement, college savings, nor house! Including these items in your day-trading nest egg increases risk a hundred-fold, and will make you much more emotional and less rational about your day trading. It isn't a good place to go.

Daily Specials

Teenie-scalping, when applied correctly, can be a low-risk day-trading strategy if you have the time and tools to watch and trade close to the market. Teenie-scalping gets *much more risky* if you aren't disciplined about closing out bad trades before they become worse.

Teenie-scalping and most momentum trading are both pretty time-consuming professions. Both require real-time concentration and quick trigger fingers. But the true amount of time consumed can depend on the number of stocks you are playing and their volatility.

Market Appetite

Do you really love this stuff? Do price movements and market behaviors excite you? Do you constantly monitor the "most active," "ups and downs" lists? Do exchange-floor reports and up-to-the-minute commentary get your adrenaline going? Are you a ticker addict, waiting for just one more "print" to go by before you get in the shower (for us West-coasters)?

Most of us can't wait to find out how our own trades work out. But there are enthusiasts out there who take it all in regardless of their own trading positions. (Of course, they're shopping for trades all the while....)

Like most interests, either you're interested or you aren't. It's hard to change that. Maybe what we're really talking about, as a style point, is dedication. Which is related to time. Can you/will you dedicate yourself to watching all the key shows, reading all the key papers, checking out all the key Web sites?

Greater commitment probably widens your horizons, your "activity zone." If you watch the whole market and 120 stocks closely, more opportunities will probably emerge, but it takes time and will tax your three eyes! Or you can focus on a few stocks and become a "guru," knowing their every movement, their every closing price and volume, and the next four earnings report dates.

Daily Specials

Day trading without looking. You can also trade "blindly"—to a limited extent. Buy Amazon at the opening (watch out for gaps), set a limit "buy" order a point higher and a limit or stop "sell" order a quarter lower. Do this daily, and if point-higher moves exceed quarter–down moves by more than a 4:1 ratio (well, 3:1 or so with commissions) you can make money. To a degree you are gambling, not trading on knowledge and "expert" interpretation. But this style can work in a pinch, if you're a normally active day trader but could only get a morning tee time with your buddies.

Fast Lane or Slow Lane?

You can decide how fast (and how often) you want to trade. It depends on your goals and the "style" you've determined so far. Do you want to make 200 1-minute trades every day? Or do you want to focus on 5 or 10 "really good" trades and watch them carefully as the day plays out?

This one might vary from day to day as different opportunities present themselves. If you're a three-eyed, two-monitored keyboard-macro speed freak, well, that's just what you are! You trade everything—in, out, in, out. The only time you slow down is during April when you struggle to collect all your trading records for the IRS!

Behind the Screen

Hello, did somebody say IRS? Hmmm... If you spend all day trading in and out of stocks, and each transaction generates a confirmation from your broker, and the IRS wants to know how much you made this year...sounds like the makings of a huge paperwork headache. How do day traders do it? Their taxes, that is. According to a tax season article in the *Wall Street Journal*, "Lots of people, including wide-eyed, novice 'day traders' who have never before filled out a Schedule D, showing capital gains and losses, are wrestling with a paperwork nightmare."

Do you have to report every trade?! Yes, says Martin Nissenbaum, national director of personal income-tax planning for Ernst & Young. Where can you find out more about this taxing question? TheStreet.com has a tax column called taxforum@thestreet.com that provides general tax information for traders. The Silicon Investor Web site has an active message board on the topic "Income Taxes and Recordkeeping," and a book is available, aptly named *The Trader's Tax Survival Guide*, by Ted Tesser, a CPA in Boca Raton, Florida. Good luck!

If you like a more placid approach, that's OK. You probably want to scalp NYSE slow movers and watch a few momentum trades play out.

You can choose which "lane" you want to play in. If you aren't doing well, or if it seems like there's always a truck in front of you preventing you from achieving your goals, you can always change lanes, and change back if necessary.

The Day Trader's Day

We already said that no two day traders are alike, and ditto for the day trader's *days*. It's guaranteed that no two days are alike, even for the same day trader. But there are patterns, sort of a lifestyle, that we can follow.

An Unalarming Beginning

You may set an alarm clock, especially those of you on the West Coast. The markets open at 6:30 A.M. out there, and they wait for no one. But we suspect that if you're really into this, you don't need an alarm clock, no matter where you are! You wake up with the birds, adrenaline pumped for the day ahead.

Behind the Screen

Among the many expensive investment seminars taught in hotel banquet rooms around the country are the Wade Cook seminars. Graduates of "Cook University" receive what are known as "IQ" beepers. These beepers go off every morning about an hour before the market opens, and alerts graduates of the Cook program to breaking news and potential stocks to watch. Some Cook graduates use the beeper as a de facto alarm clock, rising when summoned by the call. One such trader confessed to us that, unable to figure out how to turn the volume down and unwilling to get up that early to begin trading, she finally took to hiding the beeper under her sofa cushions.

The Morning News

You might lie in bed for awhile, listening to NPR (National Public Radio) News. You'll get a summary of market activity overnight in Europe and Japan (as related by those women reporters with plumy accents), some of the bigger business news stories of the previous day, and even a few of the current day if they are hot enough to make the national news. When your mind and body are ready, go grind a load of Starbucks and fetch the morning paper (hopefully, the *Journal* or *Investor's Business Daily*). Peruse the "companies in the news," "Money and Investing" commentary, perhaps the options pages. Turn on CNBC or Bloomberg, to see where the action is. Find out what the S&P 500 futures are doing. Get a reminder of what important economic data will be released today and when, and what time Alan Greenspan gives his "Open Market Committee" speech.

Turn On, Tune In

Time to boot up your computer. Check the newswires for stories or press releases on stocks you follow. Check your own numbers and charts for those stocks. Look for weakness and strength vs. their recent past, their industry group, the market as a whole.

Start creating a "what to watch today" list.

Ding … And They're Off

The market opens, and almost immediately interesting things start to happen. Gaps up, gaps down. NYSE delayed openings and order imbalances. Floor reports on active issues, "Squawk Box" reports. Fast and furious market maker activity on Level II.

Indexes up or down, TICK and ARMS up or down. You get a broad view of market strength and weakness, and a close-up view of where the stock action is today.

Decide Your Daily Fate

Now it's time to make some trading decisions (you've probably made a few already). Are you going to trade heavy or go light? (Some days are cut out for day traders, some just aren't.) Can you see the strength? Are some stocks behaving better than others? Are market makers consistent in their behavior? Do at least a few things look predictable? Make your list, and check it twice.

Trade, Trade, Trade

Of course, anything could happen here. You make a few trades; they work or they don't. You quickly close out the ones that don't but may "double" into some of the ones you do. Once your positions are out there, you track them like a hawk, ready to close out at a moment's saturation, always before they reverse. You record everything you do for later, unless you have an advanced platform that does it for you.

Midday Breather

The markets usually slow down mid-day and price movements attenuate. Good time for a leg stretch, maybe a little lunch. (That's what most pros are doing, too, which may be why it slows down!)

Getting Ready to Close

Things start humming again at the end of the day. Pro money starts to come in (or go out). Traders (including you) close out their positions. You make some decisions. You might want to hold on to some "winners" overnight, especially with a strong close. Watch for the gap-up opening tomorrow. Or, you might want to close out while ahead. Never hold a loser. You can't "hope" it back to life tomorrow.

Day Is Done

You close, and the market closes. Time to reflect on what happened that day. Look at your records or trade monitor, and count up the winners and losers. Think about what went right and why, and what went wrong and why.

Aftermath

If you had a good day, and especially if you're on the West Coast, there's time for 18 holes or a visit to your kid's day care. Unwind with an afternoon talk show, Flintstones cartoons, or whatever. Your brain will automatically reprocess what went wrong and what went right and why. You might want to study charts and news a little more closely. And you might want to prepare yourself for the next trading day.

Finally, when all that's over, relax! Don't dwell on what happened. Refresh yourself. You'll need the vigor, energy, stamina, and concentration for the next day.

Personal and Practical

The following personal behavior "gems" come from experience and readings about day traders and their stories.

➤ Stay detached. Don't get emotionally involved; Emotions work against your game plan.

➤ Don't think that "the market is stupid." The market is always right.

➤ Don't *hope*.

➤ Don't form opinions. You don't have time, and they let in emotion.

➤ Don't get angry.

➤ Don't wish for revenge. Revenge doesn't happen.

➤ Eliminate the fear of losing. Scared money never wins.

➤ Accept your losses and move on.

➤ Assume responsibility for your losses. Nobody else "did it to you."

➤ Always think positive.

➤ Hit singles and doubles—don't always swing for the fences.

➤ Don't try to hit tops and bottoms.

➤ Don't try to win on *every* trade. It's the *amount* that counts, not the *number* of wins.

➤ Remember, it's real money. Work for it.

➤ It's *not* a game and it's not gambling.

➤ Set goals.

➤ Recover from a bad day—learn from it and put it behind you.

➤ Always keep score. Analyze your results. *Learn from burn, learn from earn.*

➤ Don't expect to be an expert right away. As in all other professions, you will pay your dues.

➤ Don't expect to come out ahead, especially in your first 3-6 months. Be patient.

➤ Don't try to focus on everything. You can't. Do what you're good at.

➤ Don't expect this to be easy. It's hard work. Profits are *earned*. Maybe not the "old fashioned" way, but they *are* earned.

➤ Decide each day how much risk you want to take.

➤ Decide each day how "involved" you want to be. Some days are better than others.

➤ Remember that different strategies suit different days, different stocks, different traders, different market makers.

➤ Press winners, cut losers.

➤ Expand when you are winning, contract when you aren't. Don't try to "get it all back at once."

➤ Always follow your escape routes.

➤ Learn when you can rely on instinct vs. analysis.

➤ Stay focused.

➤ Stay disciplined.

➤ Have fun and look forward to Mondays!

The Least You Need to Know

➤ Critical day trading personality traits are: detached emotions, passion, discipline, a positive attitude, and a willingness to learn from both mistakes and successes.

➤ Among the factors to consider when developing a day trading style are: your tolerance for risk versus reward, time commitment, market appetite, and trading speed.

➤ Although day trading has inherent risk, day traders can actively manage the amount of risk they are willing to take.

➤ Risk-averse day traders can stick to less volatile stocks, scalping small amounts as a core strategy.

➤ Serious day trading requires a time commitment before, during, and after market hours. It's difficult to do while doing something else—like a full-time job.

Chapter 23

Trading at the Speed of Thought

In This Chapter

➤ Boiling it down to technique, psychology, and money management

➤ A short course in managing your money

➤ How to get started—shop, set up, practice

➤ Training your brain—by *doing*

➤ Final comments and some thoughts on the future

High-performance, information-intensive, real-time, do-it-yourself, disintermediated electronic securities trading. Not investing, but trading—*day* trading. For 22 chapters, you've been immersed in the details. In this concluding chapter, let's step back a little and take a broader look at day trading and at *you*, the day trader.

A Bigger Picture

Early on we described the elements that make day trading *possible*: rule changes, improvements in personal technology, and real-time access to information and trading. We also described market environments favorable to day trading: high liquidity, volume, and volatility. We went through the major trading strategies and a long list of trading tactics and personal habits that make day traders successful.

Where does that leave us? Aren't we about done?

Yes! You could probably put this book down and walk into a trading room or speak to a trading firm with an intelligent understanding of the basics. You know about Level II screens, market makers, ECNs, limit orders, momentum trading, and what an ax is.

But there's still a little ways to go. A book can only teach you the techniques and tactics of day trading up to a certain point. True day trading, especially the high-performance variety, becomes more a matter of mental reflex and fast response to a number of simultaneous stimuli. It's really a form of mental athletics that requires concentration, stamina, conditioned reflexes, and even the hand-eye coordination of the greatest sports.

Like most athletic endeavors, you'll only get good by doing it, gaining experience, learning from failure, and trying again. No sport was learned from a book. Not even chess.

So you've struggled through 22 chapters, and we wait until *now* to declare you can't get the hang of it by reading a book? Well, we still think there's an opportunity to share wisdom and perspective to help you get off on the right foot. But it's true, this book is only a part of your learning process.

Daily Specials

Just like any sport, getting good at day trading requires conditioning—mental conditioning. Concentration, stamina, quick reflexes, and hand-eye coordination all come into play.

The Day Trader's Trifecta

Don't worry, we won't introduce horse racing as a form of day trading! We'll stick to common stocks.

Common day-trader wisdom holds that successful day trading really boils down to three things:

➤ Technique

➤ Psychology

➤ Money management

What does that mean, exactly? Technique refers to understanding markets, information, trading, and analysis tools to make fast, rational, well informed, ahead-of-the-pack decisions. Psychology refers to some of the personal tactics and habits necessary to keep yourself in the game and keep your eye on the ball. Detachment, discipline, ability to act, ability to move on, and knowing yourself all play into psychology.

Of these three things, the one we haven't really addressed yet is money management.

A Question of Balance

You probably saw this coming, but here it is anyway: All three—technique, psychology, money management—must be present and accounted for to trade successfully. With *balance*. The best technician in the world won't succeed if he can't overcome fear or handle money. The most cold-blooded, steel-eyed mental tough won't win if he/she doesn't understand the tools or manage money. The former accountant who keeps track of every penny won't succeed either without...well, you get the point.

Every day trader should work relentlessly to develop technique, persona and style, and effective money management *simultaneously*. The best in the business all have good rhythm and balance between these important facets.

Counting Your Chips

OK, we'll admit it. We've been so caught up presenting techniques, tools, strategies, analysis, and trading style that we almost forgot money management. Shame on us. So let's examine some new principles in this final, concluding chapter.

Money management can include a lot of things. It's sort of personal finance for day trading—budgeting, knowing when and how to spend (or invest), keeping track, setting goals, making plans, knowing when to change your plan. It's a critical element of day-trading success, but it so often gets put on the back burner in training and in the heat of battle, often with disastrous results.

Poor money management leads to reckless trading and bad decisions. Every trading room or trading company has a list of clients who've gotten stuck in bad positions. It's like moving an army into battle without a proper head count, fuel supplies, or food rations. You might win, but risk and uncertainty accelerate to intolerable levels.

Money management for day trading includes:

➤ Keeping track of results

➤ Setting aside "risk" capital

➤ Diversification

➤ Knowing when to get bigger, smaller, or when to quit

These points seem simple enough. Let's examine each one in detail to see why they are so critical to your success.

> **Trading Terms**
>
> **Risk capital** is money that you can *afford to lose*, above and beyond the money that you need for everyday survival.

Keeping Track

Keeping track of results. This one sounds so simple, but again, in the heat of battle, it often gets cast aside. Hey, who has time to stop and keep track of something so mundane as results?

Any investor or trader, no matter how big or small, long-term or short-term, should track results. Somehow. Doesn't have to be anything fancy—a daily scoresheet kept on a KFC napkin is OK if that's the way you do things. Who has time to stop and keep track of results? You do.

We recommend a daily trade log and cumulative position tracker (many advanced platforms provide this). You want to know how far ahead or behind you are, to the second if possible. This helps guide your next move, and helps you decide how much risk you want to (or can afford to) take.

Behind the Screen

Keeping a day-trading diary can be a powerful tool for improving your skills, as well as for getting a better understanding of yourself and how you react in certain situations. Looking back over a week's worth of trades—some good, some not so good—can help you spot the moments when your stress level clouded your judgment. Or when you panicked and pulled the trigger too soon. By identifying these behavioral patterns, you'll be better able to react when the same situation arises.

We also recommend a cumulative diary. At the end of each trading day, enter your trades, successful and unsuccessful. Look back over these as you would a flight log to remember what you did, remember what situations you encountered and how you managed them, and see if there are situations that seem to repeat themselves. Good day traders learn from experience, and your daily log gives the most factual record of your experience. And don't forget, it might come in handy at tax time.

Setting Aside Risk Capital

We don't have to paint the grim picture of the trader who loses the vacation fund, house down payment, or child's college fund, then comes home at the end of the trading day to explain it to the (now more) significant other. You've read the same message over and over in this book: *Don't day trade with money you can't afford to lose.*

Daily Specials

Keep your trading styles a bit mixed: Don't always do the same thing over and over—but having said that, make sure you think through any style and strategy changes, and carry them out with discipline. Undisciplined, random "experimentation" usually leads to bad trading.

Funds set aside for day trading should be looked at as venture capital. Venture capital is capital set aside to pursue an idea that may—or may not—work. It is distinctly separate from your own personal working or investing capital. It should be treated like capital you would use to try out any other business idea.

Diversification

This may look like the same point as above: Don't put all your eggs in the day-trading basket. By now that's obvious. But diversification can take another dimension.

You can diversify among trading styles, among stocks, or among what you invest in. You can, for instance, day trade for bull moves in a stock, but at the same time, buy some short- or intermediate-term put options to give you some protection in case a move falls apart. Or trade indices or index futures. Or diversify into day, swing, and short-term position trades. There are innumerable ways to mix it up, all with the same objective: To balance risk and come out ahead in a greater number of the possible market outcomes.

Knowing When to Get Big

All of this sounds like poker, eh? Bet what you can afford to lose, know how many chips you have, don't bet it all on one hand. Right. It *is* a little like poker; poker being a game of chance that is parlayed into a game of skill through betting, and yes, money-management skills. Most good poker players don't consider poker to be gambling. Their money-management skills make the difference.

Carrying this analogy one step farther, we can now talk about getting bigger ("raising"), getting smaller, or folding altogether. The good player knows exactly when to do all three.

Likewise, the good day trader will "get bigger" on successful trades and get smaller when it just doesn't seem to be working. "Getting smaller" can refer to trading less money, smaller size or whatever, or closing out investments early or partially. Or it can refer to taking the afternoon off, which many a day trader has done after deciding it just wasn't their day. If you *can't* just walk away from time to time, that's *a sure sign* of trouble.

Alarm Bells

There will be days when it's better to turn off the computer and walk away. If you can't walk away from time to time, that's a danger sign.

Dealing Yourself In

Let's talk a little about how to get started.

Five-Card Draw or Seven-Card Stud?

First step: Plan your approach. What learning experience is best for you? A methodical, take-the-class, walk-before-you-run approach? Or a jump into the deep end? It depends on your objectives, your style of learning, your tolerance for risk, and level of commitment. We won't recommend any single approach, but we *insist* that you pick one before starting. You can always change it later if it turns out to be the wrong fit.

Choices

Do you want to dabble part time with Internet brokers and information sources? Do you want to try one of the advanced power-info feeds but still do your trading with an Internet broker? Or do you want to "go for it," signing up with a local trading firm or setting up an advanced platform in your home? It's your choice.

Learn by Doing

We already said you can't 100-percent "get it" by reading a book. (Not even ours!) You have to experience it, feel it, see it in action. Regardless of what approach you take, even a conservative "dabbling" one, the experience you gain will be important.

If the dabbling approach achieves your objectives, that's fine. But if you aim to become a serious or full-time professional day trader, eventually you need to experience and get a feel for high-performance trading systems and style. As with sports, you can *start* by watching, but sooner or later you have to *do* it. And the sooner the better, so you can get the feel as quickly as possible, learn from your mistakes, and develop a successful style. It's OK to take five cards and fold away your ante for awhile—so long as you're getting the experience you need by watching cards (and maybe, by watching others).

Once you decide on your approach, it's time to start signing up for stuff, and, where required, making investments in the right tools, equipment, and training.

Once you have the tools, it's time to practice.

Tool Catalogs

We've already discussed the myriad trading tools at some length, so we won't repeat it all here. Suffice it to say you should shop carefully before making choices. Spend your money—*invest it*—as you would for any other tool or piece of capital equipment vital to a business. Test drive where you can—use free trial periods and simulations where possible.

It's important that you have what you need to support your trading style. Maybe a little *more* than you need—in the interest of getting exposure and experience to more advanced styles and tools. But avoid overkill. A high-end platform with four Level II windows simply isn't necessary if you plan to swing trade NYSE stocks from your desk at work. It will cost money, confuse you, and compromise your concentration on both your trading and your job.

Computer Considerations

If you decide to trade from home, having the appropriate computer equipment is a must. Let's talk computer-ese.

We won't go into too much detail here—things change and everyone's needs are different. Different companies and software packages will have different requirements. But you should probably have the following for home high-performance day trading:

➤ Modern Pentium PC (200 mhz or higher), expandable, Win95 or better

➤ The biggest monitor you can afford. 19" good, 21" better

➤ Minimum 32mb memory, 64mb, 96mb better

➤ Second PC helps for redundancy; second Internet connection, money management, maybe a game or two when things are slow

Connections:

➤ Minimum 56K modem

➤ ISDN, DSL, cable, or direct connect (T1/frame relay) better. Depends on your budget, level of commitment, and what's available in your area.

➤ Second ISP for redundancy

➤ Cable TV not a bad idea, for CNBC, etc.

For Internet-based trading without power-push information feeds or direct-access trading, you probably don't need the large monitor.

For a discussion on computer setups, check your broker or platform provider, look into chat rooms, and check www.phactor.com. Some high-performance platform providers go further than recommending computer equipment: They team with suppliers (Dell mostly) to offer specially priced bundles designed just for day traders.

Practice Hands

It's been mentioned a few times, but can't be mentioned too often: Practice "on paper" before you bet real money.

Most day-trading platforms and trading firms allow simulated, or "paper" trading. Do it, and take it seriously. Try as much as you can to make it seem or feel like real money. Day trading provides this opportunity like few other activities—imagine your buddies letting you play poker with matchsticks while they nickel-dime-quarter away. Moral: Get good while it's free!

Good on Paper, Bad on Paper

Keep close track of your paper-trading results. Conventional wisdom says that good paper traders *may or may not* make good day traders, depending on how they respond to "live ammo." On the other hand, bad paper traders will almost always be bad day traders.

If you can't get it together on paper, keep trying, keep learning. Eventually, your brain may get wrapped around this thing, or maybe it won't. The simple fact is that not everyone is cut out to be a day trader.

If paper trading works out for you, don't get cocky. It doesn't guarantee that you will succeed at the real thing. Funny things start happening when real dollars start coming and going. Be ready for this, and be ready to slow down or quit and go back to paper trading if you need to.

Alarm Bells

One more time: Good paper traders may or may not become good day traders. Bad paper traders almost certainly will fail at the real thing.

Going Back

Going back to paper trading isn't—or shouldn't be—like putting the training wheels back on after your first bicycle wreck as a five year old. Nobody will (or should) snicker or call you a klutz. Any mature day trader will pause for practice or to "sharpen the saw" many times during his/her day-trading pursuits.

Many experienced traders will even paper trade if away for awhile, on vacation or whatever. If you're trading a new type of security, a new stock, or a new trading platform, paper trade until you learn its behavior.

Second Best for Awhile

Every poker player, and most athletes, have experienced it: second best. In poker, second best is the very worst place to be. You had a good hand, a bettable hand, but it wasn't good enough to win. You followed it anyway. You couldn't *not* follow it. It's hard not to bet on a full house even if the other guy might have four of a kind. You lost, but you gave it your best shot. And you learned.

Alarm Bells

You will lose at first. It's part of the learning process. Be ready for it.

In the Red

Invariably this will happen in day trading, and unless you have incredible beginner's luck, it will happen to *you*. Your best trading picks will go south (or north, if you bet south). Most day traders lose money for the first three to six months—a new car's worth, or a couple of good used cars. It just happens, and it's part of the learning process.

Staying at the Table

Good technique, psychology, and money management should get you out of the morass. Learn from mistakes, but don't "reach" to try to get it all back at once. Stick to your strategies and tactics or adjust slightly for better performance. Don't throw them out the window. Check your discipline: Are you getting out of bad trades as fast as you should? Get bigger or smaller where you should.

And for goodness' sake, don't be afraid to get more instruction, coaching, chat-room interaction, or paper-trading experience. Don't get mad, don't get down, don't blame others, don't seek revenge, don't sulk, don't get *overly* conservative. Stick to sound day-trading principles and practices. Keep technique, psychology, and money management in balance. The market will become "second best," and you'll become a winner.

Brain Training

We've admittedly taken a pretty deliberate approach to preparing you as a day trader. Rules, markets, information tools, trading tools, strategies, tactics, styles. Like hitting a fastball or a golf ball, there are so many little elements and mechanics you can't possibly think of during your swing—and when you do, the results can be comical!

As your day-trading technique, psychology, and money-management skills all mature, you'll find day trading to be less cognitive and more of a reflex or "action" skill. When this happens, you're starting to arrive.

Brain-Eye Coordination

You could say that skilled day trading requires "brain-eye" coordination. As your three eyes scan the screenscape and listen to CNBC drone on in the background, your brain picks up things and makes instant semi-conscious decisions. "Haven't I seen Dell do this before?" you'll quickly think, or, "Looks like upward pressure is building on the S&P 500." You find yourself visualizing the future in very small, fast increments. You'll be able to pick up the rotation of the ball before you swing.

Daily Specials

There's also an element of *hand-eye* coordination for the high-powered trader. Fast, split-second trading decisions are useless if you have to hunt and peck your order to the trading floor. Placing your order — buy, ECN limit, DELL, 49$^{11}/_{16}$ can take a long time if you're all thumbs. Entering the wrong order—or the wrong price—can be a disaster. Develop your dexterity—and check your work.

Learning How Your Brain Works

Huh? Learn how your brain works? Yeah, right. This sounds silly—if anyone can figure out how your brain works, it should be *you* (with or without the help of a therapist).

Yes, *but*.... Yes, but everybody has different reflex actions and ways of interpreting stimuli. Some things can be learned, others take a long time or never come at all. Otherwise, we'd all be making millions hitting curve balls and golf balls.

As you move from *thinking* day trading to *feeling* day trading, you'll start to get an idea of what your brain does well and what it doesn't. If you simply can't see things in charts, don't use charts. If news feeds do nothing, don't use news feeds. If you can't react quickly enough to ECN alerts, don't use them. If you just can't sell a semiconductor stock...you get the idea.

"Getting the feel" is part of developing your skills and day-trading persona. You begin to sense what's going to happen based on an assortment of stimuli. Then you make a conditioned response.

What do you need to "get the feel"? Practice and more practice. Try new things. Talk to others. Watch. Keep track of what you've done and what it's done for you. And above all else, keep learning and conditioning your brain.

The Future of Day Trading

Back in Chapter 5, we touched on some of the day-trading stories that you've read in the press. Well, there are *new* news stories on day trading literally every day. The fast-moving news pendulum swings from stern warnings and threats of government regulation right back to new day-trading opportunities and expansion of services offered by exchanges, brokers, ECNs and other service providers.

"The initial press on day trading was overly optimistic," says Tom Burton of Cornerstone Securities, a day trading firm. "And then it swung way over to the opposite side and the media message on day trading was pretty alarming. But it seems to have leveled out now. Regulatory scrutiny continues throughout the industry, all the way from Internet brokers to the more sophisticated full-time day-trading shops. The firms that provide good service to their customers and closely follow regulatory procedures will continue to thrive."

So what does the future look like? Let's review what's happening.

Online Investing

Fact: The online investing boom is here to stay. In one year, online brokerage accounts have tripled to six million. The percentage of individual traders trading individual stocks (instead of mutual funds) accelerates upward. The number of trades per investor is growing exponentially. More people have more money to invest as they plan for retirement. People *like* doing it themselves, and the new tools are becoming easier to use, more reliable, cheaper, and more available to the average investor.

Nothing on the horizon, except maybe a protracted market decline, will get in the way.

High-performance day trading should grow as well. The current regulatory attitude is to *not* get in the way, but to focus on the few unscrupulous players who surface. We predict that Internet brokers will offer more day-trading products as they increase ties with ECNs (like Datek/Island and E*Trade/Archipelago). They will realize greater commission revenue and try to differentiate themselves from their competitors. Once they add their strong brand names to the mix, away we go. Wouldn't you like to be a seasoned day trader by the time that happened?

As we go to press, we're just learning of major moves by traditional full-service brokers into online trading. Merrill Lynch and Prudential have just announced major new products designed for everyone—not just big accounts—providing less expensive online trading access. Online trade commissions are $29.95 for Merrill (to which one TV commentator quipped, "Why $29.95, not $30? Who do they think they are—Wal-Mart?"), and $24.95 for Prudential. Paine Webber is rumored to be developing a similar product.

The catch: You have to sign up for their "advisory services," which can run up to 1.5% of your account value every year—costing from at least $1,500 to several thousand per year. Not bad, if you want this level of service, but these services appear largely as a way for these firms to play both sides of the fence—to capture active trader commissions while preserving the livelihood of their traditional retail brokers and analysts. At least it's a step in the right direction, and most importantly, it's a practical path into more active trading and even into day trading for the more traditional investor.

Meanwhile, E*Trade now offers a product called "Power E*Trade," which gives the active investor (30 trades or more per quarter) Level II, direct-access, and special-service privileges including personalized phone support and assistance.

Bottom line: Expect the number of active traders to grow, competition between firms to intensify, and the lines to continue to blur. Whatever happens, do-it-yourself investing appears here to stay.

Another Population Explosion?

One thing that's a little hard to predict: What happens when the number of day traders grows? Right now there are thousands of us. Will there soon be millions of us out there day tradin' away?

Throughout history, people wary of new technologies consistently turn into doom prophets. But, surprise—steam locomotives don't poison cows' milk and computers haven't taken over the world. And day trading won't collapse either. There may have to be some adaptations, as markets themselves may not be able to handle volumes otherwise. More ECNs may have to step in to take the burden off the markets. Some traders will lose, but many will win too. Who knows? Something to think about.

At Your Friendly Neighborhood ECN

Let's talk about markets. Some really exciting things are happening to expand day-trading possibilities.

ECNs are becoming more retail friendly. As mentioned above, ties to retail Internet brokers are expanding. And formerly institution-only institutions like Instinet are proposing access to retail customers, who in turn would get a shot at after-hours trading.

After the Sun Goes Down

Speaking of after hours, one of the most exciting (or scary, depending on your point of view) proposals is the extension of trading hours, first to 9PM by NASDAQ, then, who knows? We observe that 24-hour day trading, in theory, provides about four times the opportunity of today's $6^1/_2$-hour day. But when would you sleep? When would you evaluate? When would you talk to your family? How would you keep up your concentration? We know for a fact that many market professionals would prefer this didn't happen. They have families and personal lives, too!

Day Trading Across Borders

Another exciting prospect is the ability to day trade overseas markets. There are proposals for this, too. Of course, stock-market professionals have been doing this for years. But now you too, otherwise deprived the opportunity to day trade in the wee hours, can earn your Bimmer by scalping pfennigs on BMW shares.

Daily Specials

Everybody wants to get into the action. Recent stories in the business press revealed that there are plans afoot to make bond trading more transparent, thus inviting the individual trader into the once-sacred temple of bond trading!

The NYSE Wants to Play, Too

The NYSE has gained; a much-deserved reputation as the Rock of Gibraltar of the investing world. Only the best companies may apply, and strict scrutiny applies to every company and every specialist on the floor.

Not to depart from its splendid past, the NYSE is exploring greater ECN linkages, forms of negotiated markets with multiple market makers, and greater transparency. It appears the NYSE is trying to meet the needs of day and short-term traders while continuing to support its current charter and clientele. We hope this is true. Recently, however, the NYSE has decided *not* to extend trading hours, at least until mid-year 2000.

Taking It Home with You

The day trader who, for whatever reason, fails to close out his/her position at the end of the day is said to be "taking his position home." A few parting "positions" for you to take home:

Day trading is really what you make of it. If you make the effort to learn how the markets work, get access to information and good trading tools, develop a strategy, practice, develop a style, use discipline, and commit to hard work, day trading can be a rewarding endeavor, a profession. If you refuse to learn or do the work, like most other professional endeavors, you will probably fail. The day trader who simply plays hunches without doing the homework is simply a gambler.

Many of you—maybe most of you—may wish you never read this (or any other) day-trading book. You'll try this and lose, or decide it just isn't for you. But the fact you picked this book up indicates you're curious, and now you've had a chance to satisfy that curiosity and move on. Maybe you'll become successful, maybe not. But either way, we applaud the fact that you're willing to try. That's all we writers can ask.

The Least You Need to Know

➤ Successful day traders work relentlessly to develop technique, persona, style, and money management skills.

➤ You can't learn it all from a book. You must pick it up and try it. Get the feel.

➤ Bad paper traders almost never make good "real money" traders.

➤ Almost everybody loses in the beginning. Count on it.

➤ The future looks promising. Expect day trading to become more mainstream, with greater trading opportunities in more markets for longer hours.

Trading Terms

arbitrage   The simultaneous purchase and sale of substantially identical assets in order to profit from small price differences between the two assets.

ask   The price at which a market maker or specialist will sell a stock. Also known as the *offer*. If you place a market order to buy a stock you will buy it at the ask price.

at the market   A price quote equal to the highest bid or the lowest offer currently available.

away from the market   A bid lower than the highest bid currently available, or an offer higher than the lowest offer currently available.

ax   A market maker acting as a driving force at a point in time—minutes, hours, days, or longer—holding his bid or offer position or even improving it after every execution. The ax probably has a large order from the firm they are representing and are aggressively trying to acquire or dispose of stock to meet the order.

balanced market   One in which there is an equal number of buyers and sellers evenly distributed at all prices, both at and away from the inside market.

bid   The price at which a market maker or specialist is willing to buy a stock. If you place a market order to sell a stock you will sell it at the bid price.

Bollinger bands   A charting technique showing support and resistance points, or a trading range, defined by the standard deviation, or volatility, of a stock's price.

breakthrough   A stock that has been hovering for a long time just under a milestone price is said to have broken through when it closes significantly and consistently above that price. Also known as a *breakout*.

buying power   The total of free equity funds plus funds that can be borrowed within margin rules, which in turn represents the total dollar amount of stock you can control.

call option   A traded contract to purchase a specific quantity of a security at a specific price by a specific future date.

close a position   To sell out a position bought earlier, or to buy "to cover" a position sold short earlier.

coverage   When a stock is tracked and analyzed by a brokerage house it is said to be "covered." When a brokerage house announces that it will be initiating coverage on a stock for the first time, it is taken as an endorsement by the professional community.

day trading   Buying and selling stocks or other securities during the course of a single day.

delayed quotes   Price quotes that are behind the current market prices—20 minutes for NYSE, 15 minutes for NASDAQ.

direct connection   A computer connection direct to a host computer (broker or clearing house) bypassing the Internet. Also called *direct access*.

downtick   Refers to any sale price that is lower than the previous price. The stock is said to be in a downtick.

ECN   Electronic communications networks, alternate trading paths allowing NASDAQ and sometimes NYSE (on Instinet) customers to trade directly with each other or to place orders directly into the market.

figure   Trading slang for the nearest whole dollar price.

hitting the bid   Trading slang for selling a stock at the bid price.

index   Statistical aggregate measure of a market, market sector, or group of markets based on representative securities in that market. Examples include the S&P 500, Dow Jones Industrials, Russell 2000, NASDAQ 100, or Philadelphia Semiconductor Index.

inside bid and offer   The highest bid and lowest offer currently available in the market. Sometimes referred to as the *inside market*. A market maker bidding or offering at the inside bid or offer is said to be bidding *at the market*.

intraday   Events that occur within one trading day.

Level II screen   An exclusive real time screen showing the whole NASDAQ market, all posted bids and offers.

join the bid   When a market maker enters a bid at the current inside, or high-bid level.

join the offer   When a market maker enters an offer at the current inside, or low-offer level.

leave the bid   When a market maker removes its bid from the inside, or high-bid level.

leave the offer   When a market maker removes its offer from the inside, or low offer level.

Level I   Basic level NASDAQ quote, showing inside bid and ask quotes, last trade, volume, tick direction, open, high, and low for the day. Commonly available.

Level II   More advanced NASDAQ quote, showing market-maker bids and offers at *and away from* the current inside bid and ask. Available only on high-performance trading platforms or from certain brokers, usually at a charge.

Level III   Most advanced NASDAQ screen, showing Level II information and allowing market makers to post or adjust bids and offers. Only available to market makers.

leverage   The use of borrowed funds to maximize an investing position otherwise available with a given amount of cash. Increases your percentage return on an up move, but increases your percentage loss on a down move.

lifting the offer   Trading slang for buying a stock at the offered price.

limit order   A fixed price order. A "buy limit" order is to buy a stock at or below a specified purchase, or "limit," price. A "sell limit" order is an order to sell at or above a specified price.

liquidity   Refers to the availability of enough buyers and sellers to quickly and easily execute transactions in a market.

listed stocks   Stocks listed and traded on the New York Stock Exchange, American Stock Exchange or on regional stock exchanges (not NASDAQ).

long position   Your position when you initially buy a security.

margin call   A requirement to deposit funds into your account or sell securities to increase the equity percentage above the minimum maintenance requirement.

maintenance requirement   The minimum equity percentage that must be maintained at all times in your account, according to Federal Reserve Board and your broker or clearing house rules.

margin account   An account allowing a trader to borrow funds from a broker or clearing house to buy stocks and other securities on credit.

marginable securities   Securities that your broker deems appropriate for purchase with margin funds. Many Net stocks and recent IPOs may not be purchased with margin funds.

market makers   Firms licensed to buy and sell a particular security or securities on NASDAQ. These firms are usually brokers or investment banks and can be large or small. The term also refers to individual employees acting in the market on the firm's behalf. A partial list of market makers appears in Appendix B.

market order   An order to buy or sell a security "at the market," that is, with no specified fixed price.

momentum trader   Day traders who watch for stocks that are suddenly actively traded as a result of breaking news or other factors.

moving average   An average of a security's prices, calculated over a specified number of past periods, with a specified weighting of each period's price.

NASD   The National Association of Securities Dealers.

NASDAQ   The National Association of Securities Dealers Automated Quotations system.

opening delay   A stock not trading at the market open due to news events or an extreme imbalance of orders. The specialist has 15 minutes from the opening bell to indicate a price range at which the stock will begin trading. (Listed stocks only; doesn't happen on NASDAQ.)

options   A contract to buy or sell a stock, commodity, or futures contract at a particular price by a particular date.

order imbalance   An excess of buy or sell orders that makes it impossible to match orders up evenly. May cause trading to be temporarily suspended. Listed stocks only.

oscillators   Oscillators compare the current price of a stock to its trading range over a defined period of time.

paid for order flow   Paid for order flow occurs when retail brokers sell your order to another firm for execution.

paper trading   Simulated stock trading by identifying and recording hypothetical trades and keeping track of all trades and daily profit and loss. Can be done by recording trades literally on paper, or with special software simulators.

position traders   Investors who take a position in a stock based on the performance or expected performance of the company.

put option   A traded contract to sell a specific quantity of a security at a specific price by a specific future date.

real-time quotes   A price quote which shows the price at which a stock is selling at that exact moment in time.

refresh the bid   When a market maker reestablishes the bid after being hit by a SOES execution. Refreshing the offer is a similar reestablishment of the offer.

Regulation T   Specifies an initial margin requirement, that is, a minimum equity requirement for a trader to enter a position—and a maximum that can be extended by the broker in the form of margin. Currently the initial margin requirement is 50 percent.

resistance level   A price at which a stock receives considerable selling pressure.

Rule 405   The "know your customer" rule that full-service brokerage firms must comply with. Stockbrokers must be well-acquainted with their customer's financial situation and long-term goals, and may only make recommendations appropriate to those goals.

scalpers   Day traders who try to make money by trading to capture very short-term sixteenth, eighth or a quarter of a point gains. Many trades last only a minute or two.

short squeeze   A short squeeze occurs when a sizable number of short traders get pushed to the exits all at once (have to buy the stock to cover their positions). This creates momentum and the price rises further, faster.

shorting stock   Selling stock borrowed from your broker anticipating a downward price move.

size   The volume of shares in a trade or available in a limit order or market-maker quote.

size bid   On NYSE, total shares being sought by limit order buyers (or by the specialist) at the quoted bid price.

size ask   On NYSE, total shares available to be bought from limit order sellers (or from the specialist) at the quoted ask or offer price. Also called *size offer*.

slippage   The movement of the actual trade price away from the price at the time the order is placed.

SOES   Small Order Execution System—a system implemented by NASDAQ to provide automatic electronic execution for small orders from the public without the market maker's intervention. All market makers are required to participate in SOES. Specific trading rules apply.

specialist's book   An electronic record of all fixed price orders (stop, limit) and market and short sale orders that a specialist has received, and the specialist's inventory. Used to execute orders on the NYSE or AMEX.

spread   The small price difference between the bid price and the ask price, normally representing a profit margin for a market maker or specialist.

stochastics   A way to measure the position of a stock's closing price relative to its price range over a specified number of periods and relative to its overall trend.

stock ahead   Situation preventing a limit order from being filled even when the limit price is reached—there are other "stock ahead" orders chronologically ahead that may consume the available demand and supply at that price

stop order   A fixed-activation price order. An order becomes an active market order when the price reaches your specified "stop" price. A "buy stop" becomes an active market buy order when the stock rises to the stop price; a "sell stop" becomes an active market order when the stock declines to the stop price.

SuperDot   Super Designated Order Turnaround system—an automated electronic system used to route orders on the NYSE floor to the appropriate specialist. Also used to route confirmations back to the source.

support level   A price at which a stock will receive considerable buying pressure.

swing trader   A stock trader who holds onto a position for more than a day, but closes out all trades at the end of the week.

teenies   Stock-market slang for a sixteenth of a point. The cash value of a teenie is 6.25 cents per share.

trading range   A consistent price pattern characterized by definable resistance and support levels. The stock appears to bounce back and forth between these levels for a period of time.

trendline   A straight line, or two parallel straight lines bracketing highs and lows, indicating the direction in which a stock has been moving, and can be predicted to move.

unlisted stocks   Stocks that don't trade on the NYSE, but rather on the NASDAQ or OTC markets.

uptick   The opposite of a downtick, a move upwards in the price between sales. A short sale can only be opened when the market is on an uptick.

zero-plus tick   Zero-plus tick is a minor exception to the uptick rule: a zero-plus tick occurs when the last trade was made at the same price as the previous one, but the previous one was higher than two trades ago.

Market-Maker and ECN Symbols

Here are the big financial guns behind the four-letter abbreviations you'll see flashing across the Level II screen: (for a more complete list see www.nasdaqtrader.com)

ABSB	Alex Brown & Sons	GVRC	GVR Co.
AGED	A.G. Edwards	HMQT	Hambrecht & Quist, Inc.
AGIS	Aegis Capital Corp.	HRZG	Herzog,Heine,Geduld
BARC	Barclay Investments	JANY	Janney Montgomery Scott
BARD	Robert L. Baird, Inc.	JEFF	Jeffries Co., Inc.
BEST	Bear Stearns & Co.	JOSE	Josephthal & Co
BTAB	BT Alex Brown, Inc.	JPMS	JP Morgan Securities
BTSC	BT Securities Corp.	KEMP	Kemper Securities, Inc.
CANT	Cantor Fitzgerald & Co.	KPCO	Kidder Peabody & Co
CIBC	CIBC Oppenheimer	LEGG	Legg Mason Wood
CJDB	CJLawrence/Deutsche		Walker, Inc.
CLYN	Carlin Equities Corp.	LEHM	Lehman Brothers
COST	Coastal Securities	MADF	Bernard Madoff
COWN	Societe Generale Securities	MASH	Mayer Schweitzer, Inc.
DAIN	Dain Rauscher, Inc.	MHMY	MH Meyerson & Co.
DEAN	Dean Witter Reynolds	MLCO	Merrill Lynch & Co.
DLJP	Donaldson,Lufkin,Jenrette	MONT	Montgomery Securities
DOMS	Domestic Securities	MSCO	Morgan Stanley
DONC	Donald & Co. Securities	MWSE	Midwest Stock Exchange
EVRN	Everen Securities	NAWE	Nash Weiss
EXPO	Exponential Capital	NEED	Needham & Co.
FACT	First Albany Corp.	NITE	Knight Securities
FAHN	Fahnestock & Co.	NMRA	Nomura Securities Intl.
FBCO	CS First Boston	OLDE	Olde Discount Corp.
FPKI	Fox-Pitt, Kelton, Inc.	PERT	Pershing Trading Co.
GRUN	Gruntal & Co.	PIPR	Piper Jaffray, Inc.
GSCO	Goldman Sachs & Co.	PRCS	Prime Capital Services, Inc.

PRUS	Prudential Securities
PWJC	Paine Webber
RSSF	BancBoston Robertson Stephens & Co.
SALB	Salomon Brothers
SBNY	Sands Brothers, Inc.
SBSH	Smith Barney Shearson
SELZ	Baring Furman Selz, Inc.
SHWD	Sherwood Securities Corp.
SLKC	Speer Leeds & Kellogg
SNDV	Soundview Technology Group
SUTR	Sutro & Co, Inc.
SWST	Southwest Securities
TUCK	Tucker Anthony, Inc.
TVAN	Teevan & Co.
VOLP	Volpe Welty
WARB	S.G. Warburg
WARR	Warburg Dillon Read

WATL	A.B. Watley
WAYG	Grayson Financial
WBLR	William Blair & Co.
WDCO	Wilson-Davis & Co
WEAT	Wheat First Securities, Inc.
WEDB	Wedbush Morgan Securities
WEED	Weeden & Co.
WSEI	Wallstreet Equities, Inc.
WSLS	WeselsArnold & Henderson
WSTI	Westphalia Investments

Here are four-letter symbols for the major ECNs:

ATTN	Attain
BTRD	B-Trade
INCA	Instinet
ISLD	Island
REDI	RediBook
TNTO	Archipelago

"Plain Talk About Online Investing"

Remarks of U.S. Securities & Exchange Commission Chairman Arthur Levitt at the National Press Club, May 4, 1999

Author note: This speech is a must-read for anybody involved in day or short-term online investing. It is excellent, insightful commentary on the new on line investing paradigm including the risks, responsibilities, and inherent problems with Internet trading—and how the SEC is responding. While the SEC is committing far more resources to maintaining market integrity and combating fraud, they recognize the "democratization of our markets as a desirable development that regulators should not frustrate." Read on....

Today, you can hardly pick up a newspaper, turn on a television, overhear a conversation, or talk to a friend without mention of the Internet. It has done nothing short of change the way our world works and the way our nation invests. And overall, it has changed us for the better.

I'm here today not to extol the Internet's virtues—as they are self-evident—or to raise a red flag of danger. Instead, I want to talk plainly and sensibly about the challenges it presents in the most practical ways.

Last week, I visited Martin Luther King High School in New York City to talk about the importance of financial literacy. The first question I got was from a young student who asked, "What Internet stock should I buy?" We are living in a time when the stock market is more a part of the American consciousness than ever before. After years of nothing but "up" markets and empowering technology, the investor psyche has gone through a lot of changes. Memories have shortened and important points may have gotten lost in the excitement.

We—as a nation, as investors, as businesses, and as regulators—should not get manic about the mania. One day, a little-known company stock soars 38,000 percent after online investors invest using the wrong ticker symbol. Another day, someone fabricates a news story by copying a Web page of a news organization and the stock in question rises 32 percent. Or, sadly, it's an investor who didn't take the time to appreciate what he was getting into and ended up losing his life savings in one fell swoop. It seems that with every passing day, we come across one story more amazing than the other.

As clichéd as it may be, fundamentals still apply. I want to review them here—whether they take the form of advice to investors, guidance to brokers, or reasoned action for regulators.

I want to discuss a number of important issues that should give all of us sufficient pause. First to investors, I want to talk about your responsibilities when investing over the Internet; second, to online brokerages, in the enthusiasm over online trading, you can never lose sight of the fundamental obligations to customers; and third, I want to discuss how the SEC is responding to these rapid changes to protect investors and help maintain market integrity.

By one account, more than seven million Americans trade online—comprising 25 percent of all trades made by individual investors. In 1994, not one person traded over the Internet. In the next few years, the number of online brokerage accounts will roughly equal the metropolitan populations of Seattle, San Francisco, Boston, Dallas, Denver, Miami, Atlanta, and Chicago, combined.

The breadth and pace of change prompted by the Internet are phenomenal. But, while it changes the way millions of Americans invest, online investing does not alter the basic framework that has governed our markets for the past 65 years.

The laws regulating our markets are a product of the New Deal era. To me, their concepts are as indelible as the Constitution. They have weathered challenge after challenge, decade after decade, and are every bit as relevant and effective today as they were the day they were written. Companies offering their shares—whether off a Web site or through a paper prospectus—still have to disclose what they are selling and why. Brokers—whether traditional or online—still have the same obligations to their customers. And fraud—whether perpetrated over the Internet, on the phone, or in-person—is still fraud.

Consequently, I am not convinced it's necessary for the SEC to pronounce a totally new and radical scheme of regulation specifically tailored to online investing. Yet, I don't rule out the possibility that there may come a time when the SEC sees a need for new approaches to better meet the imperatives of the Internet.

What must occur now is a greater recognition by investors of their individual responsibility. I'm talking specifically about an individual investor's duty to understand and control the level of risk he or she is assuming. That level can vary with the type of activity an investor undertakes. On one end of the spectrum lie investors who trade occasionally online and hold their investments for the longer term. They are basically retail investors who manage their portfolios through online accounts.

On the other end of that spectrum are so-called "day traders" whose time horizon for moving in and out of stock positions is measured by minutes, if not seconds. Some argue day trading is really nothing more than speculation. And, speculation is not new to our markets. Personally, I don't think day traders are speculating because traditional speculation requires some market knowledge. They are instead gambling, which doesn't. Historically, short-term trading has been an activity filled by a relatively small number of professional traders.

I am concerned that more and more people may be undertaking day trading strategies without a full appreciation of the risk and difficulty involved. No one should have any illusions of what he is getting involved in. I know of one state that recently found that 67 out of 68 day traders at a firm had in fact lost money.

Somewhere in the middle of this spectrum—with long-term investors on one side and day traders on the other—is an increasing number of Americans who use their online accounts both to invest longer term and to trade short term on momentum or small changes in the price of a stock. Call this mixed strategy day trading "light."

I'm concerned about the great influx of new and relatively inexperienced investors who may be so seduced by the ease and speed of Internet trading that they may be trading in a way that does not match their specific goals and risk tolerance. I also wonder about many of these investors who have never experienced a down market. On the other hand, a greater number of Americans investing for their futures and helping to raise capital is, in the long-term, good for our markets and good for our country.

Individual Responsibility

As far as I'm concerned, for most individuals, the stock market is best used for investing, not trading. And, it's important to make that distinction. Online trading may be quick and easy; online investing—and I emphasize investing—requires the same old-fashioned elbow grease like researching a company or making the time to appreciate the level of risk. I'm often surprised by investors who spend more time deciding what movie they'll rent than on which stock to buy.

Regardless of how frequently a person trades or invests, the opportunity to make these decisions comes with the responsibility to take the time to understand the implications of those decisions. We have noticed four common misconceptions that investors have about online trading.

The first is that although the Internet makes it seem as if you have a direct connection to the securities markets, you don't. When you push that enter key, your order is sent to your broker, who then sends it to a market to be executed. This process is usually seamless and electronic; it is not, however, guaranteed. Lines may clog; systems may break; orders may back-up.

Even when automated systems can handle a lot of investors who want to buy or sell the same stock at the same time, a line often forms. Price quotes are only for a limited number of shares; some investors may not receive the currently quoted price. And, as you would expect, the price of that stock will then go up if there are more buyers and down if there are more sellers. By the time you get to the front of the line, the price of the stock could be very different.

So, how do investors protect themselves from a rapid change in the price of a stock? One way is to use a limit order. That's the second thing every online investor needs to know. A limit order buys or sells a security at a specific price. In other words, the order can be executed only if the market price has not moved past a certain level. On the other hand, a market order buys or sells the stock at whatever price the security is at the time the order reaches the market. So, if you place a market order to buy an IPO stock at $9, you could end up paying $90 by the time your order is executed.

This isn't theoretical. More than a few investors have lost most of their savings—thousands and thousands of dollars—because they failed to limit their price. Now, sometimes limit orders may not get executed in a fast moving market and some firms may charge more for them. But, at the very least, I'd rather not own a stock or pay a little more upfront than be totally unprepared or incapable of paying a whole lot more later. My goals as an investor may be different from yours, but considering the costs and benefits of a limit order is part of responsible investing in today's market.

The third misconception is that an order is canceled when you hit "cancel" on your computer. But the fact is, it's canceled only when the market receives the cancellation. You may get an electronic confirmation, but that may only mean your request to cancel was received—not that your order was actually canceled. Recently, one major brokerage wasn't able to process 20 percent of the cancellation orders on a fast moving IPO. One investor placed an online order for 2,000 shares of the stock—thought she canceled it—and then placed another order for 1,000 shares.

After realizing that she had two orders outstanding, she tried to cancel both. Instead, she owed her broker over a quarter-million dollars for 3,000 shares after wanting to invest roughly $18,000. Most cases may not be this exceptional, but I urge investors to contact their firms to see how they can ensure a cancellation order actually worked.

Fourth, if you plan to borrow money to buy a stock, you also need to know the terms of the loan your broker gave you. This is called margin. When you buy on margin, the stock you purchase is collateral for that loan. In volatile markets, investors who put up an initial margin payment for a stock may find themselves required to provide additional cash if the price of the stock falls.

But, some investors have been shocked to find out that, if they don't meet the margin call, the brokerage firm has the right to sell their securities—without any notification and potentially at a substantial loss to the investor. Others investors have been surprised to learn that they are lending to or borrowing from other customers in their firm through excess balances in their margin accounts. It's clear that if an investor fails to understand the use and consequences of a margin account, he does so at his own peril.

You also may have heard about plans by the major markets to extend their trading hours into the evening. That's another way the markets are being responsive to ever-changing investment patterns brought about by individual investors. But with this new flexibility comes a catch—the price you pay or receive might be affected by the fewer number of people in the market at that hour. That's simply a product of the law of supply and demand.

The Cardinal Rule of Acting in the Customer's Interest

Let me turn to some of the concerns I have about the role of online firms. Firms should remember that while online trading may place significantly more responsibility in the hands of investors, it doesn't absolve the firms of their obligations to customers. Most firms are doing a pretty good job—especially in light of the dramatic growth they are experiencing. But as the Internet rapidly becomes more and more an integral part of investing for more and more Americans, I ask brokerage firms to help protect the integrity of it for the long-run.

First, firms need to ensure that their ability to provide effective customer service keeps pace with their growth. If you're marketing your firm to new customers, you'd better be able to provide them service when they do business with you. Firms are opening roughly 15,000 new accounts a day. That means 15,000 new potential complaints a day—especially if a system goes down. Are investors having a hard time getting their e-mails answered? Are customer service 800 numbers always busy? Are complaints about failures or delays in order execution, account accessibility, and other issues overwhelming the firm's compliance department?

If the answer to any of these questions is "yes," then what are firms doing about it? It doesn't take a regulator to tell you what unhappy customers mean to a company's future, or more broadly, to the future of online investing.

Second, all firms—whether online, discount or full service—have an obligation to ensure the best execution of their customers' orders. That's not just good business practice; it's a legal obligation. Firms have this same duty to their customers to find the best prices—whether they charge $10 per trade or $100 per trade.

The commission has long stressed to firms the importance of obtaining the best possible price when they route their customers' orders. They simply can't let payment for order flow or other relationships or inducements determine where they do business. That's why I have directed our examiners to focus in on firms' order routing practices in an examination sweep. I urge all firms now to review their practices to ensure they're doing right by their customers.

Third, firms need to communicate more clearly to investors. We have reviewed the disclosure in account agreements both on paper and on web pages. Overall, we found that most firms address the different types of orders available, fewer firms discuss how market volatility and the use of margin can affect online investors, and almost none talk about the risks or what to do in the event of system capacity and outage problems. I know that customers' orders can be slowed down for reasons outside of a firm's control. But explaining clearly to customers rather than merely disclaiming liability through complex and legalistic language would go a long way toward reducing the complaints pouring into the SEC, Congress, and firms.

So, to every online firm I challenge you to meaningfully communicate with your customers. Talk in realistic terms; let them know their options; and focus on the quality of your disclosure in your agreements, instead of just the acceptability of them.

Lastly, I worry about how some online firms advertise. Quite frankly, some advertisements more closely resemble commercials for the lottery than anything else. When firms, again and again, tell investors that online investing can make them rich, it creates unrealistic expectations. And, when firms sow those grandiose and unrealistic expectations, they stand a good chance of reaping the adverse results when many of them go unmet.

Now, in today's Bull Market, there may be an increasing population of tow-truck drivers who now own their own islands as a result of online investing. Assuming there's not, I don't rule out the fact that some of these commercials are tongue-in-cheek. But, in a market environment where many investors are susceptible to quixotic euphoria, I'm worried these commercials step over the line and border on irresponsibility.

I recently saw one commercial that showed two women rushing in from their jog to trade before the stock market closed. After a few clicks of the mouse, one woman proclaims, "I just made $1,700." The other woman sheepishly replies by admitting she invests in mutual funds. What's the implication of the message here? Has it become passé to invest for the longer-term and to diversify your risk?

Now, some may argue that we shouldn't tell firms how to sell their products as long as its lawful. I agree. But selling securities is not like selling soap. Brokers have always had duties to their customers that go beyond simply "buyer beware."

I've asked the NASD regulatory unit to hold a roundtable on advertising to add to the work they're already doing to improve fairness in advertising. I call on all of the firms to join in this effort. I've also asked Jay Chiat, former head of the advertising firm, Chiat Day, to work with the NASD and industry leaders to consider the public interest issues this type of advertising implicates.

What the SEC Is Doing

Today, I've talked about what investors need to be aware of if they invest over the Internet and I've also discussed some of the issues firms should be addressing. As technology recasts our markets and helps attract more and more investors than ever before, the SEC's mission to protect investors and maintain market integrity remains absolute.

Securities fraud perpetrated over the Internet represents a signal challenge for the SEC. While the scams we have seen on the Internet are the same basic frauds that have always accompanied the flow of money, the Internet's speed, low cost, and relative anonymity give con artists access to an unprecedented number of innocent investors.

Policing this marketplace will require more resources, more manpower, and more money. Nevertheless, we are prepared to do whatever is necessary to help protect investors. While we contend with the Internet's growing presence, it offers us important tools to track down and catch criminals. Law enforcement will tell you that it's a lot easier to catch someone who uses the Internet than the telephone. For example, although the individual who perpetrated last month's news hoax about a corporate takeover tried to cover up his footprints, we tracked him down within a week.

Last year, we created the SEC's Cyberforce—a specially trained nationwide corps of 125 attorneys, accountants and analysts tasked with searching for Internet fraud. This year, we will increase that number by 100 percent. For next year, the commission has asked for an $11 million increase to expand our efforts to combat fraud. And, with the support and insight of congressional and administration leaders, we will continue to step up our efforts in the future.

In the meantime, we are vigilantly pursuing those who seek to take advantage of innocent investors. In the next two weeks, the SEC's Enforcement Division will present a number of cases charging fraudulent offerings over the Internet. These cases would charge issuers and promoters with making false claims about companies or offering investments in entirely fictitious companies. We have also been working with the FBI on a project called "Operation InvestNet"—a nationwide initiative to address fraudulent securities activities taking place over the Internet.

Second, the SEC's Office of Compliance and Inspections will continue to inspect firms offering online trading. We've already conducted inspections of firms that represent 80 percent of the market share. Based on our initial findings, I sent a letter this morning to all of the online brokerage firms asking them to improve the quality of their disclosure to investors. When firms achieve the highest quality of service and continually act in the interests of their customers, they create a customer for life—instead of just another short-term trading opportunity.

The SEC and the self-regulatory agencies are also inspecting all of the brokerage firms that specialize in day trading. Clearly providing day trading opportunities is not itself against the law, but these firms should be on notice that they are still broker-dealers and must operate within the existing rules. That means complying with disclosure, capital, margin, and best execution requirements as well as maintaining updated and comprehensive books and records. And any firm, whether day trading or online, that recommends a type of investment strategy or customizes research should ensure that it is suitable for its customers.

Third, I'm announcing today the formation of a formal SEC private sector Advisory Committee on Technology. The Advisory Committee's mandate will be a broad one. It will encompass not only how the commission might better leverage its resources to protect investors and safeguard market integrity, but also examine issues specifically relating to online trading. I've asked General Ken Minihan, former head of the National Security Agency and Bran Ferren, a true innovator in technology, to lead this effort in lending cutting edge expertise to the SEC.

As its first priority, I will ask the committee to convene a group of industry executives to hear their thoughts and concerns about how technology will affect our markets and its participants.

Fourth, the commission is unveiling its new Investor Education Web Page. The Web site is www.sec.gov/invkhome.htm. It includes detailed information and tips on online investing, how to detect fraud both on and off the Internet and other important information on saving and investing.

In addition, in the letter that I sent to online firms, I have asked them to create links from their Web sites to the SEC's investor-education site. This is an idea that came up during a Senate hearing on this subject. I hope we can all agree that an informed and knowledgeable investor is good for the industry and good for individual businesses.

Lastly, I want to raise some points about chat rooms, which increasingly have become a source of information and mis-information for many investors. They have been compared to a high-tech version of morning gossip or advice at the company water cooler. But, at least you knew your co-workers at the water cooler. That just isn't true on the Internet. And, I hope investors recognize that.

I wonder how many chat room participants realize that if someone is waxing poetic about a certain stock, that person could well be paid to do it. For the future sake of this medium, I encourage investors to take what they see over chat rooms—not with a grain of salt—but with a rock of salt. By doing so, you protect yourself and you protect the Internet.

I've asked the major Internet providers who host these chat rooms to place a link to the SEC's Web site where investors can learn more about online investing and file a complaint with us if necessary. I want everyone in a chat room to know that if some-one is taking advantage of the technology, you have the opportunity to shine the light on it. Think of it as neighborhood watch on the Internet. With the help of investors, we can get those people who have only one motivation—to ruthlessly make money at the expense of others—out of our communities.

The SEC will do everything it can to protect and inform investors during this time of great innovation and change. But, I've said many times before that investor protec-tion—at its most basic and effective level—starts with the investor. In this day and age, there simply is no substitute for a person's awareness and wariness.

Conclusion

Many of the issues I have raised today were not even a blip on the screen a few years ago. Who can confidently say what online issues will demand our time and attention in the future? But we won't stop examining and thinking about how the Internet will affect investors and our markets. Through the efforts of Commissioner Unger who is spearheading the commission's work on technology issues and the rest of the SEC staff, we are going to do our best to ensure investors remain protected and our markets remain the strongest in the world.

All of us are participants in an extraordinary social phenomena. The democratization of our markets is a desirable development which regulators should not frustrate. Our mission is not to prevent losers or to modulate the sometimes mercurial movement of our markets. The standard by which we will determine our methods of surveillance, education, market structure, disclosure and, if need be, enforcement will be an unyielding commitment to the well being of investors. I call on all market participants, the media, fellow regulators and lawmakers to help us fulfill this commitment by working together to make the 21st Century defined as much by trust as technology.

Index